Christianities
in Asia

BLACKWELL GUIDES TO GLOBAL CHRISTIANITY

The Blackwell Guides to Global Christianity chart the history, development and current state of Christianity in key geographical areas around the world. In many cases, these are areas where Christianity has had a controversial past and where the future of Christianity may yet be decided. Each book in the series will look at both the history of Christianity in an important region and consider the issues and themes which are prevalent in the lives of contemporary Christians and the Church. Accessibly written by area experts, the books will appeal to students and scholars of World Christianity and others who are interested in the history, culture and religion of around the world.

Published

Christianities in Asia   Peter Phan

Forthcoming

Christianity in China Daniel Bays
Christianity in Africa Robert Kaggwa

Christianities
in Asia

Edited by Peter C. Phan

WILEY-BLACKWELL

A John Wiley & Sons, Ltd., Publication

This edition first published 2011
© 2011 Blackwell Publishing Ltd except for editorial material and organization
© 2011 Peter C. Phan

Blackwell Publishing was acquired by John Wiley & Sons in February 2007. Blackwell's publishing program has been merged with Wiley's global Scientific, Technical, and Medical business to form Wiley-Blackwell.

Registered Office
John Wiley & Sons Ltd, The Atrium, Southern Gate, Chichester, West Sussex, PO19 8SQ, United Kingdom

Editorial Offices
350 Main Street, Malden, MA 02148-5020, USA
9600 Garsington Road, Oxford, OX4 2DQ, UK
The Atrium, Southern Gate, Chichester, West Sussex, PO19 8SQ, UK

For details of our global editorial offices, for customer services, and for information about how to apply for permission to reuse the copyright material in this book please see our website at www.wiley.com/wiley-blackwell.

The right of Peter C. Phan to be identified as the author of the editorial material in this work has been asserted in accordance with the UK Copyright, Designs and Patents Act 1988.

Wiley also publishes its books in a variety of electronic formats. Some content that appears in print may not be available in electronic books.

Designations used by companies to distinguish their products are often claimed as trademarks. All brand names and product names used in this book are trade names, service marks, trademarks or registered trademarks of their respective owners. The publisher is not associated with any product or vendor mentioned in this book. This publication is designed to provide accurate and authoritative information in regard to the subject matter covered. It is sold on the understanding that the publisher is not engaged in rendering professional services. If professional advice or other expert assistance is required, the services of a competent professional should be sought.

Library of Congress Cataloging-in-Publication Data

Phan, Peter C., 1943-
  Christianities in Asia / Peter C. Phan.
      p. cm. – (Blackwell guides to global Christianity)
  Includes bibliographical references and index.
  ISBN 978-1-4051-6089-6 (hardcover : alk. paper) – ISBN 978-1-4051-6090-2 (pbk. : alk. paper)
  1. Christianity–Asia. I. Title.
  BR1065.P43 2011
  275–dc22
                                                                        2010026659

A catalogue record for this book is available from the British Library.

Set in Sabon 10/12pt by Thomson Digital, Noida, India.
Printed in Singapore by Ho Printing Singapore Pte Ltd

1 2011

Contents

List of Maps

The editor and contributors are grateful to Pietro Lorenzo Maggioni for the initial creation of the maps.

Notes on Contributors

Edmund Kee-Fook Chia is a Malaysian and is Associate Professor at the Catholic Theological Union, Chicago, IL, USA. He has written extensively on the work of the Federation of Asian Bishops' Conferences and the Christian mission in Asia.

Lois Farag is Associate Professor of Early Church History at Luther Seminary, Saint Paul, MN, USA. She has served as Chair of the Society of Biblical Literature Consultation "Christianity in Egypt: Scripture, Tradition and Reception" and is on the editorial board for the *Coptic Encyclopedia. Her* scholarship focuses on the Early Church in Egypt.

Jose Mario C. Francisco, S.J. is President, Loyola School of Theology, Ateneo de Manila University, Loyola Heights, Quezon City, Philippines. His work focuses on the interface between religion, culture, and science, especially in the East Asian contexts. He has published critical editions of seventeenth-century manuscripts, a Tagalog-Spanish dictionary, and an anthology of Tagalog sermons.

Andrew Eungi Kim is Professor in the Division of International Studies at Korea University. His primary research interests are religion, culture, multiculturalism, and social change. His articles have appeared in various journals. He is the author of two books in preparation about Korea.

Elizabeth Koepping is Senior Lecturer in World Christianity at the University of Edinburgh. She has researched local traditions in eastern Sabah as well as Anglicanism and Lutheranism of German origin in South Australia. A priest in the Scottish Episcopal Church, she also teaches in Korea and Myanmar, and has recently completed a four-volume set of readers on World Christianity.

Lo Lung-kwong is Director of The Divinity School of Chung Chi College, The Chinese University of Hong Kong and President of The Methodist Church, Hong Kong and Macau. Recent publications include chapters on ecclesiology from the perspective of scripture in Wesleyan and Asian contexts and the historical Jesus in Hong Kong, China.

Mark R. Mullins is Professor of Religion in the Faculty of Comparative Culture, Sophia University, Tokyo, Japan. He is author and co-editor of a number of works. His research focuses on the sociology of religious minorities, particularly new religious movements and Christianity in East Asia.

John Mansford Prior teaches and researches on issues of faith and culture. He is Lecturer in Theology at Ledalero Institute of Philosophy, Maumere, Indonesia and Associate Lecturer at Yarra Theological Union, Australia. He was Consultant to the Pontifical Council for Culture 1993–2008.

Peter C. Phan is the inaugural holder of the Ignacio Ellacuría Chair of Catholic Social Thought at Georgetown University, Washington, DC (USA). He holds three earned doctorates and two honorary doctorates. He authored a dozen books, edited over 30 books, and published over 300 essays in various fields of theology and religion. Among his books are: *Christianity with an Asian Face; In Our Own Tongues; Being Religious Interreligiously; and Mission and Catechesis: Alexandre de Rhodes and Inculturation in Seventeenth-Century Vietnam.*

Jeyaraj Rasiah is a Jesuit from Sri Lanka. He has been Director of the East Asian Pastoral Institute in Manila in the Philippines and has lectured Pastoral Theology at the Institute and Philosophy at the Ateneo de Manila University. Presently he is the Provincial Superior of the Jesuits in Sri Lanka.

Ying Fuk-tsang is on the faculty of The Divinity School of Chung Chi College, His research focuses on church-state relations in China, the history of Protestant Christianity in China and Hong Kong, and contemporary Chinese Protestantism.

Preface

In 2006 Andrew Humphries, then Commissioning Editor at Blackwell Publishing, asked me if I would be interested in writing a book on Asian Christianity for a popular readership. We discussed its nature and scope and agreed that it should not simply be a historical account of Christian, mostly Western, missions in Asia, though of course such history is a necessary context to understand Asian Christianity. Rather what we envisioned is a book that presents Asian Christianity as "World Christianity," that is, Christianity that has been received and transformed into local or contextualized Christianities, with their own ecclesiastical structures, liturgy and prayers, spirituality, theology, art and architecture, music and songs and dances, etc. The intent is to present Christianity as a vibrant contemporary religious movement.

Unfortunately that is easier said than done. Whereas it is feasible for a single author to produce a scholarly volume on European or Latin American or even African Christianity, it is impossible, I pointed out to Andrew, for a single scholar to write a reasonably satisfactory introduction to Asian Christianity. The Asian histories, cultures, religious traditions, and languages in which Christianity has taken root, probably since the first century of the Christian era, are so diverse and complex, and the geographical area to be covered so immense, that no single scholar, however gifted and well trained, would be able to produce anything more than an amateurish history of Asian Christianity. The only viable solution would be a collaborative work.

Another question is to determine what is meant by "Asia." We decided to adopt the conventional geographical divisions of the continent. The umbrella term "Asia" includes the countries of *South Asia* (Afghanistan, Bangladesh, India, Nepal, Pakistan, and Sri Lanka); *South-East Asia* (Burma/Myanmar, Cambodia, Indonesia, Malaysia, Laos, the Philippines, Singapore, Thailand, and Vietnam); *North-East Asia* (China [including Hong Kong and Macau], Japan, Korea, Mongolia, Siberia, Taiwan, and Tibet); and *South-West Asia* (the Near and Middle East). Central Asia will not be considered, given the relatively small number of Christians there. This geographical division also determines the structure of the book. The regional division allows the possibility of highlighting common and overlapping histories and cultures among the countries within each region wherever these exist, whereas the country-by-country approach has the advantage of singling out the unique features of Christianity in a particular country.

My first task as editor was to request contributions from the most qualified scholars, as much as possible in Asia itself, taking into account ethnic and gender diversity. Not all my efforts were successful, especially with regard to gender, but those contacted unfailingly responded with admirable grace and generosity. Communication was not always quick and easy, even in this age of email, since in some countries access to computers was not readily available.

In planning for the volume I did not set any rigid format and theological approach for the essays. The only thing I asked of the contributors is that they present the Christianity of a particular country in the most appealing yet accurate manner possible. I suggested that they imagine a tourist coming to their countries and wishing to know what kind of Christianity is active there: What would they like the tourist to know about their Christianity's history, its most interesting figures, its liturgical and theological riches, its arts and architecture, its contributions to World Christianity, its problems (yes, these too!), and its challenges?

To help readers have an idea of what the book is about, I list below the issues I asked the contributors to keep in mind in writing their "tour guide":

(1) a brief history of Christian missions in the country;
(2) major missionary figures;
(3) salient characteristics of this imported Christianity;
(4) major churches and denominations (e.g., Roman Catholic, Protestant, Orthodox, Pentecostal, etc.);
(5) how Christianity was received;
(6) key native clerical and lay figures;
(7) male and female religious orders;
(8) the role of women and their contributions;
(9) key opposition or reform movements;
(10) martyrs;
(11) relations with other religions, e.g., Hinduism, Buddhism, Confucianism, Islam, etc.;
(12) popular devotions, especially to Mary and the saints;
(13) Bible translations;
(14) liturgical adaptations;
(15) local religious arts, e.g., painting, sculpture, architecture, music, dance; literature;
(16) spiritual and monastic traditions;
(17) theological trends and key theologians;

(18) relation between church and State; Communism; colonialism, globalization;

(19) contemporary challenges in terms of politics and economics;

(20) future prospects.

Of course, not all of these issues are of equal concern and importance for Christianity in every country, but they give a rough idea of what each chapter is about.

It remains for me the pleasant task to thank the people who have been in various ways responsible for the birth of this book. I have already mentioned Andrew Humphries, whose idea of a book on Asian Christianity lay at the conception of this volume. After Blackwell was merged with Wiley, and after Andy moved on to another company, the task of shepherding the book to completion was taken over by Rebecca Harkin and Lucy Boon. I am deeply grateful to them for their admirable professional competence and long-suffering patience, as unexpected editorial work on the manuscript forced me to miss the deadline. Two other persons deserve my deepest thanks, Nik Prowse, who oversaw the final stages of production, and Gillian Andrews, the marvelously brilliant copy editor who through countless emails took care of all the details. I also would like to thank Peter Manseau, a doctoral student in the Graduate Program in Theology and Religious Studies at Georgetown University, for his editorial work on some of the essays.

The greatest debt of gratitude, however, is owed to the contributors themselves. They have generously and unreservedly put their scholarship at the service of the church and the academy. They were patient and forgiving for the notable delay in the preparation of the manuscript. If the proverbial "Asian" gentleness has any truth to it at all, they have embodied it – to an uncommon degree.

1

Introduction: Asian Christianity/ Christianities

Peter C. Phan

"Asian Christianity" or "Asian Christianities"? Both the singular and the plural forms are correct, depending on the perspective. From the essentialist viewpoint, it is proper to speak of "Christianity" since the basic Christian beliefs and practices – as distinct from those of, for instance, Hinduism, Buddhism, and Islam, to mention just the three largest religions in Asia – are the same among all Christian communities in Asia. Historically, however, these same Christian beliefs and practices have been understood, expressed, and embodied in a dizzying variety of ways. This Christian multiformity is a function of the enormous geographical, sociopolitical, historical, cultural, and religious diversity of the continent called Asia.

Which Asia?

With two thirds of the world's six-billion population, Asia is the largest and most populous continent.[1] With Europe as a peninsula of the Eurasian landmass on its west, Asia lies, on its western limits, along the Urals, the Ural River, the Caspian Sea, the Caucasus, the Black Sea, the Bosporus and the Dardanelles straits, and the Aegean Sea. On its south-western side, it is separated from Africa by the Suez Canal between the Mediterranean Sea and the Red Sea. In its far northeastern part, i.e., Siberia, it is separated from North America by the Bering Strait. In the south, Asia is bathed by the Gulf of Aden, the Arabian Sea, and the Bay of Bengal; on the east, by the South China Sea, East China Sea, Yellow Sea, Sea of Japan, Sea of Okhotsk, and Bering Sea; and on the north, by the Arctic Ocean.

Christianities in Asia, edited by Peter C. Phan   © 2011 Blackwell Publishing Ltd except for editorial material and organization © 2011 Peter C. Phan

As a continent, Asia is conventionally divided into five regions: Central Asia (mainly the Republics of Kyrgyzstan, Tajikistan, Turkmekistan, and Uzbekistan); East Asia (mainly China Japan, Korea, and Taiwan); South Asia (mainly Bangladesh, India, Myanmar, Nepal, Pakistan, and Sri Lanka); South-East Asia (mainly Cambodia, Indonesia, Laos, the Philippines, Singapore, Thailand, and Vietnam); and South-West Asia (the countries of the Middle East, Near East, or West Asia).[2]

Asia is the land of extreme contrasts. It has both the world's highest peak, Mt. Everest, and its lowest point, the Dead Sea. Climatically, the continent ranges through all extremes, from the torrid heat of the Arabian Desert to the arctic cold of Siberia and from the torrential rains of monsoons to the bone-dry aridity of the Tarim Basin.

Asia's geographical and climactic extremes are matched by linguistic, ethnic, economic, political, cultural, and religious ones. More than 100 languages and more than 700 languages are spoken in the Philippines and Indonesia respectively, whereas only one is spoken in Korea. Ethnically, India and China are teeming with diversity, whereas Vietnam is predominantly homogeneous. Economically, Asia has one of the richest countries (Japan) and the poorest ones on Earth (e.g., North Korea, Cambodia, and Laos). Politically, it contains the largest democratic and the largest communist governments in the world, India and China respectively. Along with linguistic, ethnic, economic, and political diversity come extremely diverse cultures, which are also among the oldest and the richest. Religiously, Asia is the cradle of all world religions. Besides Christianity, other Asian religions include Bahá'í, Bön, Buddhism, Confucianism, Daoism, Hinduism, Islam, Jainism, Shinto, Sikhism, and Zoroastrianism, and innumerable tribal religions.[3]

Which Christianity?

It is within the context of these mind-boggling diversities – geographic, linguistic, ethnic, economic, political, cultural, and religious – that "Christianity in Asia" should be broached. One of the bitter ironies of Asian Christianity is that though born in (South-West) Asia, it returned to its birthplace as a foreign religion, or worse, the religion of its colonizers, and is still being widely regarded as such by many Asians. But such perception of Christianity as a Western religion imported to Asia by Portuguese and Spanish colonialists in the sixteenth century, and later by other European countries such as Britain, France, Germany, and the Netherlands, and lastly by the United States, belies the ancient roots of Christianity in Asia.

First of all, Christianity may be said to be an Asian religion since it was born in Palestine, part of West Asia or the Middle East. Furthermore, though West Asia is dominated by Islam, it was, until the Arab conquest in the seventh century, the main home of Christianity. But even Asian Christians outside West Asia can rightly boast of an ancient and glorious heritage, one that is as old as the apostolic age. The conventional image of Christianity as a Western religion, that is, one that originated in Palestine but soon moved westward, with Rome as its final destination, and from Rome as its epicenter, Western Christianity sent missionaries worldwide, ignores the fact that in the first four centuries of Christianity's existence, the most successful fields of mission were not Europe but Asia and Africa, with Syria as the center of gravity.

More specifically, Indian Christianity can claim apostolic origins, with St. Thomas and/or St. Bartholomew as its founder(s). Chinese Christianity was born in the seventh century, with the arrival of the East Syrian/Nestorian monk Aloben during the T'ang dynasty. Christianity arrived in other countries such as Japan, the Philippines, and Vietnam in the sixteenth century in the wave of Spanish and Portuguese colonialism. For Korea, on the contrary, Christianity was first brought into the country toward the end of the eighteenth century, not by foreigners but by a Korean, Peter Lee Seung-hun (or Sunghoon Ri), upon his return from Beijing. As for the Pacific Islands, Christianity reached them in the middle of the sixteenth century during the Spanish expeditions from Latin America to the Phillippines and in the late seventeenth century to the Marianas.

Today, in Asia, Christians predominate in only two countries, namely, the Philippines and the Democratic Republic of Timor-Leste (East Timor) – over 85% of their populations are Catholic. In other countries, especially China, India, and Japan, to name the most populous ones, and in countries with a Muslim majority such as Bangladesh, Indonesia, Malaysia, and Pakistan, and in those where Buddhism predominates such as Cambodia, Hong Kong, Laos, Mongolia, Myanmar, Nepal, Singapore, South Korea, Sri Lanka, Taiwan, Thailand, and Vietnam, Christians form but a minuscule portion of the population. However, despite their minority status, Christians' presence is highly influential, especially in the fields of education, health care, and social services.

In addition to its minority status, Asian Christianity is also characterized by ecclesial diversity, so that it is more accurate to use "Christianities" in the plural to describe it. Because of its past extensive missions in Asia, Roman Catholicism is the largest denomination. Within the Roman Catholic Church, of great importance is the Federation of Asian Bishops' Conferences (FABC), which has served since 1970s, through its general assemblies and several permanent offices, as a clearing house for theological reflection and pastoral initiatives. Older than the Roman Catholic Church is the Malabar Church of India ("Saint Thomas Christians"). The Orthodox Church also has a notable presence in China, Korea, and Japan. The Anglican Church (including the Anglican Church of Canada) is well represented, especially in Hong Kong, India, Malaysia, and Pakistan. Various Protestant Churches also flourish in almost all Asian countries, e.g., the Baptists (especially in North India), the Lutherans, the Mennonites, the Methodists, the Presbyterians (especially in Korea), and the Seventh-Day Adventists. In addition, the number of Pentecostals and charismatics has recently grown by leaps and bounds, particularly among ethnic minorities and disenfranchized social classes. The Yoido Full Gospel Church, located in Seoul, Korea, is the largest Pentecostal church in the world, with over half a million members. Finally, there are numerous indigenous offshoots, inspired by nationalism, charismatic leadership, or by the "Three Self Movement" (self-support, self-propagation, and self-government). Among the most famous are the Iglesia Filipina Independiente (founded by Gregorio Aglipay in 1902), and the Iglesia ni Cristo (founded by Felix Ysagun Manalo in 1914), both in the Philippines, and the China Christian Council (and within it, the Three-Self Patriotic Movement of Protestant Churches in China and the Chinese Catholic Patriotic Association, founded in 1954 and 1956 respectively).

Introducing Asian Christianities

Curiously, despite the growing importance of Asia and Asian Christianities, there has been a dearth of books that deal with Asian Christianity as a whole and as a contemporary religious movement. There are of course notable histories of Christian missions in Asia and learned monographs on the history of Christianity on individual countries. This volume intends to fill the lacuna of popular introductions to Asian Christianity by presenting a panorama of Asian Christianity as a *world religion*. It is not a history of Western missions in Asia, though such history will serve as a necessary historical context. Rather, it is on how Christians in Asia have received and transformed Christianity into a local or indigenous religion, with their own ecclesiastical structures, liturgy and prayers, spirituality, theology, art and architecture, music and song and dance, often in dialogue with Asian cultures and religions. The purpose is to help readers gain a sense of Asian Christianity/Christianities as a vibrant contemporary religion.

The chapters are grouped together in terms of geographical proximity and cultural and religious affinity. The first three deal with countries in South Asia (India and Pakistan, Bangladesh and Myanmar, and Sri Lanka). The next three describe Christianity in countries lying next to each other as collections of thousands of islands in South-East Asia (Indonesia, Malaysia and Singapore, and the Philippines). The next five consider the countries whose Christian beginnings were historically linked together: Vietnam, Cambodia, Laos, Thailand, China, Mongolia, Hong Kong, Macau, Taiwan; Japan, and Korea. The last chapter studies the countries in which Christianity has its roots, its earliest developments, and sadly, its most turbulent and uncertain history.

Despite their extreme diversities, there is a golden thread that ties these Asian countries together, and that is, their religious traditions. As mentioned above, Asia is the cradle of all major religions. Understanding how these religions – including Christianity – originated and continue to exist as living institutions in Asia is not only an intellectual obligation but also an indispensable means for peacebuilding and reconciliation in the continent which is currently wracked by violence. The roots of violent conflicts among groups and nations are always many and multiple, and while these conflicts are invariably fueled by political, economic, and military interests, religious claims are almost never absent, especially where a particular religion is adopted as the state religion and its beliefs and practices of a particular religion are imposed as the social, legal, and cultural framework of the civil society. Even when a particular war is first engaged on purely secular grounds, it will not be long before leaders on opposing sides will invoke God's name and power to justify and even bless it. The war will be painted as an apocalyptic struggle between good and evil, and religious demagogues and unscrupulous politicians will stoke religious zeal to mobilize believers for a holy war against their enemies. Participating in war is blessed as a holy service to faith and to be killed, especially in suicide bombing, is celebrated as martyrdom. This is a tragic fact in the history of Asian religions – Asian Christianity included.

But religions – including Christianity – in Asia have also contributed immensely to the spiritual and material well-being of the Asian peoples, and where there is violence and hatred, religions have functioned as an indispensable and effective partner in peacemaking and reconciliation. The so-called "conflict of civilizations" cannot be resolved without the harmony of religions. This too is a salutary and hopeful lesson of the history of Asian religions – including Asian Christianity.

Notes

1. I am aware that in terms of physical geography (landmass) and geology (tectonic plate), Europe and Asia form one "continent." In terms of human geography, however, Europe and Asia have been conventionally treated as different continents, the latter divided into East Asia (the Orient), South Asia (British India), and the Middle East (Arabia and Persia). In this book the term "continent" of Asia is used in this generic sense. As mentioned in the text below, today Asia is divided into five regions (geographers rarely speak of "'North Asia"). The adjective "Asian" is also confusing. In American English, it refers to

East Asian (Orientals), whereas in British English, it refers to South Asia (India). Sometimes, the term is restricted to countries of the Pacific Rim. Here "Asia" refers to East Asia, South Asia, South-East Asia, and the Middle (Near) East or South-West or West Asia.

2. This book will not deal with Christianity in Central Asia.

3. For a succinct presentation of the Asian context in which Christian mission is carried out, see John Paul II's apostolic exhortation *Ecclesia in Asia* (1999), nos. 5–9. The text is available in Phan, P.C. (ed.) *The Asian Synod: Texts and Commentaries*, Maryknoll, New York: Orbis Books, 2002, pp. 286–340.

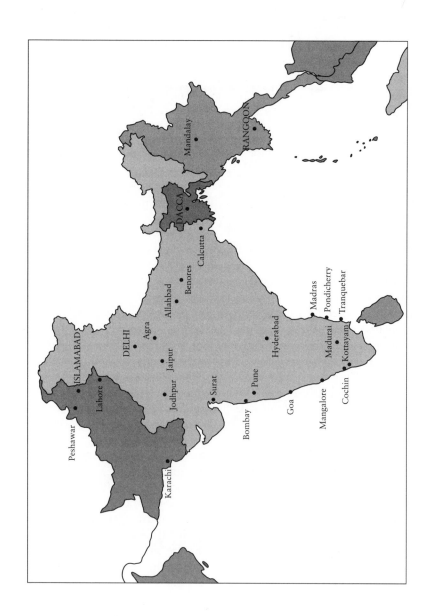

2

India, Pakistan, Bangladesh, Burma/Myanmar

Elizabeth Koepping

Caste, class, and ethnicity, local and foreign missions, contested contextualization, inter- and intra-religious pluralism, colonialism, politics, poverty, nationalism: this sample list gives some indication of the complexity of Christianity in South Asia, home to the most populous country in Asia (India), one of the poorest (Burma/Myanmar), and to two regularly threatened by floods or internal strife (Bangladesh and Pakistan). The above catalogue reflects tensions between groups of believers, and between believers and the scriptural teachings they confess.

It is important to make clear at the outset that sociological tensions and chasms between faith and practice are present in every Christian community, as in any other religious community, across the globe. However, certain elements are admittedly peculiar to South Asian Christianity: a close identification with minorities in North-East India, Bangladesh, and Burma/Myanmar; the widespread acceptance of the Vedanta caste system, especially in India and Pakistan, where four fifths of Christians are despised *dalits*; and an uncertain or clearly subordinated position for women. They are the local equivalents of the "blasphemies" associated with class, gender, race and ethnicity which form the basis of powers and principalities, ecclesial and otherwise, across the world.[1]

This chapter will focus on the socio-cultural and liturgical interaction between Christianity and its contexts in mainland South Asia. There are three reasons why this crossroads of languages, peoples, and traditions is currently one of the most important regions for sociological and theological reflection on Christianity or, more properly, a collage of contextualized Christianities.

The first, and simplest, reason is longevity. Christians have been present in South Asia longer than almost anywhere else outside the Eastern Mediterranean.[2] Orthodoxy first came to Taxila (Pakistan) and to Kerala (India) in 52 CE (or perhaps a little later), where they had to deal with the local Jewish

---

communities, just as their stay-at-home cousins in Palestine were negotiating with and, if necessary, moving away from Judaism. This ancient history and the processes of religious negotiation are not only a rich source of historical knowledge but also contain lessons of immense value for Christianity's encounter with modernity.

Secondly, all Christian denominations in their various versions are present throughout South Asia. With its firm ties both to Damascus and to the upper Kerala castes, Orthodoxy is still an economic and religious controlling force. Pentecostalism had flamed in Assam in 1905, before the Azuza Street Revival in Los Angeles, USA in 1906 claimed precedence, and is now quickly spreading through indirect influence on other mainline churches and through direct local mission and church planting. Portuguese Roman Catholicism of the early sixteenth century essayed to eliminate what they called "paganized" Orthodoxy, an adjective Jesuit missionaries readily used to describe Indian society in general, alleging its incapacity for independent thought, moral order or chastity.[3] Faltering by the early nineteenth century,[4] the Catholic Church has now resumed the contextualizing task initiated to an extent by Italian missionaries of that earlier period such as Roberto de Nobili and Constanzo Giuseppe Beschi. In the intervening years this task was forbidden across all Asia until Vatican II lifted bans on local practices and removed offensive acts such as anointing the newly baptised with the priest's saliva. Lutherans from Germany working in a Danish enclave ordained the first *sudra* pastor in 1729 and indeed the first *dalit*, and arguably offered the first Western-originating education based not on political or ecclesial aims (the Portuguese basis) but rather on the need for individuals of any social background to read the Bible in their own language. Anglicans, initially there to serve their countrymen in the East India Company and early colonial territories, became enmeshed in Empire after 1857. This could be to their advantage at times, enabling informal as well as formal ties between the missionaries and the British government, although long-term the benefits were dubious. Whether Anglican missionaries accepted or as often as not rejected the ties, they had to negotiate them, and that affected approaches to church and conversion.[5] Baptists, initially led by the brilliant linguist and missionary Carey in Bengal and Serampore, took up the baton in Lower Burma under Judson after the earlier Jesuit mission there collapsed. Together with Presbyterians, Baptists, both American and British, also missionized much of North East India and parts of the north-west of what is now Pakistan. Many denominations had and some still have a particular mission brief or region: Naga Baptists or Mizo Presbyterians within or beyond India, Kerala Pentecostals in North India, the united Churches of North and of South India, the 160 Roman Catholic dioceses across the four countries (i.e., India, Pakistan, Bangladesh, and Burma/Myanmar), the small but still important number of locally initiated or Christian-oriented independent churches.[6] (Beyond this scope of this chapter but likely to increase in importance is the

South Asian Christian diaspora, especially people originating from Pakistan and in terms of numbers those from India.)

Thirdly, while religious pluralism has suddenly become an important theological issue since Christianity in North America and Europe has had to live with difference, it is and has long been second nature in South Asia. As Wesley Ariarajah and Thomas Thangaraj have neatly stated this issue, my other-practicing neighbor and her faith is to be respected in herself and for herself, as she is, and not as conversion fodder or as an "anonymous Christian" (to use Karl Rahner's expression) who is "really" Christian without knowing it.[7] While naming traditions inevitably gives a false impression of essentialized uniformity, and can be taken advantage of by various political or religious constituencies, it may be useful to indicate something of the multi-layered nature of South Asian religious pluralism with its considerable number of options available. Pakistan and Bangladesh are the home to Muslims of various strands, accepted or abhorred by the state (e.g., the Ahmadies in Pakistan) as well as Christians and Buddhists and Hindus, and parallel or interwoven strands of those traditions. Burma/Myanmar is largely Buddhist, yet localized relations to spiritual forces predominate among the largely Christian minorities and, indeed, the Bamah Buddhist majority and small Muslim Rakhine minority. With its Hindu majority agglomerated from all the local and varied relations to the visible and less visible world, India has the third largest Muslim population in the world. Together with Buddhist, Parsi, Sikh, Jain, locally limited traditions, and 3.5% Christians, India has the broadest religious palette of the mainland South Asian region.

Local Basics

Living with religious differences has been and is normal in South Asia. Of course these differences are not always respected, and when politicized by unscrupulous leaders, they may give rise to violence. This region, therefore, with its full complement of socio-political realities, may well be crucial for understanding world religions in general and Christianity in particular, the most widespread and most numerous tradition. For Christians, in South Asia as well as elsewhere, the history of South Asian Christianity can offer epic cautionary tales.

Thoroughly Western-educated elites in South Asian countries, in common with their Euro-America mates and elsewhere, have often abandoned the often derided local or folk traditions within what we call religion and adopted the formally codified and acceptable universal codes. Actually, of course, each region in the world tends to perceive these "global codes" through somewhat local lenses, and so the break may be more imagined than real. But before swift and dramatic mobility became the norm in the last few decades for a very small number of the world's inhabitants, deluding us into assuming that it is now the norm for all,[8] people in each locality related and usually continue to relate to the spiritual forces of their own river-basin, desert, plateau or forest settlements and special sites therein. The style and detail of this relationship vary regionally and, as elsewhere in the world, exhibit an extraordinary resilience and longevity. In South Asia, the north-west is oriented more to the Persian-Indus world-view, whereas the north-east including Myanmar inclines more to South-East Asian ways of being. The South Asian heartland shares historical and cultural links with both the north eastern and western regions, yet it too has its own particular relationship to those perennial human issues of goodness, disaster, and death. Both overall and diffusely in those three Southern Asian "ways of being", we find particular physical representations of the less visible in special niches or items in homes and indeed in the very making of homes for the human and "the other"; in acts of piety and in collective rituals, frequently efficacious only when all act in concert; and in the setting aside of special places – waters, caves, tree clusters, rocks, hills and other holy sites – where the visible and less visible may be especially close.

It may be helpful to assume that South Asians (including as a third option those who have intentionally abstracted themselves from the daily round as saints and sadhus) envisage a particular relationship to place and space, and a particular relationship to people. While in no way an either-or distinction, the people could perhaps be envisioned as a vertical bounded "cylinder" enclosing family, community and ethnic group or a horizontally layered "cake" of ranked castes. The cylinders of Nagas and Mizos, Kui and Veddas, Hunza, Chin and Kachin, define the immediate locally-based or originating groups which have less resonance beyond themselves. Each layer of the cake represents a caste – Brahmin, Kshatriyas, Vaishyas, and Sudras – together with those dalits beneath the plate, and has significance beyond the residential region, to the ends of the earth. This aspect of the underlying local text, cylinder or layer, may well still be the unspoken accompaniment in the negotiating between an incoming tradition such as Christianity and a "census-defined religion" such as Hinduism, Islam, Sikhism, Buddhism, and Jainism, especially, though not exclusively, in rural areas.

The passage of time and the early arrival of Islam, (trade-led, as was Judaism) was eventually formalised in the colonizing Mogul Muslim Empire which came down from the north-west. The third wave of Christian entry into South Asia amid the burgeoning nineteenth century expansionist enterprises, negotiated with and affected all local traditions as each codified its fundamental scriptural, historical, philosophical and performed texts into definable and legally defensible streams called Islam,[9] Buddhism, Zoroastrianism,[10] and Hinduism. Such internally evolving demarcations were pushed along by expectations of census making colonists, filling in their slots. Indeed, the nineteenth-century comparative religion scholar Max Müller argued that "religious reform movements in Hinduism were the most enduring result of the [Christian] missionary effort in India."[11]

Time also brought formal European colonialism to this entire region, gradually completed with the creation of "British India" from an assemblage of principalities and localities, with Burma and the north-east (Nagaland, Mizoram, etc.) remaining as separate appendages until 1885 and 1947 respectively. The eventual dissolution of this legal, linguistic, religious and ethnic collage at Independence in 1947 into three and later four separate countries, each with its own Christian population derived from various ethnicity, history, politics, and religion, has had different effects, which will be discussed as this chapter progresses. Here I will merely point out that one outcome of the ubiquity and skill with which local and personal identity and religion (not necessarily beliefs) are merged and utilized may account for the fact that a higher percentage of South Asians are Christian now than was the case at Independence.

Given the near two millennia of Christian presence in mainland South Asia, any consideration of the relation of that faith to the region amounts to a social history of the complex religious and sociological processes of contextualization. This did not always move smoothly onward to some spiritually satisfying amalgam acceptable to all concerned, which was hardly surprising. First, the incomers tended to assume a lack of agency, interest, or capacity among South Asians. Secondly, the sheer geographical size, linguistic complexity, economic strength and political tensions in the region make for complex contexts. Thirdly, local assumptions about the non-exclusive nature of religious belonging were firmly held in the region by all but the Muslim and Jewish elites. General issues of politics, of power over people, ignorance, and racism, also played their parts.

In the second section of the chapter I discuss some processes of the early contextualizing of the Orthodox and the Roman Catholic Churches in South India. This is followed by a brief discussion of certain indigenizing patterns which developed in the north from the Indus to the Irrawaddy, and the highlighting of some Protestant approaches. The final section assesses the contemporary situation of Christianity in South Asia, with reference to church-made stumbling blocks, especially in terms of ethnicity and caste, and state-made problems leading to severe restriction and persecution.

In order to come to any conclusion about the relation of church to context at both the surface levels of architecture, dress, music, linguistic register and the deeper socio-philosophical levels with their theological challenge, a few preliminary remarks about contextualization and what is rather hopefully seen as its doppelganger, inculturation, will be helpful. In this I rely on the anthropologist Anthony Gittins.[12] Contextualization represents the minimal accommodation necessary to enable communication, such as an appropriate and comprehensible language; to reduce gratuitous and unintended offence in ritual and social interaction; and to use local forms of building, music, dress and aesthetics. A sufficiently common language is essential for conveying one's idea to another person. Avoiding offence might seem an obvious need, though the history of the church shows that "the only right way" at times overrode "the only courteous way". Local aesthetics were also not as smoothly accepted as they might have been, not only because matters of taste are often learnt slowly by missionaries, but also because certain items were regarded by the Church as belonging to the heathen practices to be rejected; they did not see their own tradition as contextualized. Moreover, as Gittins points out, a new lexicon, as a new element of material culture, sits ill, indeed can be meaningless, atop a thoroughly different underlying grammar. Inculturation is the near-revolutionary challenge posed by the Christian faith to the underlying structure in which each person and group is unreflectingly enculturated. It is a challenge which must be taken up from within a context and not one that can be done to or for that context, those people, from the outside or, indeed, by elite insiders for their subordinates.

The Early Christian Presence in Mainland South Asia

Clericalism was not yet a church feature when Syrian Christians first settled in India. Wherever it existed, the Early Church was a collection of more or less autocephalic church clusters, with no set scripture until the fourth century, with overall leadership and core doctrines either undefined or disputed.[13] Before considering Christian contextualization in South Asia, therefore, we need to appreciate that it was a pre-Ephesus (431) and pre-Chalcedonian (451) Christianity which unfolded there at some point between 52 and 356 CE. One branch of the Orthodox Church in South Asia was and is clearly Monophysite (Jacobite) – not because it is "Oriental", but simply because it is non-Chalcedonian.[14]

Given the vital importance of the Thomas Christians, as they came to be called, in my discussion of the contextualization of Christianity in South Asia, I begin with the Thomas Christians' experience in relation to the local inter-religious situation of South India. Next, I consider the vastly more difficult sixteenth-century intra-religious clashes between the local Orthodox and the incoming Roman Catholic Portuguese "brothers in Christ". The history bears out the common tendency for "family fights" to be especially unpleasant.

South Indian St Thomas Christian communities, which again saw large-scale immigrations in the ninth century, moved with the monsoon winds from Syria and Persia southward, and established a pattern of church life and relations to local political and religious ideologies which lasted until the Portuguese came in the early sixteenth century. Indeed, given that only they, among all Christians in South Asia, are regarded in contemporary India as "local", those relations arguably still endure. They followed a tradition of "religion with trade", and during the decline of the Roman Empire, they linked west and east, "furthering economic cohesion and providing suitable conditions for the first phase of globalization".[15] Agents working on behalf of church leaders had fleets of trading ships, some Roman Catholic and Orthodox churchmen being directly involved in trade.

The Syrian Orthodox in India ran their own church affairs through the Indian-based Metropolitan ("Archdeacon of all the Indies and beyond") answerable ecclesially only to Syria. They were integrated firmly into the local social system, "Syrians" fitting in at the Brahmin level, and they too could remove impurity from the polluted by a touch. While they may have shown unity externally, internally the Syrian Orthodox (similar to the Cochin Jews[16]) divided people into those tracing lineal descent through male or female directly back to the incoming Syrians (the "really pure") from people who had intermarried with Indians (the "less pure"): intermarriage between the two was excluded. Church life was run through a system of lay and clergy assemblies, *yogam*, similar to the governing pattern in Hindu temples. The general assembly dealt with overall church policies for the entire region and was chaired by the archdeacon, with local assemblies of clergy and laity in every church or parish. Any candidate for priesthood must get the formal agreement of his local *yogam,* maintaining the earlier role of the laity, which was diminished in the other "world church" at time, the Roman Catholic.

Ritual was also influenced by Hindu and Muslim custom: a worshipper bathed and put on fresh clothes before leaving for church, feet being washed anew at the door for external as well as internal purity. Before collective or private prayer, each person prostrated and kissed the floor twice. Services on feast and fast days lasted up to ten hours. Communion, in line with early church practice, was given in both kinds, rice-cakes and palm wine sometimes substituting for bread and grape wine; a leavened loaf was broken and given to all.[17]

The Thomas Christians enjoyed a certain level of independence under the Rajah of Cochin, civil delicts being dealt with by the church, not the Hindu state. In a sense the Thomas Christians were an established church in and serving a Hindu state. Part of the import-export trade from the Indian Ocean to the Red Sea, the Syrian Orthodox in India moved from importing Roman amphoras to exporting pepper, pearls, and emeralds[18] and, like the Nayars, their caste equals, they were landowners. They also acted as protectors for seventeen or eighteen categories of artisans, such as toddy tappers, who appealed to the Christians to redress any problem, and who supported them almost as their feudal lords, even at the risk of their life. Clearly stipulated in their relationship, though, was that no non-Christian worker could be asked or expected to convert, though conversion was not forbidden.

The Thomas Christians' vital pre-Portuguese niche, however, was the military, with 50 000 of them fighting for the Raja of Cochin, from whom they received privileges such as riding elephants, having gatehouses and carpets, and using umbrellas.[19] The Rajah also rewarded them by building churches, the Christians in turn sponsored Hindu temples. In fact, church and temple usually shared an adjacent block making one whole "sacred space."[20] When, for various reasons, the election of an archdeacon could not be formally confirmed by Syria, it would be confirmed the Rajah, for the church was an integral if internally separate part of the state. Apart from the fact that the Rajah was a Hindu, it was not dissimilar to the situation in Europe of the time when elected church officials had to be acceptable to the state.[21]

The First Attack on Contextualized South Asian Christianity

Acceptable though Syrian Orthodoxy was to the local polity and presumably also to the local Christians, it was challenged by the later incoming Christians who saw correct faith in Christ as given to, even owned by, them. The pattern of European and later EuroAmerican "ownership" of the correct theological, liturgical, and sociological ways of being Christian recurred throughout the second half of the last millennium in South Asia, within and beyond direct colonial control, and is worth a close look.

This tightly-knit community of inculturated Indian Christians survived easily until European Christians arrived from Portugal with their guns and Latin missals. They quickly established the *padroado* system, a papal agreement with Iberian kings allowing them to deploy clerics and run the churches in all their colonies. The small town of Goa, taken in 1507, saw Franciscans, Dominicans, Jesuits and others actively missionizing and, unlike the caste-conscious, politically dependent and cautious Thomas Christians, they tried converting Hindus where they could. Initially, Catholics accepted that the two churches shared one faith, and that local custom was not intrinsically wrong.[22] But as Portuguese power and local opposition grew, so did attacks by Catholics on both Hindus and Thomas Christians, for "anything that was not in Latin was heretical or schismatic".[23] Relations became increasingly difficult. The new comers, from the mid to the end of the sixteenth century, used all their power to eliminate "heresy," just as they eliminated Portuguese *conversos* and even some Hindus through the Inquisition, which was introduced to Goa in 1560. The line between heavy persuasion and force for Hindus to convert became increasingly thin: only Christians could use Portuguese law-courts, get government jobs, be free from forced labor, and rent state land. Some peasants converted for greater freedom, as did a large group of fishermen who thereby got Portuguese naval support against Muslim sailors.[24] Missionaries at the time and shortly thereafter saw the "favours" shown to Christians as justification for promoting conversion. Brahmins also converted, possibly to retain their power base, as a Jesuit writing a century later noted,[25] and present circumstances seem to support this view.[26] The tie made then between the two religious elite groups continues to this day in Goa.

The degree of accommodation between Roman and Orthodoxy was initially influenced by Portuguese uncertainty as well as, perhaps, by generosity. However, church reforms after the Council of Trent (1545–1563) progressively pressured the Syrians. They were forced to accept the decisions of the dubiously legal and pastorally disastrous 1599 Synod of Diamper, held to "purify all the Thomas churches of heresy, take away all their heretical books, and extinguish the Syrian language".[27] The thoroughly contextualized Thomas Christians had to adopt new doctrines and practices: veneration of icons and of the cross indicative of "respectful worship"; confirmation separate from baptism; clerical celibacy (though Syrian bishops, like all Orthodox, had been single); the doctrine of purgatory (from which the prayers of the living could deliver the dead); restriction of wine to the clergy at the Eucharist.

These prescriptions were derived from a Euro-centred view of the "correct way" of being a Christian. They affected not only long-established Churches but also mission workers trying to fit into local conditions, arguably in accordance with the apostolic precept.[28] Blaming racism (which did play a part) or sheer ignorance is inadequate. Rather the crucial factor was the ecclesial desire to control the text and its performance in all contexts, as is the assumption (still with us in recent missions within or beyond South Asia) that the power-holder's possession of "The [only way of seeing] Truth" cannot be compromised.[29]

A Second Attack on Contextualized South Asian Christianity

In Tamil Nadu, the accommodating efforts of the Jesuit De Nobili (1577–1656) led him to become a scholar of Sanskrit, write vernacular texts, live the ascetic, vegetarian life of the people whom he wished to convert, and keep all the rules of purity and separation. He succeeded in converting a segment of Brahmins and only interacted with that caste, allotting the task of converting lower castes to a separate mission group. The Italian De Nobili made clear that he was not a *Parangi* [Portuguese] but a *sannyasi* from Rome, born to a Rajah's family. He insisted that converts could follow the purity and pollution rules to the full, adding an extra "sacred thread" of the Trinity to the thread worn by all the twice born. Brahmins thus joined the Christian ranks as Brahmins, not equals of all.

Unlike his confrere Matteo Ricci (1552–1610) in China who compared the Old Testament to the Chinese classics in a prefiguring of the fulfilment theology of religion, De Nobili followed the Brahmin ways to the letter in an effective contextualizing strategy.[30] His efforts, however, were squashed in the 1744 proscription of the so-called Malabar Rites. While the Chinese Rites, also banned then, viewed the person primarily as a social-civic unit, the Malabar Rites affected the person as a unit of social purity. Practices for which de Nobili had got permission from Rome were henceforth decided upon by people who had no knowledge of India. Baptism must include breathing on the candidate and touching the lips and ears with the thumb moistened in saliva, actions locally regarded as polluting. In addition, the use of Hindu names, child marriage, public celebration of menarche, performance by Christian musicians at Hindu festivals, caste marks, and the reading of Hindu books were banned. The change was not completed overnight, but clearly "toleration" of other ways was an act of power by the tolerant, and it could be withdrawn at will and, indeed, on a whim.

De Nobili was not the only Jesuit to accommodate to the Malabar culture in liturgy and lifestyle. His compatriot Beschi (1680–1747), even more skilled in Tamil than de Nobili in Sanskrit, wrote religious rebuttals of Protestantism, specifically Lutheran Pietism, tracts against the German-Danish mission, a catechism, and a guide for catechists, the latter still used by Catholics and Protestants alike. He wrote a grammar of Tamil, and two dictionaries, Latin-Tamil and Portuguese-Tamil. His best-known Tamil texts are devotional poems, covering the Old Testament and the birth, ministry and life of Christ. Like Ricci, he too translated Tamil classics into Latin, clearly recognizing the high literary status of classical Tamil.[31] Beschi also fitted into the local lifestyle, though in his case, he emulated the rulers as he rode on decorated elephants, an umbrella held high above his beturbaned head and bejewelled body, draped in the silks and satins of a Tamil prince.

Contextualization in Early Roman Catholicism Elsewhere in South Asia

The Christian mission in the caste-influenced societies of South Asia followed the same pattern beyond South Asia during this period. One clear exception was that to Buddhist Yangon, and of course, to the Moghul (Mughal) Empire of northern South Asia centred on Agra and then Delhi. While that Empire was Muslim, it was not uninfluenced by caste.

Theology and liturgy represent but one aspect of contextualization; the material arts also have their place. Buildings that were quickly erected in South Asia for living and worshipping may well have received local influences from the masons and carpenters but they have not survived. In the more northerly part of South Asia, as in South India, there are churches, or remains of churches, in the Indus-Irrawady which echo the Gothic churches of sixteenth century Europe. Architectural plans from Europe were executed by amateur local craftsmen.

The Jesuits and the other religious orders built churches in Dhakka (1677), Lahore (1579), Delhi (decayed and then destroyed), and Madurai which combined Hindu-Muslim Bengali and Hindu Dravidian styles or included elements from those traditions. A chapel at Agra (1611) follows the plan of a Muslim tomb. That city, while still the Moghul capital, found Jesuits teaching Christianity through pictures which arguably influenced the Moghul miniatures.[32] Other churches however were straight imports from Europe, a tradition which has endured, perhaps indicating missionaries were unwilling to risk "syncretism". The proscriptions of 1744 made any attempt to build churches in the local style, had there been any, practically impossible. Adding a locally inspired trope to a European church building in South Asia was and is as irrelevant to any deeper negotiation as a frangipani-garlanded Mary addressed in alien language and gesture. It took the virtual demise of Catholicism in South Asia and its nineteenth- and twentieth-century resurgence, along with growth in other churches, for more effective contextualization to resume and begin to be visible in some church architecture of all denominations.

Protestant Contextualization – the Pietists

The theological difference between Lutheran Pietist and Tridentine Roman Catholicism was reflected in their attitude toward church formation in South India. Pietism, whether from Halle – the mission base of the first two missionaries to Malabar in 1706, Bartholomäus Ziegenbalg and Heinrich Plütschau – or the form espoused by Nicolaus von Zinzendorf (1700–1760), stressed the call by the Spirit rather than book-learning as the essential criterion for being a pastor, prayer groups and meetings rather than elaborate liturgy, and in that early period little difference between clergy and laity. The intention was to found an indigenous church. While Beschi translated catechisms, the Pietists immediately if inaccurately began to translate the Bible, print their initial version on an SPCK press from London with Tamil characters made in Halle, set up schools with translated textbooks to educate students for a trade or profession, and train catechists in a seminary. This all-round practical and biblical training arose from the demand for personal, not group conversion, the capacity for each member to read and know the Bible, and the devolution of responsibility to all members. (Later groups such as the outcaste (*dalit*) Chamars were converted en masse, but then baptized one by one.)

Ziegenbalg was competent in classical Tamil, which he could also write in a manner more accessible to the average Tamil of the area. He studied and wrote on Brahmanic Hinduism, completing his major work *Genealogie der malabarischen Götter* completed in 1713.[33] However, Ziegenbalg, as de Nobili, had problems with his European mission-sending agency, for his missionising method was not appreciated back home. His Halle director, August Francke (1663–1727) wrote scathingly that he had been sent "to extirpate heathenism not spread heathenish nonsense in Europe"; the book was not published in Germany for another 154 years. Ziegenbalg noted in passing: "I remember many learned people in Europe have written on the manner in which the heathen ought to be converted, but there was no difficulty in this [for them] as there was no one but themselves to contradict."[34]

Ziegenbalg's attitude toward other faiths was respectful, recognizing their leaders as his equals. Talking to an imam who had visited him in difficult times, he said: "If we begin by improving ourselves God will show us a way out of the corruption of the present." He made no attempt to convert or critique the imam, for "we are both priests".[35]

The first Indian pastor was ordained in 1733. In a process begun by the community in 1729, just 20 years after the mission began, he was chosen by the community – though only after the King of Denmark agreed to the process, another example of state control over church. At the meeting to start the selection process – done in the same way as back in Germany – the pastor said: "We have decided to ordain a man who belongs to you and your nation.... He will be able to deal with the people in the country more efficiently that we could ever do; he will preach the Word of God and administer the sacrament.... If a person is called and equipped by the Holy Spirit for this work, no other qualification is necessary. God is not partial."[36] Several people were available for ordination; the first chosen, Aaron, was a *sudra*. When he became ill, the possibility of ordaining Naikan, a *dalit*, arose. The mission wrote home to Halle: "We desired to ordain him priest, which we could if his work were confined to the pariahs. But the Christians of higher caste avoid coming into contact with such people. We take great pains to lessen these prejudices among Christians: but to a certain degree they must be taken into consideration. But we should hesitate to have the Lord's Supper administered by him lest it diminish the regard of Christians of higher caste for that sacrament itself."[37]

The decision not to ordain Naikan came after the Roman Catholic decision to ordain only Brahmins as priests, an example of the way the two different denominations and cultural groups (for the Pietists were not from the elite) wished or were able to pursue their goals. The work of the Pietist mission was directed to both the relative elite and the masses – which at times caused the elite no little anxiety over continued control of the "lower ranks." As in Roman Catholic church buildings, at least where these did not actually exclude the lower castes, *sudra* men sat on one side of the nave and *dalit* on the other, with the two categories of women filling each transept. Dalit children were dressed in European clothes and were named in and taught Portuguese. An effort by one Lutheran missionary to eliminate caste in church and schools failed. Used by the East India Company to supply trained clerks and doing trade-education for any attending their schools, the Pietists were integrated into the local political and social context at all levels, produced a wide variety of literature in local languages, again at all levels, and trained pastors, catechists, and mission workers.

The Baptists

So far, we have focused not only on attitudes to and of South Asian Christians as part of overall attitudes to social and ethnic otherness, but to linked processes in a South Asian Christianity wedded to Hindu-originating caste which was also evident among Muslims. The Syrian Orthodox Church benefitted from maintaining the social status quo, as did the Roman Catholic Church in its own territories and elsewhere, where religious orders such as the Capuchins did work with the *sudras* but were less involved with the *dalits*. Lutheran missionaries, who came from the middle and lower classes in Europe, saw the caste system as a theological and moral problem which they were unable to overcome in the short term.

The fourth group I shall look at are the Baptists. They deserve special consideration not only because they appear to have managed the caste issue more effectively, but also because their mission across north-ern-east South Asia included groups that are organized not by caste layers but by ethnic "cylinders." Moreover, these peoples were not part of the Sanskritic or Arabic-oriented religious traditions but rather related to the less visible world in a locally-limited manner. This is true of Lower Burma, where the American Baptist Adoniram Judson, Jr. (1788–1850) began mission work with the Chin in 1820, following on from Felix Carey, in Orissa among the Kui and Khonds from the 1830s, and later in the century in Nagaland, where American and British Baptists worked more or less together.

William Carey (1761–1834), an English Baptist cobbler, went out to Calcutta in 1793, and was given a job by a Baptist employee with the British East India Company, which prohibited mission on its lands. He soon moved to the Danish mission enclave of Serampore, where he learnt Bengali and other local languages. In 1801 he produced the first Bengali Bible, following the Protestant tradition of biblical literacy. Caste was set aside from the start, the first convert's daughter, a *sudra* carpenter, marrying a Brahmin convert. Carey became Professor of Oriental Languages at what was to become the part of the University of Calcutta. Following the Pietist and Christian Brethren pattern of pooling resources, he and his fellow Baptists used any spare money earned from outside work to support more translation work.

Mastery of the local languages and Bible translation were the key means for their learning of the new context and their significant contributions to the material and spiritual well-being of the converts.

We have seen how all church groups needed to negotiate some modus vivendi with the local power-holders, and Carey was no different. Interestingly, however, his initial secular "helpers" tended to be the East India Company soldiers who translated Gospel texts and Sunday School materials into minority languages they knew and for which they developed a writing system. The Khonds of western Orissa, for example, gained access to the new faith and to literacy in this manner, though they did not actually convert until the twentieth century, of their own volition, after the missionaries and indeed the British had departed.[38]

Indeed it is not unreasonable to suggest that in addition to the indigenization of church architecture, sacred vestments, theology and liturgy, increasingly competent translation of the Bible into local languages was both an example of contextualization and an increasingly important (if often politically unwelcome to the state) contribution to the ethnic identity of minority readers. This was especially the case for those people despised on all sides as pagan, heathen, or kaffir and confined to their locations.

Laity and the Expansion of Christianity

When mission workers, expatriate or local, began to work with people of localised rather than theoretically more universal traditions, the tendency was to regard them as less intellectually capable and less powerful. Their restricted mobility and hence their limited contacts with the outside world increased their powerlessness and scarcity of options. It is not surprising that it was only when they could assert their identity that their conversion in large numbers occurred. This moment often coincided with political independence and the departure of missionaries. Isolated peoples suddenly became a minority in a vast sea of Hindus or Muslims, and in order to establish their separate identity, these rural people, so often seen as "unthinking hicks", rationally decided to convert to Christianity.

Similar patterns developed in Lower Burma with Judson's work among the Chin from 1820 and by later missionaries among the Karen, Shan, and Kachin. The same thing was true of the work of Protestant missions in the Chittagong Hills of what is now Bangladesh, and of Welsh Presbyterians and Baptists missionizing in Mizo and Naga of North East India from 1854. In each case, the most vital agents of mission were local people.[39]

There was always, and almost everywhere, especially among so-called "animists", an attempt by missionaries to wipe out and practices regarded as belonging to religion. Prohibited were, for example, the sacred "sky-room" in the house among the Kachin, rituals which involved giving food to the less visible or spirit world, any killing of animals in a collective ritual, and usually, especially among Baptist and often other Reformed Christians, the drinking of alcohol. (Anglicans and Roman Catholics behaved similarly, though they tended to be less bothered about alcohol consumption.)

In contextualizing the Gospel, efforts by missionaries to sort out what pertains to religion and what to culture or social relations, were legion, and they were frequently if not inevitably accompanied by misunderstanding and unfortunate outcomes. For example, one practice in local religious traditions is that all who live in the place must contribute to any communal ritual, since incomplete participation reduces its efficacy. When reading the report by the earliest Naga missionary in 1891 that "For the village feasts and revels and for the old demon worship, taxes were levied on the Christians which must be paid or their property confiscated",[40] the reader should be aware that the contribution was demanded from all the residents of the village and not just Christians whose attendance was proscribed.

If the work of contextualization were to be carried out by expatriate missionaries, it would likely be based on inadequate understanding and perhaps even vitiated by the desire for control. Even a native catechist, if he or she had been educated in mission schools from an early age, would rarely understand custom fully and would, moreover, work from a natural-supernatural split. However, where catechists were fully conversant with both systems, they could be of great help in moving beyond the surface appearance to the deep structure. A catechist in Central India in 1908 saw a Gond man about to sacrifice a small goat. A foreign missionary would tend to link the action to "devil-worship and other heathen behaviour". The catechist did not but rather "explained the object of sacrifice in ancient times and that he was right to offer a kid to appease his god for his sins but that it was a symbol of Jesus who would become incarnate and shed his blood for all mankind".[41] Both actions, the local and the ancient biblical, were seen as prefiguring Christ and neither was deemed wrong for its time.

John N. Farquhar, Thomas E. Slater and other theologians who developed the "fulfilment theology" of religion in the nineteenth century might well have said the same thing had the sacrifice been in the Hindu context. But this was a local religion, which had never been sufficiently respected to be seen as a "prefiguring" of Christianity. Furthermore, the catechist was just jotting down his everyday practices as he developed them. This approach, and those of other catechists who did not accept the "devil-in-everything-local" view of some though not all foreign mission workers, lays the foundation for inculturation which engenders *faith* rather than approved liturgical *action*. Such inculturation takes place through a dynamic and critical interface between religious systems which themselves undergo change as they interact with each other and with outside events.

The growth of the Pentecostal movement in South Asia during the twentieth century was also, to a considerable extent, a result of the mobilization of lay people. It too received guidance from beyond the region. Assam had been influenced by the Welsh and early Scottish Presbyterian "spirit-led" missions from the mid-nineteenth century, which also linked this region to Korea. In Kerala and Tamil Nadu, the movement was led by two American Pentecostal ministers, Robert F. Cook (1880–1958) and George E. Berg from 1913, and by several formerly Syrian Orthodox ministers such as K.E. Abraham (1899–1974). Some of the rifts and unions in the developing Pentecostal churches related to tensions between expatriate and local ministers in the decades before Independence in 1947, while other problems concerned tension within the churches between *dalit* and Syrian streams. The early Pentecostals were so closely linked to the *dalit* that Orthodox converts who joined them were automatically regarded as belonging to a lower caste, even though they still expected to retain their superior status. As a *dalit* wrote: "when [Cook] departed, the Indian managers could not uphold the heart of the pioneer and the old baggage of Syrian traditional evils crept into the missionaries' church."[42] Simplicity of life, the rejection of caste within churches, and the prohibition of gold jewelry for women have been markers of Pentecostal adherents.[43] If, as alluded above, it is difficult to reconstruct an accurate picture of the activities of catechists alluded above, it is even more so in the case for low-ranking Pentecostal workers since it seems they did not have to keep a diary of activities for their supervisor.[44]

From the 1920s the Pentecostals also worked in Upper Burma. Healing was a core aspect of both ordained and the much commoner lay ministry, and each community was almost entirely self-supporting. Pentecostals' attitude to Buddhism as well as to local religious traditions tended to be even more negative than those of other denominations, though that of American Baptists in Burma has lasted until now. Pentecostals, however, often made use of what was they saw as a lively spirit world within locally limited tradition as a bridge to the "middle realm" of Pentecostal theology, one recent Mynamar theologian noting that "supernatural manifestations have often been the means of converting people to Jesus Christ".[45]

Contemporary Contextualisation in South Asia: Church, State, and People

Political independence of South Asia from Britain negatively affected local Christian churches as the new states formed their own identity. As laws against conversion were enacted, the growth of Christianity was restricted, foreign missions reduced if not stopped, and mission schools constrained or nationalized. In 1947, Pakistan was founded as a Muslim state with equality for all citizens and freedom of worship for all. However, 20 years after, life for non-Muslims in Pakistan became trammelled with legal restrictions negating the equality of all citizens before the law.[46] Bangladesh, founded in 1971 after the dissolution of West and East Pakistan, retained such freedoms. Burma/ Myanmar adopted Buddhism as the state religion in 1960, and though this was soon rescinded, state religion has resurfaced in different guises, with open restrictions and covert discrimination against what is seen as an alien or subversive faith of minorities.[47] India remains a secular state, and while in some instances tension (often linked to poverty) between Hindus and Muslims does not involve Christians, they suffer from the negative effects of laws against conversion which is at best tolerated.[48] Toleration, of course, far from being a gesture of justice or lack of interest, is actually an act of domination, the one who tolerates having the capacity to rescind the gesture and constrain the erstwhile beneficiary.

National independence, not only in Hindu-majority India but also in Muslim Bangladesh and Buddhist Burma/Myanmar, also affected minorities who did not see themselves as part of the new nations but rather of this or that territorially-restricted ethnic group or caste. For example, 90 to 95% of Pakistani Christians are Punjabi of the *chura (dalit)* group converted from Hinduism rather than from Islam or local religious systems. Nagaland, to take another example, was not finally made part of India until after 1947. In that year, around 50% of the Nagas were Christian. By 1971, the Indian Census showed that the number had risen to 66% and by 1991, to 87%. The desire to create a distinct identity may be one factor for such increased conversion among minorities who were thrust into a new political situation. In Burma/ Myanmar, the refusal of people of the Shan State to accept Bamar rule may also be inspired by the increased Christian presence there, which was also an issue in the states of the Chin, now 90% Christian, and the Karen, around 50%. The hill-peoples of Bangladesh such as the Khasi, Santal, Pahari also seemed to prefer Christianity to Islam for socio-cultural reasons if they wish to opt for a tradition which is viable beyond local boundaries.

In pre-Independence India covering all four contemporary countries, Christians made up .99% of the population according to the 1901 census, and 1.79 according to that of 1931, the last full census under colonial rule. While figures need to be treated with caution, India's first post-Independence census showed 2% were Christian, rising to 2.6% in 1971, and dropping back to 2.34% in 2001: Kerala has the highest proportion of Christians, at 29%. However, Indian laws stipulate that the *dalit* and other scheduled castes lose their benefits on conversion to Christianity. This legal stipulation is based on the view that Christianity other than Syrian Orthodoxy (with no conversion of *dalit* possible) is not an Indian faith tradition but an alien import. As a result, the above figures may not accurately reflect the number of those who are baptized but retain a previous adherence for official purposes and those who "follow Christ" privately. Under 2% of the Pakistan population are Christian, and similar political issues mean that there too, figures do not reflect actual adherence, for converts are at risk of life and limb: in Bangladesh the figure is less than 0.5%. Burma/Myanmar currently has the highest percentage of Christians of pre-1947 India, at 5% of the population, with several minorities being overwhelmingly Christian.

Violent Attacks Against Christian Churches

Recent events in South Asia, especially in Pakistan and certain areas of India such as Orissa, have certainly affected the willingness of people to identify themselves formally as Christian. Such anxiety would not have been seen as normal in the past, though the events of the Partition of India in 1947 should stop us from assuming that the different faiths inevitably rub along nicely.

At the level of the neighborhood, communities, however, religious differences do not generally create problems, with people sharing different foods, rituals, and festivals. Indeed the idea that only one religion is right and all others wrong was largely an alien concept in the region until rather recently. It is not espoused by Hinduism, the Sufi-influenced Islam of South Asia, or Buddhism. Orthopraxis was usually demanded only by locally-limited religious systems as a condition for common residence.

However, in the last twenty to thirty years, religion in the region has been heavily politicized as part of the local response to economic problems. Religious conflicts have also been fomented by certain segments of the Muslim and Hindu communities, such as Wahhabism and diaspora ideologies, in India and Pakistan and, minimally, in Bangladesh. New agendas have the potential to turn violent. Attacks against Christians as "alien outsiders" increased after Zia Ul Haq's tenure in Pakistan, and persecution in that country, exacerbated by the ease of "blasphemy" accusations and the extreme difficulty for non-Muslims to defend themselves, increases year by year.[49] Violence in parts of India, especially Gujarat and Orissa, accompanied the growth of political groups such as Rashtriya Swayamsevak Sangh (RSS) and Bharatiya Janata Party (BJP), which have at times expressly encouraged attacks on Christians accused of forcing conversions.[50] Both Indian and Pakistani Christians regularly face demands from Hindutva or Islamist groups to convert, or "revert," by a set date to avoid death. Religious conflicts have also been brought about by Buddhist rulers in Burma/Myanmar, Yangon's military suppression of minorities in eastern Burma, and earlier in Chin state, also including attacks against Christians. This particularly affects devout Christian youth, who feel their future prospects within the country will be limited by their faith.

Certain Pentecostal-Charismatic Churches or "mainline" mission-workers from some countries that have recently come to or evolved in India and

Burma/Myanmar (less often Pakistan and Bangladesh) tend to promote the view that only Jesus saves in a very strident, even aggressive, manner. Moreover, they not only preach that no other religion is efficacious, but that all other religions are of the devil – and this may include established Christian traditions. While certainly such views could be heard in the past from mainline churches, such crudities would be rare now. Needless to say, loud antagonistic attitudes worsen the often already difficult life of long-established Christians.

One of the consequences of these tensions is that Christians tend to keep a low profile. Christians in Burma/Myanmar, for example, did not march in Yangon in September 2007 in solidarity with Buddhist monks, in part in order for the church to survive. Nevertheless, the head of the main seminary there urges Christians to "continuously engage aggressively (though not violently) in combating the oppressive structures and evil systems of militarism and globalisation that ruin Myanmar society".[51] Christians in Pakistan do not join other oppressed groups such as the Ahmadies, or Hindus, or secular Muslims in opposing the catch-all laws on blasphemy, and nor did Christian women join other Pakistani women pushing to change Zia ul Haq's misogynist laws.[52] While expecting the worst, they rather hope to survive by avoiding trouble.

While the politicization of social life in South Asia produces tension between States and religious or ethnic minorities, the process of conversion and the accumulation of wealth over the millennia also create conflicts among Christian groups and occasionally make for odd alliances. Major churches in India are great land-owners, especially the Roman Catholic Church and the Church of South India, and this can affect praxis and, one might surmise, theology. Perhaps the most striking result of the unequal distribution of wealth among Christians is exemplified in Goa, which sent two Brahmin Roman Catholic BJP members to the Lok Sabha (the Lower House of the Parliament of India) in 2000. The close collaboration between high caste Hindus [and Catholics] who control the state and high caste Catholics who control the Church leaves little room for the average Goan – and replicates the pattern established five hundred years ago. As Gomes says, Christian Brahmins in Goa continue to be "a dominant caste who occupy some of the highest positions in the administration, clergy and the liberal professions".[53]

Theological, Ecclesial, and Liturgical Contextualization

Given the above-mentioned issues of colonial history and nascent statehood, together with the growing understanding of the need – seen as practically if not always theologically vital – to embed Christianity in the locality, efforts were made by Anglican, the Roman Catholic and some other mainline

Churches in South Asia to contextualize Christianity in the period leading up to Independence.

It was a task fraught then as now, with dangers. "Culture" is so riven with fissures and fractures that drawing a line around it to define "sameness" unavoidably becomes an exercise in power. So it is with the Church, especially ones which had for centuries been defined and controlled from overseas. Monteiro sharply points out that "for the emergence of an alternative [non-hierarchical] model, the church would have to break down boundaries separating the different groups of people; the caste barriers that segregate Christians as high and low; the frontier that cuts off the tribals [minority ethnies] from the mainstream of life, and the biased mentality that relegates women".[54]

If the task is to be done, who decides what is appropriate and what is not? Who wields the power? Where are the dangers? Clearly this is not a new issue, as the boundaries of what is appropriate has already been squabbled over in the various Epistles of Peter and Paul. In a fledgling church, teachers, catechists and clerics will make decisions as they go – neatly ordering the process post hoc in memoirs! But as a group becomes established, formality grows and the charisma accompanying the first months and years is formalized to substantiate the long-held knowledge of the leaders (of whatever group) and, perhaps, to fit into the context.

This is an especially acute problem for a worldwide church that has central authorities with little or no understanding of the local situation. Knowledge according to the centre becomes normative for all, whether the headquarters are located in Paris, Lambeth, Rome, Seoul, Boston or, indeed, Delhi, Yangon, Dhaka or Islamabad. The dangers of contextualization beyond that minimum required for communication are actually less those of "syncretism", that useful slander for whatever is unclear, new, confused or merged. Rather the danger is that of worshiping the culture as defined by the local stake-holders. This is part of the universal history of the church, whether episcopally or congregationally organized. Such worship and maintenance of the local becomes an act of power because it will inevitably exclude those of a different and lesser group, each locality being riven with fissions and fractures, with elites and subordinates.[55] If faith is to become part of life for a group of people, rather than mere outward presentation and performance, and if that is the purpose of ministry and mission, then inculturation must challenge each and every local context. Such a process is risky and involves a loss of power and of authority for certain groups. In comparison, reifying and deifying a "culture" as defined by the stake-holders is a much more pleasant option.

The problem is illuminated most clearly in relation to India, where Roman Catholic, Anglican and some other mainline churches began somewhat unreflectingly using Sanskrit-Vedanta texts and images as equivalent, or a first step, to the Old Testament. The problem with this, however, was that though this philosophical tradition was indeed Indian, it was also the tradition that condemned the *dalit* to their outcaste status. Thus, for those who had become Christian precisely to be equal to other humans, such as the south Indians around Travancore who had been slaves until freed by the churches,[56] the contextualizing church was extolling the instruments of their previous oppression. *Dalit* theology, initiated by Nirmal and others, began to challenge that unfortunate contextualising approach – but change was slow. Contextualising from across the whole spectrum of a group or community, and what may merely look like that process, therefore needs careful examination. The SVD priest and classical dancer Barboza, for example, who tries to express the Gospel in dance, may seem a perfect example of contextualizing. Yet his Sanskrit-based gestures easily become offensive to the *dalit* audience, whose dance and music draw on quite different frames.[57]

This issue is likely to be especially acute in churches with a large proportion of *dalit* members and very few *dalit* church leaders. The Roman Catholic Church has 160 bishops, only six of whom are *dalit*. The Church of South India has 26 bishops, 14 of whom are *dalit*. Moreover these bishops's voice carries less weight than that of those belonging to the *sudra*, just as voices of upper *dalit* are listened to more than those from the bottom of the heap. In theory, Christians in Pakistan should have the least difficulty in this regard given that the origin of most is from *dalit* groups – but in rank-organized societies, rank can always find its way.

But caste is not the only area of tension in inculturation. Ethnicity is another. Where church leaders are drawn from one ethnic group, others are easily left out. Thus any attempt at inculturation is skewed in favour of the churches of the leaders. For instance, if inculuration for Baptists in Burma/Myanmar is done by the Chin, it will reflect their particular understanding of the male-female relationship, females being legally less well off and more potentially polluting than their Karen sisters. This can lead to a plethora of separate churches which each reflect and maintain their own view of life and exclude others. Yet even where such ethnically based churches do expand to other groups, they replicate the early European mission churches, which insisted on fluency in English or another imported language for church work and often worship, by insisting, for example, that all leaders are fluent Mizo speakers. Presbyterians of Mizoram and to a lesser extent Baptists of Nagaland are replicating their particular cultural traditions, just as earlier expatriate missionaries had done with theirs. Recent research makes this abundantly clear:

Hnatlang [core Mizo ideology] created problems in the foreign mission field by its inherent tendency to be the dominating force behind all efforts in the field. Mizo missionaries felt they are the owners of the gospel; they play administration and leadership roles; they manage finance and control construction works. Thus indigenous mission workers and Christians not only lack ownership of the property, finance and authority, but also the gospel.[58]

Pastor Hlawndo writes as an aware Mizo mission worker: the doctoral thesis of a Chin Presbyterian pastor, Lal Tin Hre, over the border in Burma sets out in painful detail just how dominating Mizo ideology and language is for his own non-Mizo group, and, indeed, the constricting effects this has on Presbyterian church growth in Burma.[59]

In addition to the wide reach of caste and territorial expension from an ethnic base, both of which impact on contextualization and any hope of inculturation, the difference between town and country can be another source of tension within churches and for church life. Even where efforts are being made to contextualize, the problem so often is: what is the yard-stick. In India, for example, those *dalit* theologians working in town tend to base their inculturation on an urban understanding and to view country people as both deficient and contaminated with rural gods.

A consequence of all this is a profound dissatisfaction with the inculturating efforts made by mainline churches, especially but not only Protestant, despite continued efforts made by Roman Catholics after Vatican II and by Protestant and Orthodox in World Council of Churches. Where most people in a particular area are Christian, as in certain regions in India and Myanmar, and any of them have an "all things being equal" opportunity to be leaders, conflicts arise less from contextualization as such but from the conflicts in social life. But where contextualization is directed and controlled by an elite who assume they represent the whole community but in fact only their own clique, the problems arising from such a process profoundly undermine the entire church, especially the respect that church members have for one another. This is an issue for both Episcopal and congregational systems.

It may seen unfair to single out one incident as example of stubborn resistance of the elite when challenged by what one might call basic Christian ideals, but the appointment of a *dalit* archbishop to the archbishopric of Hyderabad by the Vatican in 2000 offers the perfect illustration. Of a high caste, the retiring head of the church in Andhra Pradesh, Arulappa, said that his *dalit* successor would work only for the *dalit,* who make up 80% of the archdiocese population. As a *dalit* commentator noted: "Is his comment not a reflection of his own strategy by which he has been supporting his own caste men and women during his 28 year tenure?"[60] Three years passed before Archbishop Joji could function fully to care for his people.

Similarly, a *dalit* man in the Church of South India in Tamil Nadu explained to a theologian-researcher:

We were Untouchables in Hinduism. We came to Christianity hoping for a better life. But there is no equality or respect; we only got a different sort of untouchability and slavery. The priest doesn't care for us and nor do the other since we have nothing to give. We thought that by believing in Yesusami we might be treated as equal human beings with respect, but we don't even get to sit in the same place at church! Our hopes are crushed. When will we have a new life? When will we be included?[61]

The same thing, of course, can be said of women, both within – or below- the caste rankings and in ethnically-organized groups. Women in the Roman Catholic or Orthodox Churches have no realistic expectation of ordination, though some do still hope. As a letter from a group of Indian nuns to Pope John Paul II in 1994 states: "Priests make use of inequality [between us] to their maximum benefit by extracting cheap labour from us.... Doctrines are made out of a culture of dominance and subservience."[62] Churches which ordain women in other parts of the world also ordain them in India, but not in Pakistan, Bangladesh and Burma/Myanmar. Yet even in India, ordained women do not always function as "ministers of word and sacrament" or their equivalents for all but minister exclusively to other women and children. As one side in a squabble in a community of the Church of South India puts it: "The Revd Monica was not to conduct the service from the altar, preach from the pulpit nor celebrate and assist in sacraments."[63] Women in Pakistan and Bangladesh are not yet ordained, out of deference, it is said, to the Muslim majorities.

Chin and Kachin Baptist women in Burma/Myanmar may be ordained if they are and remain single, although married women over the age of 45 may also be ordained; Karen are rather more flexible. The rationale for this policy is the alleged inability of the church to pay for childcare if the minister is a mother. However, given the prevalence of childcare by grandparents, this seems a thin excuse.[64] The cultural-ethnicity argument is also used by leading Anglican clergy there to defend their refusal to ordain women, even though women's ordination was accepted in principle in 1973. A leading Burmese Anglican pointed out in 2007 that women priest were unsuitable in "our Burmese culture."

Seventy percent of Burma/Myanmar's population are Bamah, almost all of whom are Buddhist and with whom Christians do not always have a close tie. Most Burmese Anglicans are Karen, an ethnic group with equal land-owning for males and females, equal access to moveable and heirloom property and the maintenance of ties to a woman's natal group. When I asked the above-mentioned Anglican clergyman what the "cultural problem" would be in such context, I was not surprised by his response: "Well, the women really have to push more if they want to be ordained." He added that for any change in church practice to take place, it must be approved by the synod. Since membership of the synod is half clergy and half lay, 95% of the latter being male, change is not likely to come, despite the church's efforts to have a larger representation of women and youth at the synod.

His appeal to culture having failed to convince, the clergyman then blamed the presence of missionaries, saying that "it will need a revolution to change. When we've gone, the generation of clergy trained by the missionaries, they can change." Given the fact that the decision regarding the theological acceptability of woman ordination in the then Diocese of Rangoon was taken 11 years after the last foreign church staff had left, and by people all of whom had been trained by missionaries, this pretext is hardly more convincing. This is even truer especially now, since almost all the leadership has been trained by local personnel. Yet "culture," this "coherent, cohesive, agreed whole" was nevertheless the clergyman's first and last appeal. That, in South Asia as elsewhere in the world, is unfortunately rather common.[65]

There are situations where even if the church wishes to "speak to the people" in a way they relate to and hear, government prevents it. The Roman Catholic church in the Karen are of Burma/Myanmar, under the leadership of Archbishop Gabriel in the 1970s, was so constrained, perhaps wishing to divide communities by religion. A Karen, the Archbishop established a traditional Karen puppet group, which went round that state playing Gospel stories to all-comers, Christian and Buddhist alike. While security problems could easily be invoked to stop the practice, the understanding is that it was the blurring of boundaries between faith traditions which was the primary cause of objection. That this may well be the case is suggested by a similar outcome when Anglicans in mid-Burma, also in the 1970s, used traditional song-styles and language for community outreach. Any effort by contemporary Myanmar Christians to include Buddhist ways of being a person and practicing faith in Christian liturgy is avoided as part of keeping a low profile, for it is firmly opposed by the authorities.

As we have seen with both caste and gender, in contextualizing the Christian faith the church runs the risk of uncritically accepting local cultural mores and moulding the faith to them. This is clearly the case with regard to caste in the churches of India and Pakistan. Of course, missionaries were not always aware of the contextualized nature of the faith they brought to other countries which is never culturally pure. But they were not the only nor the last people "making the faith" in mission lands in their enculturated image. It is equally possible and equally easy to for local Christians to replicate their local practices in the church.

This practice of uncritically replicating the local culture seen as a single unit in contextualizing the Christian faith has enormous consequences. For instance, a theology student in Bangalore, who is no doubt a firmly contextualized Christian, insisted that beating his wife is an acceptable behavior because it is allowed by his "culture".[66] In this case, clearly, the deep structure challenge to local mores on issues such as gender rank and ethnicity, without which inculturating faith is unlikely, has not been accepted. Not that that is not an issue elsewhere in the world.

The Performance of Christianity in South Asia

Developing an indigenous theology and church organization in South Asia is as complex in South Asia as anywhere else, but no doubt the difficulties here are compounded by the minority and sometimes persecuted status of the various churches. Such development is of course multifaceted, and it is only possible to mention a few aspects here. In terms of translation into local languages, the enterprise, as pointed out above, was highly successful. But church life is not just about reading and hearing words, it also has to do with music, buildings, and the performance of liturgy.

Music, together with musical instruments and songs, are essential parts of the local cultures and, where there is no split between the sacred and the profane, music often draws on and expresses a religious understanding of the world. Unfortunately, in the past, foreign missionaries not infrequently out-lawed musical instruments and songs that were judged to be inspired by the local "pagan" culture and imposed instead their own European music and song. Local people did not oppose such practice if they had accepted, at that time at least, that anything from their religious past was sinful. Pastor Jamir, writing on folk and church music among the Nagas, reports that according to most of his interviewees, early Naga Christians themselves had wanted to cut themselves off from their past folk music lest it "take them back" to their old pagan ways. This attitude, to the extent that it was correctly reported, seems to have been influenced by the missionaries' view that the old music and folk songs were "unclean." Jamir holds both the expatriate missionaries and the local Christians responsible for this loss of the indigenous music. In the early stages of mission, some folk songs were used by the missionaries – until they learnt that such songs, as a Naga pastor said, "stimulated the people to go to war and created enmity, immorality, etc."[67] Similar negative attitudes are also found among other communities in Burma/Myanmar and Bangladesh as well as among the *adivāsi* (aboriginals) in India.

I have already noted the problems for the *dalit* when Sanskritized materials were introduced into the churches as part of the contextualizing process. The South Indian theologian James Appavoo wrote music for the Tamil *dalit*, reclaiming their folk music and rural cultural traditions for use in Christian liturgy. Wishing to convert people not so much to the Christian faith as to what he calls the "kingdom values of love equality and justice", Appavoo uses *dalit* drumming in the liturgy, despite the fact that it is believed that local spirits use drumming to make people go into trance and that drumming brings about ritual pollution. Insistently bringing the allegedly polluting sound of drumming into the church, Appavoo intends to make the music of the oppressed locals heard again. His music is not an addendum to liturgical and theological inculturation by the rural *dalit* in Tamil Nadu: it is crucially part of it. While Appavoo suggests that the silencing of indigenous music was done primarily by Western missionaries, it appears that its exclusion from the churches was also supported by those who stood to gain from it.[68] This music, long embedded in the everyday life of the *dalit*, is only now being brought back to life with great difficulty in Christian Tamil Nadu – and there are still opponents, especially though not only in the more Protestant or the more town-led churches.

Indigenous music was also largely eliminated from the church among minority peoples in North East India and in Burma/Myanmar. The attempt to "allow" drums and gongs in Baptist, Presbyterian and Anglican worship in Myanmar is fraught with problems, from the rather common "We should do it, but it is not quite the right time" of an Anglican Kachin musician[69] to the "We can have some drums in some churches but not gongs" of Chin Baptists – who do use gongs in the countryside, held outwith the church, to announce a death. As so often when an issue is still contested, the blame for exiling local musical instruments and styles is attributed to "the American Baptist missionaries who converted us": the fact of their departure some 50 years ago is ignored. The issue has been largely dealt with in the Roman Catholic church in Myanmar, drums, gongs and flutes (nose and mouth) being part of rural services – though not until after Vatican II, local Roman Catholics before that period having a not dissimilar and equally dark view of local ways.[70] The fact that hymns have been a largely post Vatican II addition to that liturgy has been helpful, it being easier to fit new hymns to local scales and tunes from the start than change long-used and much-loved organ or piano-led hymns to local melodies and scales.

The final example of music takes us back to the first organization of church life in South India, that of Syrian Orthodox Christians. The Syrian tradition still remains in South Asia. But, there as well as elsewhere, it has evolved into new forms that have gone some way to challenging the caste basis of Syrian Orthodoxy. This is true of, for instance, the Mar Thoma Church. Philip Wickeri describes one such church in Kerala, a community of 85 families who work in the rubber plantations.[71] As elsewhere in South Asia, shoes are taken off at the entrance of the church,[72] women sit on the right and men on the left, members of the same caste background being together.[73] The Holy Qurbana, or Eucharist, was retained as the key part of liturgical worship when the Mar Thoma Church evolved from the Syrian Orthodox Church in the nineteenth century, with the sermon having a more important place than in the Syrian tradition.

A combination of change and continuity characterizes the Mar Thoma Church: the individual piety of the Lutheran tradition and the liturgical richness of the Syrian tradition; the prime role of the laity in the liturgy and the ritual performance of the priest and the three deacons at the elaborate altar; the use of the vernacular in all speech and the sung liturgy in Malayalam. Yet the overall impression is that of an Orthodox service, *especially* in the music that evolved from Syrian roots but which fits thoroughly into the South Indian melodic pattern. Again, in a fitting revision of the early Roman Catholic distain of the local, Catholic churches in South India, and elsewhere in South Asia, commonly use Indian melodies and liturgical styles. Yet, as I have cautioned above, we must be careful not to assume the "surface grammar" of music, dress and movement is relating to and challenging the deeper levels of locality, history and ways of being.

Toward a Conclusion

To sum up the present and predict the future state of this "faith in the making" in South Asia would take rather more hubris if not sheer crystal-gazing than is sane. The generals in Myanmar may alter course next month; the Hindu parties in India may rise up more widely next year; the beleaguered Talibans may turn their attention from blowing up schools for Muslim girls in Pakistan to an even more meticulous destruction of Christian buildings and Christian lives. Yet Christians too will make decisions, individually and collectively, as they negotiate their way in relation both to the socio-political context as they now experience it and to memories of the past and paths for the future. Directions are rather uncertain – yet one point is not: while Christianity in South Asia can and does function as an admired (if at times distrusted) social welfare movement, a source of external links, a source of deep personal faith, it can also function like the stuffed sheep in an Afghan polo game, there to be hit.

Rather than predicting what might be, I would prefer here to reflect on three points. Firstly, the longevity of the faith, the plethora of denominations and the pluralism with which this chapter began. Secondly, the extent to which Christianity in South Asia ingests or spits out the layered cake of castes and the territorial cylinders of ethnicity. Thirdly, the extent to which South Asian churches, whoever controls them, do have particular problems with defining what is acceptable and what not, which Christian is an equal before God and which is a nothing.

As we have seen, it is not the case, contrary to many contemporary teaching texts in colonialism or World Christianity, that Christianity first arrived in Asia in the nineteenth century, however useful this historical version is to some contemporary political views in South Asia. Orthodox communities in Kerala over the last two thousand years exemplify something of the process of integration, symbiosis, and syncretism with the local faith tradition which Christianity underwent in Europe – but without eliminating it in India. The maintenance of Christianity in South Asia has been erratic, dependent on church decisions made in Rome or briefly in Copenhagen, and on political and territorial decisions in various European centers – but it endures and even expands, driven by its own internal momentum.

Denominations also increase from within by inner mission; after schism, as part of control over people or ideas; through internet links and formal teaching, or with returning migrants, just as early Pentecostalism came to Italy with returning emigrants from America. There were few comity agreements between mission agencies in nineteenth-century South Asia compared with, for example, those in Korea; rather, direct competition was more common, and is still the case. It is, as I noted above, a cause of current concern which, given the attitudes of certain mission groups both towards other faiths and toward other varieties of the Christian palette, makes "keeping a low profile" for those with nowhere else to go a very difficult endeavor.

South Asia has, on the whole, long been *the* context for a "live and let live" pluralism, of parallel living of the various traditions. This does not always survive modern state politics, exacerbated by the sometimes divisive attitudes of diaspora South Asians, some of whom, in North America and to a lesser extent in Britain, incite separation in a homeland in which they no longer have to live. This affects the pluralism of everyday life, curtailing the sharing of the sacred space, of festival foods, and of joy and sorrow. Yet that apart, it is perhaps not chance that several leading Roman Catholic exponents of pluralism such as Jacques Dupuis and Raimon Panikkar spent much of their working life in India – and are deeply unpopular in Rome. Would that the EuroAmerican world, only now living with many traditions, were willing to learn from South Asian tradition in this regard!

The second point for reflection is this: just as the introduction of locally based church music was easier for the Roman Catholic Church in South Asia as they imported little music before Vatican II, we might suggest that the extension of Christianity after 1880–1920 in areas untouched by that or any other world tradition was rather easier and numerically very much more effective than in earlier areas settled by local or foreign missions. Yet in these northern hills of India, Bangladesh and Burma/Myanmar, issues of power over believers and potential converts are not absent, and ethnicity in these regions can be as much a bane and eventual constraint as a blessing.

In areas where it existed, the layered caste cake is still there in all aspects of life. Attendance at specific churches in the town or links to a particular diocese will still stamp a person not only as a *dalit*, for example, but as a particular sort of *dalit* or person of a particular caste. Yet, abhorrent though caste segregation is, its effect is scarcely different from church life elsewhere, so neatly patterned after the prevailing class, color and cultural mode.

Nor is segregation by gender unique to South Asia. Yet there too, women begin to speak loudly and claim their place as equals, not only in Protestant but also in Roman Catholic churches, whatever their male leaders say. Husbands, however, are another matter, and in terms of safety at home, violence by Christian men against their wives relates closely to the norm for each region than to an idealized Christian pattern of peace.

The final point along this path of reflection on Christianity in South Asia is that of the power to name, to make boundaries, to include this or that drum, song, thought, action, gesture, translation, and exclude others. It is not uncommon to find outsiders blamed for silencing the drums and drowning the voices – yet as I have set out in this chapter, such a simple dichotomy is inadequate. Where groups are deciding if they wish to claim the voices of their forebears – or indeed to reject them – there will be several interest-groups with which to negotiate, and the outcome will satisfy some and sadden others.

In this, as in the complex dramas which make up Christianity in South Asia, it is perhaps reasonable to suggest that South Asia exemplifies both the power which can be so appalling in church life and organization and a creative inculturation of faith which goes beyond the locally decorative and socially safe. Indeed this vast area of languages, peoples and faiths could contribute much to the ecclesial world beyond South Asia – would that their voices were heard!

Notes

1. Writing as an anthropologist working in both religious studies and theology, I say this so clearly not to blame Christians in particular for such shortfalls, but merely to point out the normal state of affairs, the normal gulf between theory and practice, in any value system. "Blasphemy" is based on Galatians 3:26–28.
2. See Kurikilamkatt, J. *First Voyage of the Apostle Thomas to India*, Bangalore: ATC, 2005.
3. See Županov, I. "Lust, marriage and free will; Jesuit critique of Paganism in seventeenth century South India," *Studies in History*, 16:2, 2000, 199–220.
4. "There is not at present in the country more than a third of the Christians who were to be found eighty years ago, and they diminish every day by apostasy" Dubois, J. [1823], in Koschorke, K. (ed.) *A History of Christianity in Asia, Africa and Latin America, 1450–1990*, Grand Rapids: Eerdmans, 2007.
5. Andrews, C.F. *The Sermon on the Mount*, New York: Collier, 1962 [1941]. G Viswanathan, *Outside the Fold: Conversion, Modernity and Belief*, Princeton: PUP, 1998.

6. Including Islamic Christian groups such as in Bangadesh: see Jorgensen, Jonas P.A. Jesus Imanders and Christ Bhaktas: A Qualitative and Theological Study of Syncretism and Identity in Global Christianity, Ph.D., Copenhagen: Univ. of Copenhagen, 2006 and also resistance groups against, but influenced by, Christianity such as Heraka in Nagaland and Pau Chin Hau in Myanmar/ Burma.

7. Ariarajah, W. *Not Without My Neighbour*, Geneva, WCC. Thomas Thangaraj also discusses this issue with great sensitivity in his *Relating to People of Other Religions*, Nashville, Abingdon, 1997.

8. The past 150 years has seen considerable inter-continental movement of people, yet we might reasonably assume settled people live out their lives in a radius of ten to twenty miles. Media links, internet and TV certainly expand knowledge, but not for all rural dwellers.

9. J. Openshaw's *The Bauls of Bengal* (Cambridge: CUP, 2004) shows the inanity of labeling as Muslim these players who transcend as they reject both "Hindu" and "Muslim" categories.

10. It was the conversion of a Parsi boy at a mission school in the Bombay of the 1840s which encouraged Parsi codification of doctrine. See Palsetia, J. "Parsi and Hindu Traditional and Nontraditional Responses to Christian Conversion in Bombay, 1839–45," *Journal of the American Academy of Religion,* 2006, 74:3, 615–645.

11. See in van der Veer, P. *Imperial Encounters in India and Britain*, Princeton: PUP, 2001, p. 110.

12. See Gittins, A. "Beyond Liturgical Inculturation," *Irish Theological Quarterly*, 69, 2004, 47–72.

13. Cyprian, third century, noted "each Bishop is autonomous in his diocese answerable only to God". Victor, an early Bishop of Rome in 190 CE, was forced by Bishop Irenaeus of Lyon to withdraw his threat to excommunicate all who rejected his date for Easter, Irenaeus regarding the church as a communion of churches of equal standing, similar to the current Orthodox view.

14. See Atiya, A. *History of Eastern Christianity*, Notre Dame: Notre Dame Press, 1968.

15. Dark, quoted in Tomber, R. *Indo-Roman Trade: from Pots to Pepper*, London: Duckworth, 2008, p. 169.

16. See Katz, N. and Goldberg, E. *Kasrut, Caste and Kaballah*, Delhi: Manohar, 2005.

17. Aerthayil, J. *The Spiritual Heritage of the St Thomas Christians* Bangalore: Dharmaran, 2001, pp. 128–135.

18. Tomber, R. *Indo-Roman Trade: from Pots to Pepper*, London: Duckworth, 2008, p. 170.

19. See Aerthayil, J. *The Spiritual Heritage of the St Thomas Christians*, Bangalore: Dharmaran, 2001, p. 57.

20. See Bayley, S. *Saints Goddesses and Kings: Muslims and Christians in South Indian Society 1700–1900*, Cambridge: CUP, 1989.

21. Padinjarekutt, I., *Christianity through the Centuries*, Mumbai: Bombay St. Paul Society, 2005: p. 7 gives an early example of the Copper Plates of Kerala given by the then king to two bishops and a merchant in 800 citing their privileges.

22. The then Pope wrote that, "Although we desire they agree (with us) we permit you to maintain the customs and the old rites which of course can be proved to be legitimate provided in sacraments and other things pertaining to faith and necessary to salvation you follow the Roman Church." Quoted in Thaliath, *The Synod of Diamper*, Bangalore: Dharmaram, 1999 [1958].

23. Aerthayil, J. *The Spiritual Heritage of the St Thomas Christians*, Bangalore: Dharmaran, 2001, p. 23.

24. Texeira, P., S.J. [1580] in Koschorke, K. (ed.) *A History of Christianity in Asia, Africa and Latin America, 1450–1990*, Grand Rapids: Eerdmans, 2007, pp. 24–26.

25. de Trindade, P., 1634.

26. See Gomes, J. "Portuguese Mission in Goa; Conflict and Collaboration between Colonial and Brahmanical Power," *Bangalore Theological Forum*, 32, 2000, 125–142. "Today the Goan Catholic hierarchy of priests and especially bishops is dominated by Brahmin clergy...there is absolutely no communal conflict between Catholics and Hindus in Goa today. Rather the conflict between high caste Catholic and [lower caste or *dalit*] Pentecostals is intense." At p. 137.

27. Firth, C. *An Introduction to Indian Church History*, Delhi: ISPCK, 2005 [1961].

28. See 1 Corinthians 9: 19–23.

29. South Indian mission to Northern India, and more especially Mizo and Naga mission beyond India, are each facing opposition from potential converts due to the assumption that converts need in effect to become Mizo or Naga: the earlier blinkered vision of the Vatican or the Halle Mission Board in Germany, the arguments of Peter and Paul in Acts and 1 Corinthians, seem doomed to eternal return!

30. An effort was made in the Ezoram Vedam of 1778 to find a prefigured Jesus and make at least the second book of the Vedas into an Old Testament equivalent, but apart from the fact that the text, attributed to de Nobili, was a forgery, there were and are great problems with this approach, discussed below. See also Mohan, J. "La civilisation la plus antique; Voltaire's Images of India," *Journal of World History*, 16:2.

31. See Rajarigam, D. *The History of Tamil Christian Literature*, Tranquebar: Tamilnadu Christian Council, 1958, pp. 19–21.

32. See Butler, J.F. "Nineteen Centuries of Christian Missionary Architecture," *The Journal of the Society of Architectural Historians*, 21:1, 1962, 3–17, and

his "The Theology of Church Building in India," *The Indian Journal of Theology*, 2, 1956, 1–20.

33. English translation: Genealogy of the South Indian Deities: An English Translation of Bartholomäus Ziegenbald's Original German Manuscript, with Textual Analysis and Glossary (London: RoutledgeCurzon, 2003).

34. Irschick, E. "Conversations in Tarangambadi," *Comparative Studies of South Asia, Africa and the Middle East*, 23:1&2, 2003, 260.

35. In Irschick, E. "Conversations in Tarangambadi," *Comparative Studies of South Asia, Africa and the Middle East*, 23:1&2, 2003, p. 261.

36. Ziegenbalg letter in Koschorke, K. (ed.) *A History of Christianity in Asia, Africa and Latin America, 1450–1990*, Grand Rapids: Eerdmans, 2007, p. 54.

37. In Paul, R. *The Cross over India*, London: SCM, 1952, p. 67. Naikan continued working as a catechist supported by five under-catechists: his wife succeeded to his job on his death.

38. See Santra, J. Christian Communication and Indigenous Agents of Conversion among the Kui People of Orissa, 1835–1970, unpublished Ph.D., Univ. of Edinburgh, 2004.

39. This is of course relevant in any mission context, though records tend to downplay local contribution to the actual mission process. See Dube, S. "Conversion to translation: Colonial registers of a vernacular translation," *South Atlantic Quarterly*, 101:4, 2002, pp. 807–837.

40. Quoted in Bendangyabang, A. *History of Christianity in Nagaland*, Mokokchung: Shalom, 1998, p. 127. However, the act of contributing "covers" every member of the household with the ritual benefit.

41. In Dube, S. "Conversion to translation: Colonial registers of a vernacular translation," *South Atlantic Quarterly*, 101:4, 2002, at 811.

42. Dalit Tribute to Robert F. Cook: Pentecostal Pioneer. Revd J. Yesunatha Das. www.pneumafoundation.org/resources/in_depth.jsp?article=/YDas...xml

43. Personal communication: Rev. Dr Joseph George, who suggests these markers do not survive emigration to North America.

44. See also Pulikottil, P., "Ramankutty Paul: A *dalit* contribution to Pentacostalism," in Anderson, A. and Tang, E. (eds.) *Asian and Pentecostal*, Oxford: Regnum, 2005, pp. 245–257.

45. Chin, K.K. "The Assemblies of God and Pentecostalism in Myanmar," in Anderson, A. and Tang, E. *Asian and Pentecostal*, Oxford: Regnum, 2005, p. 269.

46. The evidence of one man is worth that of two women, of one Muslim that of two Christians: so offences against Christians, especially in cases of blasphemy and rape, and especially against Christian women, have little chance of being punished.

47. See Ling, S.N. "Reading Amos' Justice message in the Myanmar context," *Rays; MIT Journal of Theology*, 8, 2007, 32, 38.

48. See Kim, S. *In Search of Identity*, Delhi: Oxford, 2003.
49. Walbridge, L. *Christians of Pakistan: The Passion of Bishop John Joseph*, London: Routledge, 2002.
50. Esteves, S. "Violence against the Cross," in Puniyani, R. (ed.) *Religion, Power and Violence*, Delhi: Sage, 2005, pp. 277–289.
51. Ling, S.N. "Reading Amos' Justice message in the Myanmar context," *Rays; MIT Journal of Theology*, 8, 2007, p. 38. Catholic and Protestant (mainly Baptist) alike keep going under considerable restrictions – though interestingly the government was more than willing to let the Anglicans retain the School for the Blind in Yangon.
52. Abdullah, T. "Women and Christian-Muslim Relations," in Amjad-Ali, C. (ed.) *Developing Christian Theology in the Context of Islam,* Rawalpindi: CCC, 1996, pp. 63–64.
53. Olivinho Gomes in "Villages in Goa." See also Robinson, R. *Christians in India*, Delhi: Sage, 2003.
54. Monteiro, E. "Towards Partnership," in her (ed.) *Concerns of Women: An Indian Theological Response*, Bangalore: Dharmaram, 2005, p. 114.
55. This is least evident in locally-limited traditions, where there is no development of an elite and a "folk" tradition. "World" traditions writers usually miss this point.
56. See Manickam, S. *Slavery in the Tamil Country*, Madras: CTL, 1892.
57. Barboza, F.P. *Christianity in Indian Dance Forms*, Delhi: Sri Satguru, 1991.
58. Hlawndo, Z. personal communication, 2009.
59. See Hre, L.T. Reformed Ecclesiology and its role within the Chin reformed churches in Burma: an analysis of the Independent Church of Burma and the Presbyterian Church of Burma, 1938–1984, unpublished Ph.D. Lutheran Theological Seminary, Hong Kong. Discussions with other Presbyterian ministers in Burma support Hre's view.
60. "Problems and Struggles": www.dalitchristians.com/Html/arulappa.htm.
61. Jeremiah, A. Lived Religion among Rural Pariahs of South India, unpublished Ph.D., Univ. of Edinburgh, 2009, p. 276.
62. "14 Indian Sisters' Letter to Pope in 1994 on Ordinatio Sacerdotalis," in Kottoor, J. (ed.) *Woman Why are you Weeping*, Delhi: Media House 2002.
63. "Should a woman lead the Church?" in Wilson, H.S. (ed.) *Pastoral Theology from a Global Perspective*, Maryknoll, New York: Orbis, 2001.
64. Menstrual pollution may well be relevant here.
65. See my *Food Friends and Funerals: on Lived Religion*, Berlin: Lit, 2008.
66. Gnanadason, A. *No Longer a Secret*, Geneva: WCC, 1995, p. 51.
67. Temjen Jamir, A. *Popularisation of Folk Music in Christian Worship*, Aolijen: CTC, 2001, pp. 36–40.
68. See Sherinian, Z. "Dalit theology in Tamil Christian Folk Music: A transformative liturgy by James Appavoo," in Raj, S. and Dempsey, C. *Popular Christianity in India*, Albany: SUNY, 2002.

69. This comment may well reflect political concerns which restricted Roman Catholic puppet theatre among the Karen, Kachin songs being linked to resistance.
70. When all foreign missionaries and priests were expelled by Burma in 1962, those present at Independence were allowed to stay, which included a cohort of Italians, some of whom are still (at time of writing, 2009) in continuous rural post.
71. Wickeri, P. "The Mar Thoma Christians of Kerala," in Farhadian, C. *Christian Worship Worldwide*, Grand Rapids: Eerdmans, 2007.
72. Myanmar is again rather different: in town, shoes are removed in the pew before approaching the altar for Communion, and thus not removed in a prayer-only service.
73. *Dalit* as members of Mar Thoma churches do experience some discrimination, yet the concern for social justice in the church assists internal efforts in facing the issue.

Further Reading

Aerthayil, J. *The Spiritual Heritage of the St Thomas Christians*, Bangalore: Dharmaran, 2001, pp. 128–135.

Amjad-Ali, C. (ed.) *Developing Christian Theology in the Context of Islam*, Rawalpindi: CCC, 1996.

Anderson, A.and Tang, E. *Asian and Pentecostal*, Oxford: Regnum, 2005.

Atiya, A. *History of Eastern Christianity*, Notre Dame: Notre Dame Press, 1968.

Bayley, S. *Saints Goddesses and Kings: Muslims and Christians in South Indian Society 1700-1900*, Cambridge: CUP, 1989.

Frykenberg, R. *Christianity in India*, Oxford: OUP, 2008.

Kim, S. *In Search of Identity*, Delhi: OUP, 2003.

Koschorke, K., Delgado, M.and Lutz, F. *A History of Christianity in Asia, Africa and Latin America, 1450-1990* (ed.), Grand Rapids: Eerdmans, 2007.

Massey, J. *Dalits in India: Religion as Bondage or Liberation with Special Reference to Christians*, Delhi: Manohar, 1999.

Monteiro, E. (ed.) *Concerns of Women: An Indian Theological Response*, Bangalore: Dharmaram, 2005.

Raj, S.and Dempsey, C. *Popular Christianity in India*, Albany: SUNY, 2002.

Robinson, R. *Christians in India*, Delhi: Sage, 2003.

Viswanathan, G. *Outside the Fold: Conversion, Modernity and Belief*, Princeton: PUP, 1998.

Walbridge, L. *Christians of Pakistan: The Passion of Bishop John Joseph*, London: Routledge, 2002.

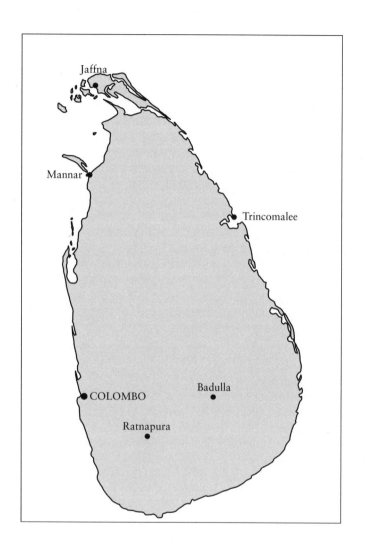

3

Sri Lanka

Jeyaraj Rasiah

The Land, its Make Up and the People

The Democratic Socialist Republic of Sri Lanka, formally Ceylon, is a teardrop shaped island off the south-eastern coast of the Indian subcontinent, separated from India by the Palk Strait and Gulf of Mannar. Its maximum distance from north to south is about 440 kilometers (approximately 273 miles) and from east to west about 220 kilometers (approximately 137 miles) with the total area of 65 610 square kilometers (25 332 square miles). The contour of the island is mountainous as the land rises from the coastal sandy beaches to a central plateau covered with lush tea plantations providing an idyllic landscape.

The first settlers on the island are generally believed to have been of Mesolithic Age proto-Austroloid ethnic group that was absorbed by the Indo-Europeans who migrated around the sixth century BCE. These new-comers from North India developed into present day majority Sinhalese population. The present day minority Tamils, who are Hindus, most likely descend from a wave of migration from South India 500 years later, beginning around the first century BCE.

While this geneaology of settlement is usually accepted, the identities of the original inhabitants and the first arrivals in Sri Lanka remain disputed questions. The recorded history of the island spans over 2500 years, even before the arrival of Buddhism in the third century BCE, according to the religio-mythical narrative *Mahavamsa* (literally, Great Genealogy or Dynasty). This chronicle compiled in the sixth century in Pali, the language of Theravada Buddhism, forms the bedrock of Sinhala ethos. Though the chronicle is not considered a sacred text in the Buddhist mind, it carries a certain canonical authority. Its underlying motif portrays Sri Lanka as the land chosen by the Buddha himself to preserve Theravada Buddhism in its purity. While there is evidence of the presence of Christians in the sixth and seventh centuries, Christianity as it today exists in Sri Lanka traces its origins to the 1505 arrival of the Portuguese, who ruled parts of the island till 1658.

From the time of first contact with Europeans, Sri Lanka endured four centuries of Western domination. This era can be divided into three periods, which have been seen in both negative and positive lights. Negatively, the roughly 400 years of Western influence can be described as a Portuguese period of colonial aggression, a Dutch period of indifference and harassment, and a British period of moderate imperialism. More benign descriptions recount the same periods as 110 years of Portuguese imperial patronage and Catholic evangelization, 150 years of Dutch Protestant neglect and commercial exploitation, and 150 years of British religious toleration, Western education, and benign but self-interested economic improvement.[1] Yet the fact is that Christianity and Western culture in all these different shades entered the island with influence of each foreign power.

The Portuguese Period

When the Portuguese arrived in their pursuit of the Eastern spice trade, the island was divided into three kingdoms: Kotte, in the South; Kandy, at the center; and Jaffna, on the north of the island. A Franciscan priest, Fr. Vincente, who arrived with the Portuguese traders, said Mass and left with them. In 1518, a second Portuguese expedition brought a chaplain, who remained to minister to the garrison and make the contacts with the local people. The first Portuguese missionaries (five Franciscans) arrived on the island in 1546 as a delayed response to the request of the king in 1543.

After the death of the king, he was succeeded in 1551 by his grandson,[2] popularly known as Dharmapala, who was later converted to Christianity. Along with the new king, his household, his courtiers and many common people (altogether around three thousand) embraced Christianity. King Dharmapala, who was also known by the Christian name Dom Joao Periya Pandar, bequeathed his kingdom to the King of Portugal in 1580. He also granted properties of some of the Buddhist temples to the Franciscans. By then, the Portuguese had become sufficiently entangled in local politics that they hoped to gain control of other kingdoms in the south of the Island.

While the south was caught up in power struggle between the local kings and the Portuguese, in the north, on the Island of Mannar, which was part of the kingdom of Jaffna, hundreds were converted to Christianity by a secular priest sent by St. Francis Xavier from India. To deal with these converts, the enraged King of Jaffna sent a company of soldiers who put to death at least 600 of the new Christians, the first martyrs on the island.

When a Portuguese expedition sent by the Governor of Goa in 1560 to avenge the slaughtering of Christians was beaten back by the King of Jaffna, the retreating Portuguese took control of the Island of Mannar and fortified it for a possible future invasion. The Jesuits who had gone with the army remained in Mannar and began organizing a Christian community there.

Another Portuguese invasion of the kingdom of Jaffna in 1591 gave them a foothold, and in 1618 Jaffna became a Portuguese possession. The Franciscans entered the kingdom for missionary work soon after. The kingdom, much under the Portuguese influence, if not control, gave ample scope for evangelization. The Jesuits were invited from India to Colombo in 1602 to open a college. They were followed by the Dominicans in 1605 and the Augustinians in 1606. By the end of the Portuguese period in 1658, it is estimated that there must have been between 100 000 and 150 000 Catholics on the island, served by about 100 missionaries.

The Dutch Period

The Dutch who arrived on the island allied themselves with the King of Kandy, the only independent kingdom under the Portuguese. Hoping to drive away the former masters and to wrestle control of administration, they issued multiple decrees calling for the allegiance of the Catholics. When these failed to win the alliance of the island's Christians, the Dutch began rounding up priests and shipping them to India. Laws imposed by the Dutch forbade, under pain of death, concealment of priests, and prohibited public or private assemblies of Catholics. According to mission reports, there were four periods of persecution between the years 1689 to 1729: the first in Jaffna, the second in Colombo and Negombo, the third in Jaffna and Mannar, and the last in Colombo.[3] These measures, rather than discouraging and suppressing the Catholics, helped them to grow in different ways.

When the King of Kandy later fell out with the Dutch, he invited the Catholics to his kingdom, thus allowing Catholicism to survive on at least part of the island. In both Sinhalese and Tamil communities within Dutch territories, some Catholics maintained their faith outwardly while conforming to the Dutch regulations, while others reverted to Buddhism, or became Calvinists or Baptists, at least externally.

The first Presbyterian minister appointed to the island died en route, making the 1643 arrival of Johannes Stertemius the earliest recorded encounter with the Reformed church. However, it would be several years until Reformed Christian communities were established. In the congregations organized by Philip Baldaues in Jaffna between 1658 and 1661, the Reformed Christians did not feel the need to build churches as they took away the Catholic churches, transforming the structures for worship on the Sabbath and for schools during the week. In this manner, the Franciscan church of St. Francis in Colombo became the official church of the Dutch.[4]

The Dutch period in Sri Lankan history was complicated by the arrival of a young Catholic priest from Goa, India, by the name Joseph Vaz. Disguised as a beggar, he entered the Island in 1687 and made his way to Jaffna. After having worked there for some time, hunted by the Dutch, he traveled to the kingdom of Kandy. Overcoming initial setbacks, he was allowed full freedom to carry out his zealous ministry from there to other parts of the island, even inviting members of his Oratory in Goa.

Withstanding the harassment of the Dutch, Catholicism spread far and wide on the island due to the hard work of the Oratorians, based in the kingdom of Kandy, who learnt well the local languages and wrote books to instruct the new Catholics and sustain the former ones. The Bible was available in Tamil from 1708 and in Sinhalese from 1722.

However, the freedom enjoyed by the Catholics in the kingdom of Kandy came to an end with the end of the Sinhala dynasty in 1739. When Nayakkar, from South India, the brother of the then queen, took over the reins of the kingdom of Kandy, he bent to the influence of the Dutch and the Buddhist revivalists, and banished the Oratorians.

The Oratorians found refuge with a petty ruler in the Vanny region and continued their evangelizing mission. The shifting ground of loyalties during the Dutch period soon found banished Oratorians along with the Sinhala Catholics offering help to the Dutch in their attempt to invade the kingdom of Kandy. This brought greater freedom to the Catholics under the Dutch, evidence of which can be seen in the first baptismal registries of the island, which date to this period in 1763. These changed conditions also brought about changed attitude and lifestyle of the Oratorians. Though they continued to be venerated by the people, there were also accusations of many kinds levelled against them. The ignorance of the local languages on the part of the new arrivals may have contributed to this situation.

The British Period

Replacing the Dutch East India Company, the English East India Company became the masters of the Maritime Provinces of Sri Lanka in 1796. Six year later, the British Government took over the Island from the Company and made it a Crown Colony with a Governor representing the British Sovereign. Finally, in 1815, the English conquered the kingdom of Kandy and became the sole masters of the whole Island.

With the arrival of the British, the Catholics began to breathe freely. All restrictions previously imposed by the Dutch were removed in 1806. This religious freedom was further enlarged eight years later. Though Anglicanism was the new state religion, the government still recognized the Presbyterians of the Dutch Reformed Church as the "ecclesiastical establishment of the colony". As for the Buddhists, the 1815 treaty that ended the independence of the Buddhist kingdom of Kandy guaranteed support to its national religion, which was declared "inviolate and is to be maintained and protected." In 1853, the authorities dissociated themselves from governmental administration of Buddhist affairs. This paved the way for Christian missionaries to move about without hindrance administering to the faithful, even though some had fallen back to Buddhism or Hinduism.

Other missionary bodies such as the Baptists (1812), Wesleyan Methodists (1814), American Board of Commissioners for Foreign Missions (1816), and Church Missionary Society (1818) soon arrived to carry out the evangelizing mission by setting up schools, hospitals, printing establishments, and churches. This trend continued and still more missions such as the Salvation Army (1883), the Seventh-day Adventists (1904), and Assembly of God (1923) also arrived to carry out their missions. In the second half of the twentieth century, after the political independence of the island, there was a proliferation of such independent and foreign-affiliated missions. The arrival of these churches and missionary societies has been a great blessing to Sri Lanka in the field of education, as the many schools and colleges begun by these organizations continues to witness.

The early stage of missionary activity was marked by cordiality when compared to the later stages. For example, the Baptists and the Wesleyans shared one another's places of worship and frequently shared the same platforms.[5] A major contributive factor to this state of affairs was that the different denominations and churches were assigned different territories, and thus continued their missionary activities without any interference. However, the relationship between the Catholic Church and the other churches was distinctly unfriendly. Added to this, the privileged position enjoyed by the Anglican Church eventually created bickering and squabbles within the Christian fold.

A survey of 1838 reveals that there were about 74 787 active Christians on the island attending services of whom 72 870 were Catholics. The adherents of the Dutch Reformed Church, though once large, had dwindled for they were nothing but nominal Christians. The Portuguese and the Dutch who were more interested in commerce had not affected much the lives of the people. The old values have remained intact, also the administrative structure and the village organization. However, with the advent of British influence, the old values gradually began changing as the isolation of the villages was eliminated and a centralized administrative structure was introduced. Equal opportunity, including government jobs, lured many to English education, which in turn fostered a unified administrative structure. English education was provided by a government college, which later became the Royal College, and by Anglican and Wesleyan colleges run by these churches.

In response to the development of Christian culture on the island, the second half of nineteenth century saw a Buddhist revival begun by some monks educated in Christian schools. These devout Buddhists challenged the missionaries to debate, and defeated them.

The great Panadura debate of 1873 exemplified this clash of cultures and the climate of the time. As one of the accepted rules of such debates was that the opponents should attempt to prove each other's religious beliefs false, these events proved to be most polemical. On the Christian side at Panadura was David Wickrametilleke de Silva, a convert from Buddhism with a reputation as a Pali scholar. His counterpart on the Buddhist side was Mohottivatte Gunananda, a militant monk whose oratory attracted thousands of listeners. It was estimated that the first day of the debate attracted and audience of 6000, and the second day brought 2000 more.

While both sides claimed victory, misrepresenting each other's religious claims and beliefs in an attempt to impress their own followers, the true winner seemed to have been the Buddhists, given the sentiments of the populace.[6] About the same time, the arrival of members of the Theosophical Society from Europe and America further challenged Christian cultural dominance by fostering Buddhism and beginning Buddhist schools, adding foreign support to the Buddhist revival which had been begun by the locals.

Among Christians, the desire for European missionaries and for English schools remained strong. The call for further Catholic influence was answered when Rome named Sri Lanka an Apostolic Vicariate in 1836, with the Oratorian Vicente do Rosario as the first apostolic vicar. He was succeeded by another Oratorian, Caetano Antonio in 1843, and yet another Oratorian, Orazio Bettacchini, who was appointed coadjutor to Caetano in 1845 with the assigned task of special care of Jaffna.

The same year, the Sylvestrine Joseph Maria Bravi and two Cistercians arrived on the island. While the former remained in Colombo the two Cistercians proceeded to Jaffna. In 1857, Jaffna became an apostolic vicariate with Bettacchini as Apostolic Vicar and Bravi replaced him in Colombo. Bettacchini invited the Oblates of Mary Immaculate to serve in the newly erected vicariate and obtained four of them, one of whom, Fr. Stephen Semeria, who in 1856 was ordained coadjutor to Bettacchini, became the Apostolic Vicar of Jaffna after the demise of the latter the following year.

Thus the vicariate of Jaffna became the responsibility of the Oblates of Mary Immaculate, who developed the area with special attention to education by multiplying the schools for boys, and inviting the Sisters of the Holy Family of Bordeaux to do the same for girls. In the Vicariate of Colombo, Bravi fell ill and set sail to Europe in 1860 to recuperate, but passed away during the journey. In 1863, the Sylvestrine Abbot Sillani was appointed apostolic vicar of Colombo after a gap of three years. Sillani encouraged the work of education by opening up parish level Catholic schools. He himself built the St. Benedict's Institute and entrusted it to the Brothers of the Christian Schools and invited the Sisters of the Congregation of the Good Shepherd to open up schools for the education of the girls. These developments led to the establishment of the hierarchy in Sri Lanka in January 1887, with Colombo as archdiocese and the dioceses of Jaffna and Kandy as suffragans.

After the establishment of the hierarchy, a permanent Apostolic Delegate was appointed for India and Sri Lanka, in the person of Msgr. Agliardi, who was succeeded by A. Aiuti, who was followed by L. Zaleski. The latter founded the papal seminary in Kandy, which continues to serve the church today. He also created two other new dioceses in 1893, inviting the Jesuits. The twentieth century saw many changes in the Island, the chief of which being the political independence in 1948 which gave greater impetus to the Church to become fully indigenous. There are presently 11 dioceses entrusted to the diocesan clergy helped by 19 religious families of priests and brothers, and more than 26 religious families of nuns of whom 5 are contemplatives, the majority of whom are indigenous.

The growth of the Anglicans remained relatively steady as the statistics of the Church Missionary Society (CMS) reveal: in 1848 there were 10 foreign missionaries and 2 native clergy with 3000 adherents. After 20 years foreign missionaries were 11 and the native clergy were 7, and in 1899, there were 57 foreign missionaries and 23 native clergy with about 9300 adherents.[7]

As populations of individual Christian churches rose and fell, the inter-church relationship remained a matter of concern for many churchmen. Each church carried on its activities in its own way, even though there was an organization known as the "Christian Alliance." With Rev. J.A. Spear as its first President, the group met for prayer, fellowship, and exchange of views, and struggled to prevent disagreement among the denominations.

The Decennial Conference of 1902 in Madras, India, which brought together 250 delegates from over 50 different Missionary Societies, was a path breaking venture in this regard. The conference sought to reduce tension among the various missionary societies and churches by encouraging the delegates to work on the principles of division of labor and comity. While the World Missionary Conference held in Edinburgh in 1910 gave the needed impetus in the direction of union among churches, the visit of Dr. John R. Mott to Colombo in 1912 led to the formation of the National Christian Council of Ceylon. Further practical steps were taken in the same direction in founding the Ceylon Training Colony in 1914 by the Anglican, Methodist, and the Baptist Churches, and the erecting of a chapel in the Peradeniya Training Colony.

A further move was made in 1934 when church leaders met at Trinity College, Kandy to discuss the problems related to church union. Forming a society called "Friends of Reunion," the leadership assembled a Joint Committee on Church Union in 1940. The Union Scheme worked out by the Committee was first printed in 1949 and successively reprinted with amendments; the third such printing came out in 1964. Though the scheme was still open for amendments and suggestions to be incorporated after the Union, it was voted upon favorably in 1971, and a schedule was drawn up for events to follow.

However, a small minority of those vociferously opposed to the union challenged the vote in the courts, and an injunction against the union was obtained. Though the judgment of the court was given on June 20, 1974, stating that it was not a "suitable case to grant a declaration restraining the plaintiffs action with costs," the intended church union was not realized even years later.[8] In 1998, eight member churches of the island's National Christian Council decided to revive the unity efforts but were unable to bring about any substantial outcome. In November 2005, 65 years after the initial initiatives, church leaders from Anglican, Baptist, Dutch Reformed, Methodist, Presbyterian, Salvation Army, and Church of South India assembled at the Anglican cathedral in Colombo for the service to mark the anniversary. At this meeting, Narme F. Wickremesinghe, coordinator of the Franciscan Communion, which describes itself as a forum of concerned lay Christians, lamented: "We are still waiting for fruition of the dialogue initiated by visionary church leaders."[9]

Independent Sri Lanka

The relationship of Christians to Buddhists in independent Sri Lanka has been marked by bitterness and suspicion for half a century, except for a brief period of incipient dialogue and co-operation following the Vatican Council II.[10]

After three successive foreign dominations, when the Sinhala Buddhist majority took the reins of the island by democratic election in 1948, they brought with them the contention, not without foundation, that those who embraced the new religion had been unduly favored by the colonial powers. The Oxford-educated Anglican S.W.R.D. Bandaranaike became Prime Minister in 1956 on a wave of Sinhala Buddhist nationalism after converting from Christianity to Buddhism and promising to make Sinhala the only official language within 24 hours. At the time, the English educated people from all communities were in positions of power and prestige while the Sinhala Buddhist majority educated in vernacular felt marginalized. Further, while those who embraced the new religion owed their allegiance to a foreign power, the patronage offered to Buddhism was, slowly but steadily, withdrawn.

To redress this imbalance certain measures were introduced: in 1956 Christian nuns were prohibited from working in government hospitals, Christian Schools were nationalized in 1961, the constitutions of 1972 and 1978 accorded a privileged position to Buddhism, and since 1966 up to the present certain unsuccessful attempts are being made to prevent conversion to another religion with the accusation that unethical means have been used to lure people from one religion to another. Recent years have witnessed a sharp rise in violence such as the burning of Christian churches in reaction to the perceived threat of conversion.

These measures went hand in hand with a process of internal revival within the Buddhist community, by which they "became better organized, self-confident, and intellectually sophisticated." This paved the way for a certain type of "Buddhist nationalism"[11] and turned out to be a reactionary movement against all forces perceived as being opposed to Buddhism which included "missionaries and the colonially favored Christians of the past era of foreign domination creating insecurity in the minds of the Tamils and the Christians."

The period from the late 1960s to the 1970s, inspired by the openness of Vatican Council II, was a period of incipient dialogue and co-operation as many groups and individuals of notable influence in the Sri Lankan churches (Catholic and others) took the initiative and were successful to some measure. There were three factors to this openness of the Catholic Church in Sri Lanka: (1) initiatives already taken (even before the Council) by individuals from Christian churches; (2) the nationalization of schools; and (3) the youth revolt of 1971. Notwithstanding the lukewarm support of the official church, these individual initiatives portrayed the church as a servant church in dialogue with people of all walks of life.

Unfortunately, the period that followed, from the 1980s to the 1990s, brought with it other factors which further strengthened the previous mistrust and suspicion at the official levels on both sides, even while mutual understanding and cooperation among the poorer sections of the masses continued. One of the factors that contributed to this deterioration of the relationship between the Buddhists and the Christians was the Open Economic policy of the J.R. Jayawardana Government. Begun in 1977, this policy aided some fundamentalist Christian groups with heavy funding from the West to bring about conversions from Buddhism in a rather aggressive manner. As a result, Buddhists became suspicious that the inter-religious dialogue initiated by the Christians was merely a ploy for proselytism. A further factor was the widening of the ethnic divide between the majority Sinhalese and the minority Tamils, especially after the ethnic riots of 1983. The involvement of Tamil Christians in their struggle for safety and security was viewed by Sinhala Buddhists as connected to the church's anti-Buddhist posture and interpreted as anti-nationalistic. Added to these factors was the Catholic Church's call for New Evangelization, which created greater animosity due to certain high-handed methods adopted by some church authorities.

A different story can be told of Christian-Hindu relations. Under British rule there was the real danger of the Tamils losing their language, their culture, their way of life, and their Hindu beliefs. Arumuga Navalar (1822–1879), a pioneer of Tamil prose and champion of Hinduism (Saivism), checkmated the efforts of the missionaries, giving birth to Hindu Renaissance among the Tamils of Sri Lanka. At the same time, Arumuga Navalar collaborated with Rev. Percival, who was a Wesleyan missionary teacher at Jaffna Central College, in translating Christian material including the Bible into Tamil.[12] This attitude of openness, religious tolerance and broad-mindedness of Navalar seems to have influenced the psyche of the Tamils. Though a period of bitter religious feuds followed between Christian missionaries and Hindu scholars, it seems not to have left long-lasting residues of religious animosity in the minds and hearts of the majority of Tamils, thanks to the religious tolerance of Hinduism and the people who had imbibed that spirit.

On the Catholic side, Fathers S. Gnanapiragasar (1875–1947) from Nallur, David Singarajar, and Thaninayagam did yeomen service to the Tamil language which was gratefully recognized by the Tamil community irrespective of their religious affiliation. Even though Fr. Gnanapiragasar seems to have converted thousands of Hindus to Christianity, his research in Tamil language and culture is not equalled by many. Fr. Singarajar continued his predecessor's research into Tamil philology and lexicon. Fr. Thaninayagam, even in his lifetime known as the roving ambassador of Tamil, was solely responsible for the creation of the International Association for Tamil Research in 1964, which continues even today bringing scholars together from all over the world. Due to these contributions to the advancement of Tamil language and literature, the community as such does not look at the Christians as aliens, or as a force opposed to Tamil nationalism.

In the political arena, the safety and security of the Tamil minority community deteriorated gradually after independence as a result of the measures adopted by successive repressive Sinhala Governments. This sense of insecurity combined with lack of equal opportunities in various fields gave birth to Tamil nationalism. The roots of Tamil nationalism may be traced back to 1959, when C. Suntheralingam M.P. for Vavuniya, formed the *Eela Tamil Ottrumai Munnani* (Unity Front of Eelam Tamils) and called for a '*Eela* Tamil Struggle for Independence' in the aftermath of the 'Sinhala-only' official language law of 1956, the 1958 abrogation of the 'Bandaranaike-Chelvanayakam Pact' and the first racial riots of 1958.

The call for Tamil nationalism came into public focus in 1972, when the United Front government under Prime Minister Sirimavo Bandaranaike repealed the independence constitution and introduced the Republican constitution. This constitution, while consolidating all the gains the Sinhala-Buddhists had made in asserting their supremacy, and so excluding the Tamils from any power sharing, emphasized the rejection of Tamil demands for federal autonomy, regional devolution of powers, and Tamil as the official language of the north and east, where they live in majority.

Amidst the fast growing insecurity for the Tamils, the Tamil political leadership formed the Tamil United Liberation Front (TULF) in 1976. At its inaugural convention, presided over by S.J.V. Chelvanayakam, the TULF resolved to restore and reconstitute the state of Tamil Eelam. When Tamil nationalism reached its militant stage as a historical necessity, due to oppressive successive Sinhala Governments, specially at the initial stages, several Catholic priests were suspected by the government of aiding and abetting Tamil 'terrorism,' and were incarcerated, tortured and even murdered. At the later stages subsequently, the Tamil Catholic Church openly opposed state terrorism and gave international publicity to the plight of the Tamils. While on the one hand, these factors helped the Tamil community to stay together without divisions in terms of religious affiliations, on the other hand, Tamil nationalism has divided the Catholic Church of Sri Lanka in terms of Sinhala and Tamil ethnicity.

At the Turn of the Century

When Sirimavo Bandaranaike's daughter, Chandrika Kumaratunga, became president in 1994 with the mandate to find a political solution to the ethnic issue, she formed a coalition government with the left wing and nationalist Sinhalese *Janatha Vimukthi Peramuna* (JVP), a formerly outlawed Marxist party. Their stance of Sinhala Buddhist identity, which opposes any form of devolution of power to the minorities, makes any viable solution to the ethnic question a distant dream. For a brief period, the opposition United National Party government brought in a ray of hope with the ceasefire agreement brokered by Norway in 2002. However, the situation worsened, not only as to the ethnic question but also in the religious front, after a divided election of April 2004, which marked the official entry of nationalist Buddhist monks into politics under the *Jathika Hela Urumaya* (JHU) banner with their anti-Christian stance. This all monks' party introduced an anti-conversion bill, which would in effect criminalize all attempts at religious conversion as "unethical," by which they mean paying the poor to become Christians. It may be acknowledged that there may have been some cases of cultural insensitivity that have given the church a bad image. Some extreme Christian groups likewise may have contributed to the spread of allegations by using very aggressive methods of evangelization. It cannot also be denied that some such groups who are relative late-comers compared to the mainline churches continue to project Christianity as a foreign religion. It is such a scenario which "justifies" the burning of churches and attacks on the faithful.

The Present Scenario

The Presidential election of 2005 brought to power, by a slender majority, President Mahinda Rajapaksha. From the deep south of the island, from the very beginning he consistently projected a pro-Sinhala Buddhist stance and sought a military solution to the ethnic issue. Even while accusations of human rights violations mounted against the Government from the international community, with the support of certain neighboring nations he fought a bloody war against the separatist militants and brought to an end the protracted war in May 2009. Obviously, the war left thousands killed and maimed on both sides of the ethnic divide. Church organizations, alone or along with certain NGOs, and the Government are making every effort at resettlement and rehabilitation of the war-ravaged zones. Christianity seems better equipped in many ways than other religions to bring about peace and reconciliation after decades of suspicion and animosity. Building up a united Sri Lanka is an uphill task.

Process of Inculturation and Contextualized Theology

The process of inculturation may be said to have been begun with the missionary activities of Fr. Joseph Vaz and his Oratorian companions. These early Catholic missionaries learned the local languages of Sinhala and Tamil well, produced books of Christian instruction, and made available Tamil and Sinhala versions of the Bible in the early part of the eighteenth century. However, it was the impetus given by Vatican Council II that brought the vernacularization of liturgy and the adaptation of some of the cultural symbols. Furthermore, at least in certain instances Buddhist and Hindu festivals began to be celebrated jointly by Christians, Buddhists, and Hindus.

From the beginnings of the Christian presence on the island, there has been a long history of being faithful to the Christian tradition on the one hand, and on the other hand articulating the faith experience in the local context in the actual life situations. However, with the heightened nationalism after the political independence in 1948, there began a proliferation of nationalist writings by authors from both communities. These reflections have also led to the formation of centers for social action to address the inequalities in the society. Two valuable source materials in this regard are *The Radical*

Tradition[13] (1985) by N. Abeyasingha and *Asian Christian Theologies*[14] Vol. 1 (2002) edited by John C. England *et al*. Both these volumes not only trace the development of local theology but also, especially the latter, detail a host of local theologians and their basic insights along with a list of institutions which have combined local theological reflection with social action for the uplift of the poor and the needy.

Whither Sri Lanka?

The future seems bleak. There is no denial of the fact that the island is fragmented along ethnic as well as religious lines. Any attempt at reconciliation and peaceful political settlement of the ethnic question, uniting well-intended moderates irrespective of religious affiliations, has been malignly interpreted as selling off the Island to the minority Tamils by some sections of the Sinhala Buddhist community. At the same time, any Christian initiatives, either social or political, are also construed as a sinister plan for pan-Christian domination. The JHU and the JVP with their anti-conversion and anti-Tamil stance do not seem to be realistic or are manipulating for short term political gains. The Sinhala Buddhist identity which they want to foster argues against the very fabric of the Sri Lankan society, which has always been multi-cultural and multi-religious.

According to the 1998 statistics, the population of Sri Lanka is 18.774 million, of which the Sinhalese account for 74%, Sri Lankan Tamils for 12.6%, Indian Tamils for 5.5%, Moors for 7.1%, and others for 0.8%. Religiously, Buddhism is the religion of the majority with 69.3%, while Hindus make up 15.5%, Christians 7.6%, Muslims 7.5% and others 0.1% of the total population. While the majority of Sinhalese are Buddhists and the majority of Tamils are Hindus, Christians are found among both ethnic communities and from all castes. As seen, Sri Lanka can boast of having the four major religions of the world. Yet this variegated richness of the island is being threatened at present.

It cannot be denied that due to historical developments, Buddhism and Sinhala identity are fused together to a great extent. However, they should not be and cannot be identified as one. Christianity, though a latecomer to the island compared to Buddhism and Hinduism, has existed for the past five centuries and today Christians form 7.6% of the total population of the land. Unless the multi-cultural and multi-religious identity is accepted, Sri Lanka cannot hope to pull through this stalemate.

Accepting and respecting such a plurality, will it be possible to construct a national identity comprising all Sri Lankans, irrespective of ethnic and religious affiliations? This is a million dollar question. The history of the island in general, especially the past half a century and the signs of the times at present, seems to suggest the negative.

Granting the presence of two ethnic groups that may not come together to form a national identity, given the decades' old suspicion, animosity, violence and war, we may be able to speak of a Sinhala identity and a Tamil identity. In this scenario, Christianity seems better placed than Buddhism and Hinduism as it gathers members of both the communities to play a vital role in bringing about better understanding and thus reducing racial tensions.

Can the Church succeed in her mission of being a bridge builder and bring about peace and reconciliation? In order to do so, the Church needs to go through a change of heart, shedding her own superiority and becoming a servant Church. She needs to acknowledge her own past sins and find new ways of being the leaven in a land blessed with four major religions of the world.

Notes

1. Moffett, S.H. *A History of Christianity in Asia*, Vol. II: *1500 to 1900*, American Society of Missiology Series, No. 36, Maryknoll, New York: Orbis Books, 1998, p. 336.
2. See Moffett, S.H. *A History of Christianity in Asia*, Vol. II: *1500 to 1900*, American Society of Missiology Series, No. 36, Maryknoll, New York: Orbis Books, 1998, p. 39.
3. Cited in Moffett, S.H. *A History of Christianity in Asia*, Vol. II: *1500 to 1900*, American Society of Missiology Series, No. 36, Maryknoll, New York: Orbis Books, 1998, p. 224.
4. See Moffett, S.H. *A History of Christianity in Asia*, Vol. II: *1500 to 1900*, American Society of Missiology Series, No. 36, Maryknoll, New York: Orbis Books, 1998, p. 226.
5. See Kanagasabai Wilson, D. *The Christian Church in Sri Lanka*, Colombo: The Study Centre for Religion and Society, 1975, p. 43.
6. See Moffett, S.H. *A History of Christianity in Asia*, Vol. II: *1500 to 1900*, American Society of Missiology Series, No. 36, Maryknoll, New York: Orbis Books, 1998, pp. 581–582.
7. See Moffett, S.H. *A History of Christianity in Asia*, Vol. II: *1500 to 1900*, American Society of Missiology Series, No. 36, Maryknoll, New York: Orbis Books, 1998, pp. 582–583.
8. See Moffett, S.H. *A History of Christianity in Asia*, Vol. II: *1500 to 1900*, American Society of Missiology Series, No. 36, Maryknoll, New York: Orbis Books, 1998, pp. 46–57.
9. Ecumenical News International, ©World Alliance of Reformed Churches News-System powered by Johannes a Lasco Library. Available from http://

www.warc.jalb.de/warcajsp/side.jsp?news_id=656&part_id=0&navi=5; accessed August 4, 2007.

10. Pieris, A. *Buddhism and Christianity: Interaction between East and West*, Colombo: Goethe Institute, 1995, pp. 192– 213.

11. *Buddhist Nationalism and Sri Lanka's Christian Minority*. The Institute for Global Engagement, 2004. Available from http://www.globalengage.org/issues/2004/12/srilanka-2.htm; accessed on April 2, 2006.

12. See Eelaventhan, M.K. "*Arumuga Navalar* 1822–1878; Pioneer of Tamil prose and champion of Hinduism, 1996." Available from http://www.tamil-brisbane.com/doc/TAQ_NewsLetter2007.pdf; accessed on April 2, 2006.

13. Abeyasingha, N. *The Radical Tradition: The Changing Shape of Theological Reflection in Sri Lanka*, Colombo, Sri Lanka: The Ecumenical Institute, 1985.

14. England, J.C., Kuttianimattathil, J., Prior, J.M., Quintos, L.A., Suh Kwang-Sun, D., and Wickeri, J. (eds.) *Asian Christian Theologies: A Research Guide to Authors, Movements, Sources*, Vol. 1, Maryknoll, New York: ISPCK/Claretian Publishers/Orbis Books, 2002.

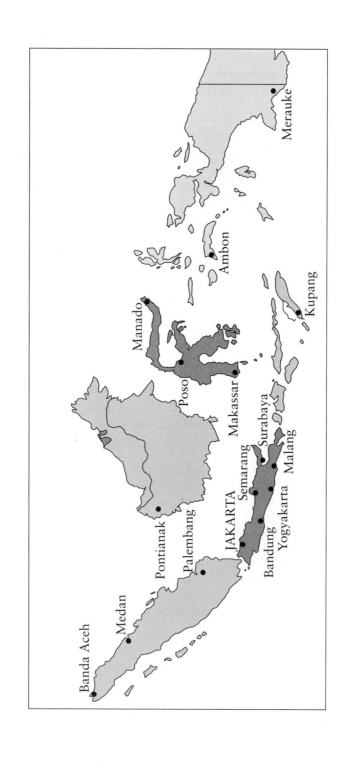

4

Indonesia

John Prior

You would see very little jetting the 3200 miles from east to west high above the 13 000 inhabited islands of the Indonesian archipelago, scattered across the equator between Australia and Malaysia. You need to board a low flying aeroplane to note how dry the smaller isles are to the south and east and how lush the tropical forests on the larger ones to the north and west. Spot every type of sea craft from dugout canoes on the rivers of Papua to the latest semi-automated tankers on the high seas. Observe environmental-friendly traditional dry-land farming, but also the flooded thousand-year-old rice terraces of Bali. View the gold, copper, tin, and coal opencast mines in Papua and Kalimantan that are polluting rivers and destroying nature. Catch a glimpse of several of the 128 volcanoes in this equatorial "ring of fire", one at least will be lighting up the night sky.

Language

Land on islands at random and pause for a while. You will hear some of the 350 distinct local languages while everywhere people will also speak the national tongue of *bahasa Indonesia*. This modern language has matured from the thousand-year-old inter-island lingua franca of Malay, absorbing vocabulary from merchants, mystics, and migrant settlers who spoke Sanskrit, Arabic, Portuguese, Dutch, or English. From time immemorial the islands of Indonesia have been ports of call to seafarers plying their trade between South Asia and Southern China, establishing trading centres and so enriching the ever increasing variety of peoples, cultures, and religious beliefs.

Cultural Diversity

Politely ask to photograph half a dozen Indonesians hailing from different islands, and you will not immediately recognize them as coming from a single

Christianities in Asia, edited by Peter C. Phan © 2011 Blackwell Publishing Ltd except for editorial material and organization © 2011 Peter C. Phan

nation. Make out the varied features from Malay to Papuan, from tribal to Chinese. The 225 million multi-ethnic population enjoys over 30 major cultural domains, the majority, some 60%, coming from Java and Madura. Many worldviews swirl within these islands for each island cluster has developed its own linguistic, cultural, religious, and physical characteristics. Aptly enough Indonesia's national motto reads: *bhinneka tunggal ika* – unity in diversity, a unity recreated by each generation through ongoing tensions oscillating between centre and periphery, the majority and myriad minorities.

Christian Diversity

Given the thousands of islands and hundreds of cultural domains, as well as the strategic site the archipelago holds for seafarers and the fortunes of history, unsurprisingly each of the island clusters has developed Christianity in its own unique way. This diversity has been entrenched through the Dutch colonial policy of not allowing more than one church tradition to work on each island. Thus the Dutch Reformed Church (Presbyterian) began in the Moluccas but today has its largest membership on West Timor. The Dutch Re-reformed Church (Gereformeerde or Congregationalist) is significant on the neighboring island of Sumba, while Catholics have a majority on nearby Flores. Lutherans gave birth to what is now the largest Protestant Church in the Bataklands of north Sumatra. Catholics first came with the Portuguese in 1534, Calvinists with the Dutch in 1605, Lutherans with the Danish/Germans in 1862. Pentecostals began with a single house church in 1924. Church growth took place in quite different ways also: the outer isles witnessed mass conversions while the villages of Java and the Chinese minority in the cities have seen more individual conversions. Each denominational and cultural mix has worked out differently.

The largest number of conversions took place in the decades immediately preceding and following independence (1945/1949). Christianity is not just rooted in local cultures, it is also answers the need for a renewed identity in a rapidly changing world.

Outward Form, Inner Spirit

While the formal thinking and organization of the churches seem Western, their heart is Asian, their soul indigenous. Christian faith and values are expressed in Indonesian painting and sculpture, architecture and theatre, music, and dance, literature and poetry, in both classical and modern styles. While Western liturgical forms function as an identity marker for many Protestants, the spirit of the liturgy is intimately Indonesian as are many of the hymns and musical instruments.

Christians and Muslims

As you across the archipelago do not be surprised at how churches and mosques nestle side by side, for customary celebrations bond neighbourhoods together. The extended family, with members from different faith traditions through local cultural celebrations help maintain inter-religious harmony. While 87% of Indonesians declare themselves Muslim, 9.5% are Christian of which almost 7% are Protestant and 2.5% Catholic, with a growing Pentecostal/charismatic presence. Meanwhile 2% are Hindu, mainly on the island of Bali, 0.9% Buddhist or Confucians, mostly among Chinese Indonesians, with just 0.6% classed as "other." Indonesia possesses the largest Muslim *umma* (community) anywhere and has one of the larger Christian minorities of any Muslim country.

All is not harmonious today. For centuries Christians studiously ignored the Muslim majority; today they can no longer do so. Until the 1980s Christians claimed that only 40% of Indonesians were "real" Muslims, the other 47% merely "nominal" adherences. The recent Islamic resurgence has given lie to this claim. Meanwhile rapid social change and mass migration have weakened social ties. As families have become more individualized, local cultures more globalized, and the values of a competitive market more central, so inter-ethnic and religious strife has erupted. Open conflicts in the late 1990s have forced the pace of a long delayed rapprochement. And so if you were to pop into Ambon in the Moluccas or Poso in central Sulawesi today you would hear of the 1999–2002 conflict with inter-ethnic and inter-religious overtones; and in Jayapura and Banda Aceh you might learn of long-standing separatist struggles. From the air, Indonesia is a tropical paradise; on the land, we face the challenge of nurturing the vision of unity in diversity, of a common future in the face of widening communal fractures.

Papua: Dignity and Identity

We begin our tour where the sun first rises, in Papua, the western half of the island shared with Papua New Guinea. Indonesian Papua now has as many (mainly Muslim) migrant settlers as native Papuans of whom the large majority are Christian. Christianity came almost a century before West Papua was integrated into Indonesia in 1969; they converted collectively as clan and village communities. Christianity brought the modern world to Papua and is today central to the peoples' dignity and identity as they are being overwhelmed by Javanese migrants. Pentecostal movements often sweep across the island Melanesian style. Ancestors continue to be acknowledged and cosmic rituals persist, for local traditions and biblical Christianity have merged. Local congregations are lively while their church leaders are vocal on human rights and environmental issues. As the dominant religious group in northern Papua, Protestants support autonomy if not independence, while Catholics, who dominate the south, limit their advocacy to human rights abuses. Despite difficulties in maintaining educational standards in such mountainous terrain, the neighbouring Protestant and Catholic faculties of theology in Abepura are well attended. Papua has produced a number of Christian theologians of note. One such is Karel Phil Erari (b. 1947) who researches environmental ethics, with particular reference to land issues. He maintains that the peoples of Papua have components within their cultures that could lay the foundation for a contextual eco-theology. After teaching theology in Abepura (1976–1984), Erari became General Secretary of the Papuan Synod (1984–1992), director of research for the Communion of Churches in Jakarta (1988–2001), and then returned to Abepura to direct the postgraduate program in theology.

Ambon: Conflict and Reconciliation

From Papua we call in at Ambon among the famed spice isles of the Moluccas. Here the Catholic Church was born in 1534 but whose members were drawn into the Protestant Church by the Dutch after their arrival in 1605. Protestants remained the dominant group until rapid economic development since the 1970s which brought in a large influx of Muslims. Social unrest accompanied the collapse of Soeharto's regime in 1998, when common norms collapsed, traditional family ties loosened, and religion became increasingly politicized. The ethnic-religious patchwork that survived for almost two centuries was rent asunder when Muslims rivalled Protestants for local hegemony. Violence broke out in January 1999 subsiding only in 2002 after some 5000 deaths. Triggered by rival local elites, the conflict was kept aflame by elements of the police and the army who took opposing sides. Involvement by national politicians prolonged the crisis. The sickness was in Ambon, the virus in Jakarta. Reconciliation was brought about through the extraordinary bravery of groups like the "Movement of Concerned Women" founded by a Protestant Pastor, a Catholic Sister, and a leading Muslim lady. Visitors need to listen to peacemakers, to those who refuse to allow their religion and race to be manipulated by politicians and the military.

Sulawesi: Vibrant and Vocal

And so we move further west to Sulawesi, one of the five larger islands of Indonesia, where we find strong minority Christian communities in the north and centre and staunchly Muslim communities in the south. Manado district is dotted with churches. The outstanding church choirs can be heard on any of the numerous local Christian radio stations. The Protestant Church of Minahasa (GMIM), as well as the Catholic Church, has a comprehensive school system from kindergarten to university. Theological faculties in north, central, and south Sulawesi educate church leaders, lay and ordained.

The Protestant churches of Sulawesi have given birth to some remarkable women. Henriette Marianne Katoppo (1943–2007) was Indonesia's first internationally recognized woman theologian. A freelance theologian, novelist, journalist, and translator, she was independent and forthright and conversant in a dozen Asian and European languages. Her most explicitly Christian novel is *Raumanen* (1977), her most well-known theological work *Compassionate and Free* (1979). Meanwhile Sientje Merentek-Abram (b. 1947) is a biblical theologian and ordained minister in GMIM (1981). She has worked in theological education for both the WCC and in South-East Asia as well as chairing the General Synod of the churches of north and central Sulawesi. Another outstanding woman, Agustina Lumentut (1937–2002) hailed from the Central Sulawesi Church. One of the first women to be ordained (1959), Lumentut worked for the Indonesian Communion of Churches in Jakarta (1985–1989). Back in Sulawesi she was elected the first woman president of her church (1989–1996) apart from also working for the Christian Conference of Asia (CCA) and the WCC. She was a key mediator during the ethnic-religiously driven conflicts in Poso (1999–2002). Here as elsewhere, conflicts arose where a community felt politically silenced, socially ostracized, culturally belittled, and economically sidelined. When on top of this the community is religiously harassed, then dignity and identity tend to be defended with much aggression.

Of a younger generation, Septemmy Eucharistia Lakawa (b. 1970) teaches theology in Jakarta. She has been General Secretary of PERWATI (Association of Theological Schools) and was the founding editor of *Sophia*, the first feminist theological journal in Indonesia (2000).

Henriett Tabita Hutabarat-Lebang, universally known as Ibu Ery (b. 1952), is yet another of the outstanding women from the Sulawesi churches. She was born in the southern city of Makasar and ordained in the Toraja Church (1992). After heading the women's desk of the Communion of Churches in Indonesia (1984–1986), she became Programme Co-ordinator of the CCA in Hong Kong. As with other women theologians, Hutabarat's work has been developed with teams of colleagues and published jointly. She is probably the most influential Indonesian woman theological thinker today.

In Sulawesi as elsewhere, many of the more creative theological scholars are working outside theological faculties and seminaries; they are evolving their theology as writers, journalists, novelists, and in broad ecumenical networks.

East Nusa Tenggara: Christian Heartlands

And so we move south to the islands of Nusa Tenggara. In these Austronesian cultures Christianity is woven into the very fabric of the peoples' identity. For the majority, to be Timorese, Sumbanese or Florenese is to be Christian, whether Presbyterian (Timor), Congregationalist (Sumba) or Catholic (Flores). Cultural values such as hospitality, generosity and accepting everyone as they are, have readily inter-pollinated with Christian virtues. Similarly, pre-modern religious rites, modern education, and post-modern global horizons intermix in both individuals and communities. For instance, you can witness how cosmic marriage rituals handed down from the ancestors form a single process with the church blessing at its climax. Similarly, widely-scattered extended families fly in from neighbouring islands and countries to attend funerals, replete with ancestral rites. Visitors pour into East Flores to take part in the annual Holy Week processions, introduced by Portuguese Dominicans 400 years previously.

Magnificent hand-woven *ikat* cloth, lively rhythmic singing in local tongues, and graceful dancing are all integral elements of major Christian liturgies which are often celebrated in the open due to the number of worshipers.

The mass conversion of Flores and Timor took place in the first half of the twentieth century although Catholics proudly trace their origins to the late sixteenth and Protestants to the early seventeenth centuries. Flores, and much of Timor, remained under Portuguese influence until sold to the Dutch in 1859. West Timor has the second largest Protestant Church in Indonesia (GMIT), while over 30% of Indonesia's Catholics live on these islands. In East Nusa Tenggara Muslims form a small minority. Rooted in a popular religiosity, church leaders collaborate closely with both cultural leaders and government officials, most of whom are Christian. This tends to mute the church's prophetic voice.

Tens of thousands of migrants from these islands are found on every Indonesian island and beyond. These migrants not only make their voice heard in church choirs throughout the country, they are also creatively present among Jakarta's intelligentsia, in the media, the theatre, journalism, and the universities. The Nusa Tenggara school system, both Protestant (Timor and Sumba) and Catholic (Flores), begun early in the twentieth century, led to Christianity being almost identified with education. The Catholic seminary of Ledalero in Flores, celebrating its seventieth anniversary in 2007, has among its alumni 15 bishops, over a thousand priests, and 350 missioners working in 46 countries. These days the Protestant theological faculty in Kupang, Timor has more women than men studying for the ordained ministry for both Presbyterian and Congregationalist churches.

Bali: A Minority within a Minority

To the west of Sumba lie the Muslim isles of Sumbawa and Lombok and then the Hindu isle of Bali, a tourist hotspot. In Bali Christians are a tiny minority within a Hindu culture which is itself a 2% minority in the country. Although a majority of Christians are migrants from Timor, Flores, and Java, much art and sculpture, dance and flower offerings, hymns and *gamelan* percussion orchestras are Balinese. And so try to avoid the surfing beaches of Kuta and Sanur and go west to the town of Negara to the Christian village-complexes of Blimbingsari and Palasari.

The tightly knit culture of the walled villages of Bali had little space for Christians whose first converts came from the lower caste. Rejected by the village, the Protestant community established their own village complex in the western forests at Blimbingsari in the 1930s, while the Catholics built their refuge at Palasari, five kilometres away. To some extent these Christian complexes parallel the Hindu mother temple complex of *Pura Besaki* on the slopes of Mount Agung in the east. Blimbingsari centres upon an open plan church with a *candi bentar* (split gate) entrance separating the outside world from the inner sanctum. Appropriate scriptural verses give Christian significance to each construction. The large church at Catholic Palasari is recognizably Western in shape while its decoration is quintessentially Balinese.

Just north of Denpasar is Tuka village, the Narareth of the small Catholic community. Visit the small Balinese open-plan church and *Widya Wahana* Reference library next door with a collection of over 20 000 books and manuscripts on Balinese culture.

Java: Indigenous Roots

You will need time to absorb the variety of Christianities in Java, the island where more than half the population lives. Among the overwhelming Muslim majority, small Christian communities are visible in cities such as Surabaya, Malang, Yogyakarta, Semarang, Bandung, and the capital Jakarta. These vibrant congregations consist not only of Javanese and Chinese-Indonesians but also of migrants from the outer islands. Many cultural and religious layers interlock producing a great variety of churches.

Central Java has evolved a fluid religious culture with a localised Buddhist-Hindu root upon which the Islamic faith has been grafted, the whole planted in cosmic soil. One hundred and fifty years ago many Javanese were open to new spiritual paths and religious symbols to satisfy their inner need for cosmic harmony. Religious borders were porous and as individuals converted so they felt they had the right to embrace and develop Christianity according to their own feelings and inner needs. The most famous of the nineteenth-century evangelists was Kiai Sadrach Surapranata (1835–1924) who announced the gospel as *ngelmu* (esoteric knowledge) which gives inner contentment and answers the secret of life, a guide on the way to perfection. Christianity made inroads due to such inter-religious blending, where cosmic culture and popular religion merge. Cosmic religiosity is still very much alive in individuals and families. Recently, as globalization has shaken cultural roots, so local cultures have revived, and with it, Sadrach and other nineteenth-century evangelists have been appreciated anew.

Java: Education

The twentieth-century nationalist movement valued Western education, better living conditions, and political emancipation, and the churches responded by centring their outreach on schools, health, and social service. The more important cities have Christian universities and Christianity came to be identified with education and modernization. Jakarta and Yogyakarta (Jogja) are home to numerous Christian educational institutions at all levels. In Jogja visit the Protestant Duta Wacana University and the Jesuit Sanata Dharma University, both of which have ongoing relations with the State Islamic University. At postgraduate level their theology faculties educate thematically via the "pastoral circle" of insertion, social analysis, academic reflection, and practical response.

Java: Art and Music

Christian artists, composers, chorographers, dramatists, poets, literati, and architects have entered the mainstream of Indonesia's cultural life. In Jogja art, theatre, and dance interweave the traditional and the ultra-modern. Socially-engaged artists and politically-aware dramatists are creating a new language in which to re-picture the Jesus of the gospels: portraying the Incarnate Word as the heartbeat of the popular culture struggling for space to breathe, for dignity, for a meaning that overcomes death.

The most well-known artist, musician and choreographer was Bagong Kussudiardja (1928–2004). His picture of Jesus the cosmic dancer ascending to the heavens is widely appreciated. Several of his dance and theatre productions are explicitly Christian. His theatre continues with his children, one of whom, Gregory Djaduk Ferianto (b. 1964), composes multi-media productions drawing together song, poetry, declamation, dialogue, dance, acting, and lighting effects. His is a pluralistic model synthesizing Javanese culture and post-modern technology, accessible to anyone of goodwill, Christian or Muslim.

The Jesuit Audio Visual Studio sponsors artists, producing, in one program, 100 Balinese-style paintings of biblical scenes. Suryo Indratno, a young artist from central Java, painted a large (1.80 × 2.66-meter) jubilee-year hanging expressing a theology of creation and of the Spirit in the context of violent times. The studio also runs training sessions on street theatre drawing on social justice themes. For the past three decades the Jesuit Centre of Liturgical Music has composed liturgical songs according to the scales and rhythms of Indonesian musical traditions. Most hymns today are Indonesian in tone and texture.

Others deserve a mention such as Judowibowo Poerwowidagdo (b. 1942) who has worked in theological education both in Yogyakarta and Jakarta (since 2000) as well as with the World Council of Churches (1992–1998). Together with his wife, the professional artist Timur I. Poerwowidagdo, Judo has established a dance troupe who acts out scriptural narratives in Javanese style. He is also president of the Asian Christian Art Association. Timur painted a series on Christ's passion as an act of compassionate solidarity with the women raped in Jakarta as the Soeharto regime collapsed in May 1998.

Java: Movers and Shakers

Throughout Java Catholics will proudly speak of their first Indonesian bishop, the Jesuit Soegijapranata (1895–1963). An alumnus of Francis van Lith's elite teacher's training school in Muntilan (opened in 1904), Soegijapranata was one of the first generation of nationalists, lay and ordained, produced by the school. Firmly siding with the revolution (1945–1949), Soegijapranata, until his death, remained a close friend of Indonesia's first President, Soekarno.

Perhaps the bishop's most well known protégé is Yusuf Bilyarta Mangunwijaya (1929–1999). After ordination (1959) Mangun studied architecture as part of a diocesan plan to Javanise the church. Visit his open-plan *joglo* churches at Tambran-Ganjuran, Klaten, Sragen, Salam and Yogyakarta and do not fail to miss the trappist convent at Gedono. His design for the Marian pilgrimage centre at Sendangsono, birthplace of the contemporary Catholic Church (1904), focuses upon popular religiosity and natural beauty rather than formal liturgy or large-scale buildings. His use of cultural symbols (tree of life) replaces more explicitly Christian ones (e.g., the cross). Retiring from grand designs he turned to "people's architecture" and redesigned the squatters' camp by the Code River in Jogja (1980–1986) which won the (Muslim) Aga Khan Award (1992). In 11 novels, numerous newspaper articles and other writings, Mangunwijaya is the most creative theological thinker to have emerged from the Indonesian Catholic Church over the past 150 years. He died on the shoulder of the young Muslim intellectual, Mohamad Sobary. His funeral was attended by thousands, not just clergy and literati, but also rickshaw riders, squatters and street children, many of whom he knew personally.

Make an appointment with Agustina Nunuk Prasetyo Murniati (b. 1943) who lives near Gaja Madah University. Ibu Nunuk, as she is known, is a retired economist and university administrator, and is one of the first generation of Catholic women to take up theology. For Ibu Nunuk theology is conversation, an ongoing questioning process by groups of involved people. Not one-sidedly cerebral, theology is personal, birthed by the heart in music, movement, painting, architecture, meditation and asceticism. Theology brought on a faith-crisis as the pious Jesus of her upbringing was challenged by the biblical Jesus of feminist research. Ibu Nunuk is active in both national and international theological and human rights networks.

Jakarta: Pietism and Social Engagement

It is invidious to pick out a single figure from the host of major thinkers and church people in the capital, Jakarta, who have made their mark over the past half century. Nonetheless, the life and thought of Eka Darmaputera (1942–2005) sums up the rapid and radical changes the churches are undergoing. Throughout his adult life Pak Eka led a local congregation while teaching ethics at tertiary level; "Not doing theology", he disclaims, "but theology by doing", responding to ethical, political and dogmatic questions as they arise. A well-known preacher and newspaper columnist, he changed the quietist Chinese-Indonesian congregation into a socially engaged multi-ethnic church. He is one of many Indonesian theologians to study the state ideology of Pancasila (1982) which he saw as an attempt to enable traditional culture cope with contemporary problems. A "both-and" or "neither-nor" worldview leads to acceptance, not of right over wrong, but of what fits in with one's feeling and intuition. Eka found in this traditional worldview fertile soil in which to advocate basic human rights. While Christians have maintained their public profile through journalism, literature, theatre, the arts, and human rights advocacy, it is also true that some urban congregations have retreated into a more ritualistic religion that gives instant fulfillment to their followers' emotional needs rather than work for societal transformation.

Towards the end of his life Eka was critical of the increasingly charismatic style of the richer churches describing them as, "internally irrelevant and socially insignificant". Muslim resurgence over the past 30 years had drawn some to collaborate more closely, but led others to withdraw into ritual.

Sumatra: Local Roots, National Leadership

And finally our tour takes us to the northern part of Sumatra, the western-most island in the archipelago, nestling beside Singapore and the Malay peninsula. Here we find the largest Protestant Church in Indonesia, the *Huria Kristen Batak Protestan* (HKBP) which has many congregations in Jakarta also. The lively Batak people have embraced Christianity with great verve. From their beginnings in the 1860s the Lutheran Rhenish Mission announced the gospel in conscious dialogue with Batak culture. Free of both colonial rule and Islamic influence, Christianity brought security to an area as their culture was no longer capable of holding society together. Due to Ludwig Nommensen (1834–1918), the pioneering visionary, and his companion, P.H. Johannsen, the linguist and bible translator, the Bataks embraced Christianity as a development of ancestral wisdom and values (*adat*). Today, both the Toba Bataks and the Karo Bataks live side by side with Catholic Christians and Muslims in a dynamic and tolerant religious kaleidoscope, held together by the traditional bonds of custom and kinship, a pattern also found elsewhere whether by design (mission method) or appropriation (the genius of the local people). Before the rapid social-economic change of 1970s–1990s, custom and kinship were fundamental and so multi-faith families were able to keep an increasingly pluralistic society together.

This strongly Christian area of North Sumatra has produced some remarkable national figures. Tahi Bonar Simatupang (1920–1990) is not your likely international church statesman let alone ecumenical theologian. He was a guerrilla leader during the revolution (1945–1949) and after independence Chief of Staff of the Armed Forces (1951–1954). Pensioned off early by President Soekarno in 1959, Simatupang became one of the more original theological thinkers of his generation. He claimed that the church needed to become ecumenical in order to counter the ethnic composition of most local churches. He felt it vital that the churches move from a position of weakness and isolation to the centre of society. The churches should engage society, "positively, creatively, critically and realistically". He was one of the key figures who shifted pietistic congregations into the mainstream of national development in order that they develop a coherent social vision. And all this while active in the World Council of Churches.

Future Prospects

What then of the future? The continuing influence of *Kompas*, the largest circulation broadsheet and published by Catholics, the Protestant *Suara Pembaruan* newspaper,and the Islamic daily *Republika*, indicate that religion is maintaining an important role in society, although not always as the most crucial compass in life. Despite an apparent decline in values and a rise in conspicuous consumption, society maintains an important place for religious values. Religion is where people feel significant, both ritually and morally and as a distinct group. Confined largely to ritual under an authoritarian government (1966–1998), Christianity is now being challenged to live as a free and faithful minority.

Kompas and *Suara Pembaruan* are engaged in an ongoing public conversation with a resurgent Islam and revitalized local cultures within the context of a public life which is practically devoid of morality and where force rules rather than law. Columnists such as Mangunwijaya and Darmaputera in the recent past, and contemporary thinkers such as Mudji Sutrisno S.J. and A.A. Yewangoe, envisage an open, flexible, accommodating church, a future in terms of widely scattered networks of prophetically-inspired ecclesial and inter-faith communities. In a pluralistic society, Christians no longer focus upon the congregation, let alone the church institution, but rather upon the family supported by networks of base communities.

Partners on the Muslim side are intellectuals such as Nurcholish Madjid ("Cak Nur", 1939–2005) and Abdurrahman Wahid ("Gus Dur", b. 1940) who argue for a tolerant, righteous, and democratic civil society. Gus Dur is the one-time leader of the 30-million-strong Nahdlatul Ulama traditional movement, while Cak Nur worked in academic circles, coining the phrase: "Islam, yes; Islamic political parties, no."

Literati such as the Jesuit Sindhunata (b. 1952) are actively evolving the syncretistic tradition while giving voice to the victims of oppressive politics and rapacious economic development. Theirs is a universal humanism, open to the Spirit, in the language of popular culture; a vision of universal solidarity that acknowledges that everyone has been made in the image of a single creator. Such thinkers are unconcerned whether sources are Muslim, Christian or indigenous, as long as they give voice to and strengthen the cultural renewal needed to empower the marginalized. This religious-cultural syncretism at the commencement of the twenty-first century contrasts with the politicization of religion which is endeavouring to draw ever-sharper demarcations between religious institutions. The churches are having to learn how to sustain mission without the traditional support of schools, health and social outreach by nurturing Christian and inter-faith communities as "contrast cultures" where trust, honesty, transparency, mutual help, advocacy, and a social conscience can thrive.

And so, the gospel-culture encounter has become a multi-dimensional, critical, transforming dialogue, for Indonesian culture is no longer simply cosmic-holistic but also global-secular. Similarly, a gentle but firm feminism is gradually deconstructing Islam and Christianity both in their patriarchal cultures but also in their dogmatic traditions. In a pluralistic society authentic witness, rather than creedal formulation, become central. And yet both Christians and Muslims have small hardcore extremes; for people threatened by rapid change tend to reassert their impervious boundaries.

As Indonesia undergoes profound change in all sectors, the churches are having to choose between reinforcing internal cohesion, often in charismatic mode, or embracing a broadly ecumenical and inter-faith agenda to build up a society of justice and compassion where the gospel emancipates human consciousness leading to solidarity with others. The future is coming about more through an instinctive urge than by any ecclesial grand vision. This chapter hopes to have shown that Islam and Christianity do not only differ from each other; both also have a range of internal differences as well. Acceptance of internal plurality permits openness to, and collaboration with, "the other". Only thus will reality – and realism – accurately reflect Indonesia's national motto "Unity in Diversity."

Timeline	
Seventh to thirteenth centuries	Buddhist Kingdom of Srivijaya.
Ninth century	Prambanan (Hindu) and Borobudur (Buddist) temples. Small Christian enclaves on coasts of Sumatra and Java.
Thirteenth to fifteenth centuries	Hindu Kingdom of Majapahit.
Twelfth to sixteenth centuries	Peaceful conversion of Sumatra and Java to Islam.
1534	Portuguese arrived in the Moluccas; birth of the Catholic Church.
1605	Dutch established spice centre in Ambon; Protestant Church born, Catholic Church outlawed.

1807	Progressive emancipation of Catholics began.
1859	Portuguese sold Flores and Central Timor to Dutch; Catholic clergy return to Flores.
1904	Rebirth of Catholic Church at Sendangsono, central Java.
1908	Nationalists and Islam spearhead national renaissance and independence movement.
1942–1945	Japanese occupation. Protestant Churches separate from the state.
1945	Political independence declared, internationally recognized in 1949.
1949–1959	Parliamentary Democracy.
1959–1965	Guided Democracy under Soekarno.
1965–1966	Abortive coup-de-état followed by army instigated massacre.
1966–1998	The authoritarian "New Order" of General Soeharto.
1990s	Hundreds of churches bombed and fired as Soeharto's regime entered final phase.
1998	Soeharto's regime collapsed in corruption, a monetary crisis and student unrest.
Since 1998	Slow shuffle to a renewed democracy. The churches work at reforming themselves as family networks of gospel communities.
1998–2003	Christian-Muslim strife in the Moluccas and central Sulawesi.

Further Reading

Aritonang, J.S. and Steenbrink, K. (eds.) *History of Christianity in Indonesia*, 2 vols, Leiden: Brill, 2008.

Aritonang, J.S. *Sejarah Perjumpaan Kristen dan Islam di Indonesia*, Jakarta: BPK Gunung Mulia, 2004.

Boelaars, H.J.W.M. *Indonesianisasi, Het omvormingsproces van de katholieke kerk in Indonesië tot de Indonesische katholieke kerk*, Kampen: Kok, 1991 (Indonesian trans. Yogyakarta: Kanisius, 2005).

Kirk, M. *Let Justice Flow: An Asian Woman Works Creatively for the Liberation of her People*, Delhi: ISPCK, 1997.

Klinken, G. van, *Minorities, Modernity and the Emerging Nation: Christians in Indonesia, A Biographical Approach*. Leiden: KITLV Press, 2003.

Pusat Penelitian dan Pelatihan Teologi Kontekstual Fakultas Teologi Universitas Sanata Dharma, *Gereja Indonesia Pasca-Vatikan II: Refleksi dan Tantangan*, Yogyakarta: Kanisius, 1997.

Steenbrink, K. *Catholics in Indonesia 1808–1942*, 2 vols, Leiden: KITLV, 2003 and 2007 (Indonesian trans. Maumere: Penerbit Ledalero 2006).

Subangun, E., *On the Half-hearted Decolonizing Process of the (Catholic) Church in Indonesia*, Yogyakarta: Kanisius, 2003 (Indonesian ed. Yogyakarta: Kanisius 2003).

Suleeman, F., Sutama, A.A., and A. Rajendra, A. (eds.) *Bergumul dalam Pengharapan, Struggling in Hope: Buku Penghargaan untuk Pdt. Dr. Eka Darmaputera, A tribute to the Rev. Dr. Eka Darmaputera*, Jakarta: BPK Gunung Mulia, 1999.

Sumartana, Th., *Mission at the Crossroads: Indigenous Churches, European Missionaries, Islamic Association and Socio-Religious Change in Java 1812–1936*, Jakarta: BPK Gunung Mulia, 1994.

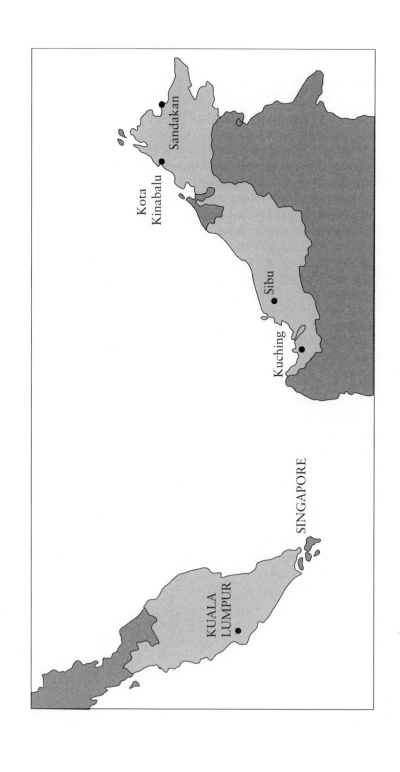

5

Malaysia and Singapore

Edmund Kee-Fook Chia

The Countries and Their People

While Malaysia and Singapore are today two distinct and independent nations they do share a common history and especially a common cultural heritage. Composed of two noncontiguous regions, Malaysia is divided into the peninsula of West Malaysia and the two East Malaysian states of Sabah and Sarawak, located in northern Borneo. Singapore, which is a city-state at the tip of the Malay peninsula, is a tiny island of 635.5 square kilometers (245 square miles).

When speaking of Malaysia and Singapore the one feature often mentioned is their distinctive multiracial, multi-ethnic, and multi-religious population. The Malays, the Chinese, and the Indians are the three dominant ethnic groups of the countries. In Malaysia the Malays are referred to as *bumiputras* (literally: "sons of the soil"), a term also used in reference to the *Orang Asli* or indigenous peoples whose communities are found mainly in East Malaysia (e.g., Kadazandusun, Iban, Murut, Melanau, etc.) but also in the peninsula (e.g., Senoi, Jakun, Semai, Negrito, etc.). While Malays make up more than half the total Malaysian population, the indigenous peoples make up more than two-thirds of East Malaysia's population. The Chinese are the dominant ethnic group in Singapore, constituting more than three-fourths its population.

Most Malays are Muslims. In fact, the Malaysian constitution defines "Malay" as one who professes the religion of Islam and practices Malay culture. Most Chinese adhere to a syncretism of the religions of Confucianism, Taoism, and Buddhism, and most Indians are adherents of Hinduism and some to Sikhism and Jainism. Christianity, a Western import, derived its converts mainly from the Chinese, the Indians, and especially the indigenous population. There is also a small Eurasian Christian community.

Christianities in Asia, edited by Peter C. Phan   © 2011 Blackwell Publishing Ltd except for editorial material and organization © 2011 Peter C. Phan

While Christians number about 9% of the total Malaysian population of 26 million, the majority (about two thirds) reside in the less developed East Malaysia where they comprise up to 20–30% of the local populations. Some East Malaysian villages are almost 100% Christian. The more populous, developed, and urbanized West Malaysia, on the other hand, has an average Christian population which is as low as 1 or 2%. Many cities, especially in the east coast of the peninsula which is predominantly Malay, have a negligible number of Christians. This means that most Malaysian Christians are from East Malaysia and that they are primarily of indigenous backgrounds residing in rural communities. Meanwhile, the metropolitan city-state of Singapore has a Christian population which number around 15% of the nation's population of about 4.5 million. Most are of Chinese, Indian, and Eurasian descent and they are almost all middle-class urban dwellers.

The difference in these demographics have as much to do with the differential movements of peoples in the region as with the deliberate interventions by those in power during the colonial era. Thus, the story of Christianity in Malaysia and Singapore can best be understood within the dynamics of the region's history, especially that of colonialism, and in the context of how race and religion interacts within the socio-political structures of the two nations.

Political, Cultural, and Religious History

The history of the Malay peninsula dates back to at least the third century BCE with records of trading activities between Indian and Chinese merchants. The region's strategic position made it a natural confluence for trade and cultures. By the beginning of the first century CE Hinduism and Buddhism were already established in the Malay archipelago. The subsequent centuries saw the region coming under the influence of various empires, the most significant of which were the Palembang-based Buddhist civilization of Srivijaya and the Javanese Hindu civilization of Majapahit.

With the spread of Islam in the thirteenth and fourteenth centuries from the Arab states and Indic subcontinent, the Malay archipelago quickly established Muslim empires. By the early fifteenth century Parameswara, a rebel Srivijayan prince, established his kingdom in Melaka and wielded power over many of the provinces of the Malay world. He became a Muslim, established a Sultanate, and made Islam the official religion. The subsequent century was to become the golden age of Malay self-rule, whereby Melaka turned into a center of great culture and learning.

At the beginning of the sixteenth century the European powers competing to open trade routes to the Far East sought to establish their own trading ports. To counter the Muslim monopoly of trade in the Malay archipelago, Alfonso de Albuquerque captured Melaka in 1511 and made it the eastern capital of the Portuguese empire. Freed from Melaka's domination, the Malay world broke up into a series of independent sultanates.

The decline of Portuguese power in the Far East towards the end of the sixteenth century was followed by the rise of Dutch power. In 1641 the Dutch captured Melaka and reigned over the region through control of the Straits of Melaka. Following the European Wars of the late eighteenth century where the Netherlands lost to France, rather than handing over some of colonies to France, the Dutch handed them over to the rising power in the East, namely, the British. With time, Britain took control of the Malay world, acquiring the island of Penang in 1786 and by 1824 had acquired Singapore, Melaka, and Province Wellesley, thus establishing British Crown colonies of what came to be known as the Straits Settlements.

It was from there that the British wielded control over the rest of the Malay world and the region became known as British Malaya. The local sultans lost practically all power except those pertaining to the Malay religion and customs. The northern part of Borneo, including East Malaysia, also came under British rule. This was to go on until the Japanese invaded the archipelago during the Second World War, following which Malaya received its independence from the British in 1957.

In 1963 the Federation of Malaya merged with Singapore, Sabah, and Sarawak to form the Federation of Malaysia. The merger was short-lived and in 1965 Singapore was expelled, forcing it to become an independent nation-state, a republic. From then on the two nations went their separate ways, with the Malaysian government thriving on race politics and Singapore on a secular ideology.

British Imperialism and Racial and Ethnic Politics

The rule of the British was not only the longest but also the most significant in that it left long-lasting marks on the social structures of the Malay world. Among the major impacts was the influx of foreign settlers into Malaya. The enhanced economic importance of the region increased labor demand, which was met first by the Arabs and later the Indians and Chinese, many of whom were brought in as indentured workers. The Malays had little role in this. Their peasant lifestyle and religious values were actually used to justify imperial rule. The imperialists' ideology was that the Malays were rural and lacked economic interests and, thus, incapable of exploiting the country's resources. The British, therefore, had to facilitate the immigration of citizens from poverty-stricken provinces of India and China to contribute to the labor force in Malaya.

By the beginning of the twentieth century the three distinct communities dominant in Malaya were divided basically along labor lines: the Malays remained as peasants and smallholders in their farmlands and *kampungs* (villages), the Indians toiled as rubber tappers in secluded rural settlements, and the Chinese worked the tin mines and controlled trade in the urban areas. This division of labor along ethnic lines reinforced the socio-cultural differences between the communities and the spatial segregation exacerbated the already tense inter-ethnic relations. When the Chinese, in view of their occupational advantage, became economically successful, the Malays felt themselves subordinate to the alien immigrant community. The British came to the "rescue" by according the Malays partial political power, while allowing the Chinese to keep the economic pie. This divide-and-rule policy helped in clouding the perception that the various local Asian communities were in fact jointly subordinate to the colonial masters.

The Second World War was the watershed for inter-ethnic relations in Malaya. Until then, there had not been any explicit tension between the ethnic groups if only because there was little occasion for interaction. With the Japanese invasion of the region the Chinese were targeted by the armed occupiers, driving many into the Communist underground. The Japanese used the Malay-populated police force to suppress them. When the British returned after the war, they were met by a nationalistic movement led mainly by the Malays. The non-Malays (who had benefited from colonial rule) were less enthusiastic about independence. The British yielded to the demands of the Malays, returned more political powers to them, accorded them full citizenship, and promised to protect Malay rights and privileges.

Sensitive to Malay demands, the British were less generous toward the Chinese and only granted citizenship to those who had both parents born in Malaya. The Chinese reacted – to the British, as well as to the Malays. They went underground again in 1948, giving rise to a period called the "Emergency." The Malay-dominated government cut off support for the Communists by resettling about a million rural Chinese in "New Villages," fencing them off within barbed wires. This further aggravated inter-ethnic relations which in the 1950s were delicate as the Malays constituted less than 50% of the population.

It was to ensure Malay dominance that when the Malayan government proposed a merger with the Chinese-populated Singapore, it also included the two states of East Malaysia with their majority Malay and indigenous population. The failed merger was also in part due to the politics of ethnicity as the Singaporean Chinese did not take well to the preferential treatment given to the Malays, an allocation enshrined in the country's constitution drafted by a British-appointed commission. Things came to head in 1969 when race riots erupted in the major cities of Malaysia.

The Malay-led government in Malaysia wasted no time in implementing affirmative action programs in favor of the majority Malays such as the New Economic Policy. Its objective was the redistribution of wealth, specifically by allowing the Malays to "catch-up" in the areas of professional life, business, and higher education. The reality, however, is that the policy has been abused and ends up discriminating against the non-Malays as it doles out financial assistance to Malays who are not necessarily poor but politically well-connected. This has further exacerbated the Malay versus non-Malay divide, a situation which has worsened over the years.

While inter-ethnic relations have played a key role in the socio-political development of the two nations, religion often compounds the situation. It is within this context that Christianity exists. Its advent and subsequent growth was due in no small part to British rule and colonial policies and the difficulties and challenges confronting it today are residual effects of the same.

Christianity: Its Beginnings and Development

Records suggest that the Malay world had contact with Christianity as far back as the seventh century when Nestorian settlements were found in the northern parts of the peninsula. By the fifteenth century there were already Christian communities, in particular those from Eastern churches such as the Armenians and Persians, living amongst the people. The arrival of Christianity to the Malay archipelago, however, is more often aligned with the arrival of the Portuguese. The conquest of de Albuquerque in 1511 was done under the banner of the *Padroado Real* through the flagship of the Military Crusading Order for Christ. Accompanying him were eight priests, including Dominicans and Franciscans, who engaged in missionary activities.

But it was with Francis Xavier that Christian mission really took on a more serious note. Not only did he emphasize preaching and Christian instruction, he also built the first school, St. Paul's College, during his five visits to Melaka from 1545 until his death in 1552. With the renewed energy of the Counter-Reformation the Catholic Church sent out more missionaries to Melaka, among them the Blackfriars, the Greyfriars, and the Augustinians. Converts to Christianity came from among the resident Chinese and even some local Muslims. But it was amongst the group of Indian Hindu merchants, who had benefited most from their association with the Portuguese, that there were large numbers of converts. It is no surprise then that there arose the perception that being Christian meant being Portuguese.

With the Dutch capture of Melaka Catholicism was suppressed as Protestantism came into ascendancy. The Dutch destroyed all the churches except for St. Paul's Hill which was converted to Dutch Presbyterianism.

Catholics continued to meet, albeit clandestinely, and were supported especially through lay groups such as the Confraternity of the Holy Rosary.

When the British came into power in the nineteenth century they encouraged the Protestant missions to flourish alongside the spread of Catholicism. Missionaries from all over Europe quickly took advantage of this and made their debut into the Malay world. It was this era which saw the foundation of a variety of churches in Malaya (see Timeline at the end of this chapter). The British also encouraged the founding of Christian mission schools, hospitals, and other forms of social outreach.

With the influx of immigrant Chinese and Indian workers to the Malay world more Christian missionaries were imported. In particular, missionaries from China, both Europeans as well as Chinese, came in great numbers, especially in the aftermath of the 1899 Boxer Rebellion, which generated a host of anti-imperialist sentiments, and also with the fall of China to the Communists in 1949. Some of these missionaries ministered to the ethnic Chinese in the New Villages set up after the Emergency and others established churches in East Malaysia, where many Chinese had already settled, not as immigrant workers but as colonizers.

The Second World War and the independence movement which followed forced Christianity into a period of soul-searching. Having for so long been associated with European imperialism Christianity was to lose much of its prestige and privilege when the Malay world sought freedom from British hegemony. The Malaysian Christians were now faced with a Muslim-led government while Christians in Singapore found themselves in a young nation motivated by a deliberately secular ideology. It was thus crucial for Christianity to take on a more indigenous character so it can be integrated into the socio-cultural and religious fabric of the two nations. Its foreign image, therefore, had to be shed.

Christianity: A Foreign Religion

That Christianity is foreign to the Malay world is obvious but that it continues to be regarded as such even after five centuries needs further discussion. In fact, the Malays sometimes refer to Christianity as *agama orang putih* (literally: "white man's religion"). This is a sore point considering that all the other religions (Islam, Buddhism, Hinduism, Taoism, Confucianism, etc.), even as they were initially foreign, have long since been considered local religions. It is only Christianity which is perceived as foreign not only in the Malay world but in the rest of Asia as well. It is regarded as having been transplanted onto Asian soil but with roots which are not only genetically European but in physical expressions as well.

Evidence of this is that many churches, even until today, are built according to European style and architecture. The entire corpus of Christianity, from its liturgical rites to its hierarchical structures to its teachings and doctrines, reflect European thought patterns. Some things such as the vestments which priests put on are no more than vestiges of Roman imperial courts. Hymns and prayers used for worship are in the main composed in the West and passed on to the local people by the missionaries. In short, there is really very little in Christianity which is local other than its membership.

Moreover, the local churches have also been overly dependent on Western missionaries for providing leadership and especially for financial support. Some liken this to a codependent relationship which is as much enforced by the foreign missionaries as desired by the local Christians. The former knew no better and saw Christianity as intrinsically linked to its Western forms of expression. The latter saw the Western modes as symbols of power and prestige, much the same way they viewed the European colonizers as the superior race, referring to them as *tuan besar* ("great master"). No doubt both parties are but well-meaning and good intentioned and simply reflecting the attitudes of the time. As Malaysian theologian Kenneth Williams suggests,

> There was a real attempt to form a native clergy but this was hampered by a mentality which suspected the moral and intellectual competence of 'the relatively weak races' and which, if it considered an indigenous episcopacy at all, saw it as serving a useful secondary function in relieving the missionaries for more productive work.[1]

The dynamics of this foreign missionary versus local Christian relationship went unquestioned for most of Christian history in the Malay world until the Second World War. The event surrounding the occupation by Japanese forces was the watershed for local consciousness. First, the local people were disillusioned that Britain failed to offer them protection, thus raising questions about its might and invincibility. Second, many European missionaries were interned by the occupying forces, forcing local Christians to step forward to take charge of the churches. Third, the local people realized that they were now controlled by an occupying force made up of people who were not white but of yellow skin, just as they were. With this the myth of Western superiority crumbled just as British colonialism crumbled all over the world. As the Union Jack descended in Malaya the search for an indigenous identity and local autonomy began to increase. This sentiment was not only shared in the socio-political realms but extends to the Christian churches as well.

The Challenge of an Indigenous Church

Developments within the Roman Catholic Church, whose members constitute about half of all Christians in the region, during this era is especially
telling. While its local ecclesiastical structures date back to the arrival of the
Paris Foreign Missions (M.E.P.) in the late eighteenth century, it was only in
the last five decades that local priests were afforded leadership roles. Dominic
Vendargon was made bishop of Kuala Lumpur and Francis Chan of Penang in
1955. As for East Malaysia, when the new government made it difficult for
missionaries to continue serving in the region Peter Chung became the first
local to be appointed bishop of the Diocese of Kota Kinabalu in 1970. Until
then the region was managed mainly by the English Mill Hill Missionaries
whose presence in Borneo dates to the late nineteenth century. Meantime, the
Catholic Church in Singapore continued to remain under the jurisdiction of
Melaka's M.E.P. French bishop until 1977 when a local priest, Gregory
Yong, was consecrated bishop for Singapore. The Protestant churches were
not much different. The Methodists had their first local bishop when Yap Kim
Hao was appointed in 1968. The first local bishop of the Anglican Diocese of
West Malaysia was Roland Yap who was elected in 1970.

The subsequent decades saw a few more local Malaysians thrust into
leadership positions. But they were all either of Chinese or Indian descent, an
understandable fact given that it was from these two immigrant communities
that many converts to Christianity came from. But that does not discount the
other fact that nearly two thirds of all Christians belong to the *Orang Asli* and
indigenous communities. It was not until 1993 that the first indigenous
Catholic, Cornelius Piong, a member of the *Kadazandusun* tribe, was
appointed bishop of the newly created Keningau diocese. One could surmise
that even here the politics of race is in play. Just as the European missionaries
were condescending toward the local Christians, the Malaysian Christians of
immigrant descent were probably as condescending toward those from the
indigenous communities. The justifications may well be the same: that they
are a "weaker" race, that they are not as educated, and that they lack the
moral and intellectual fiber to lead Christian communities.

As is obvious, the issue of race is as much alive in the church as in society. To
be sure, ethnic churches are still common in Malaysia, continuing the
tradition of yesteryear when communities were segregated. But today, aside
from church services conducted in English, Tamil, Mandarin, Cantonese, or
Iban, they are also conducted in the languages of the new immigrant workers
such as Filipino, Vietnamese, and Korean.

The use of *Bahasa Melayu* (the Malay language) was controversial from its
outset. It is not just because Christians continued to harbor anti-Malay
sentiments; they were also not particularly competent in the language. The

reality, however, is that there is no other unifying language for Malaysia and that the younger generation are simply more competent in *Bahasa Melayu*, which has become the national language. Incidentally, Singapore, with its majority Chinese population, still has *Bahasa Melayu* as its national language, though its official language includes English, Mandarin, and Tamil.

If the language issue is already so complicated, one can expect that the task of authentically inculturating Christianity in the Malay world would be even more challenging. The first challenge: which culture does Christianity identify with? There are Chinese Christians, Indian Christians, and Eurasian Christians, aside from the *Orang Asli* and indigenous Christians. The Chinese Christians who are of Confucian, Buddhist, or Taoist backgrounds are culturally quite different from the Indian Christians who are of Hindu, Sikh, or Jain backgrounds. The issue of ancestor veneration may concern the former while the issue of caste, the latter. The *Orang Asli* Christians may yet have concerns arising from their animist roots such as negotiations with *semangat* (spirits) or the role of shamans in daily living. To be sure, there is no easy solution for the inculturation of Christianity in the region.

Some suggest that Christianity ought to be inculturated into the dominant culture of the Malay world, namely, the Malay culture. The problem, however, is that historically Christianity has had little to do with the Malays, not only because the British discouraged proselytizing among them (respecting their deal with the local sultans) but also because being Malay has become synonymous with being Muslim. As such the racial antagonism of Malay versus non-Malay is often confused as a religious one, of Muslims versus the non-Muslims. Christians, therefore, generally regard the Malay culture as inherently Islam and, thus, incompatible with Christianity. Moreover, any attempts at inculturating Christianity into the Malay culture may also raise suspicion that they are but laden with ulterior proselytizing motives. Suffice to say that it would certainly have an adverse effect on Christian-Muslim relations.

The Challenge of Islamization

The Federal Constitution of Malaysia explicitly spells out Islam as the official religion. But since the same Constitution also provides for the freedom of religion interreligious relations should be peaceful and harmonious. Politics, however, has decided otherwise. When the dominant political party controlling the government, the United Malays' National Organization (UMNO), experienced in-fighting, it gave rise to the splinter group *Parti Islam SeMalaysia* (Pan Malaysian Islamic Party or PAS).

PAS operates on the premise that UMNO has become secular. PAS, therefore, champions the politics of religion and especially the establishment of an Islamic state. By this it is referring to a state based on the principles of religion, i.e., one of justice and free from the ills of corruption, cronyism, and nepotism. Because PAS is now in the opposition, UMNO has to launch counter-attacks. Both, of course, are competing for the very same electorate, namely, the Malays, since politics has been in the main along communal lines.

PAS's Islamists' ambitions are met by UMNO's Islamization policies. Thus, Islam has permeated into many areas of the public sphere and into institutions such as the media, judiciary, banks, schools, universities, etc. In a way, UMNO and PAS are simply trying to out-do one another. In the process competing interests have to be minimized. Christianity represents one such interest. Thus, for example, to facilitate the Islamization of education in schools, the de-Christianization process has to take place first. In this regard Christian schools, which have been in existence for more than a century, are slowly being phased out. On account of other governmental policies Christians are having difficulties procuring lands for the building of churches or for Christian burial grounds. Good Friday is no longer a public holiday. Open displays of Christianity, even the singing of Christmas carols in public places, can lead to problems. History is taught in schools from an Islamic perspective, including the history of Christianity and that *Nabi Isa* (prophet Jesus) did not suffer the fate of death by crucifixion. The list goes on and on. In a way, one can say that the privileges accorded Christianity by the British are slowly being taken away.

Specific laws have also been enacted to guard against proselytizing Muslims. For instance, there is a legislation which forbids non-Muslims to use lexicon items which could be mistaken for Islam, namely, Arabic words such as *Allah, Nabi, Rasul,* etc. While the law aims at protecting the simple-minded Muslim from thinking that Christianity and Islam are one since Christians address God the same way as Muslims do, it of course impinges upon the rights of Christians (as well as members of other religions) to use the words in their own worship sessions. Likewise, the law which forbids a Malay or Iban translation of the Bible – aimed at preventing Malay Muslims and Iban Muslims from gaining access to the Bible readily – also impinges upon the rights of Christians to read the Bible in the Malay or Iban language. Of course, where the faith of no Muslim is at stake the practical reality is that these laws are seldom enforced, and so churches continue to use the Arabic words and the Iban or Malay Bible.

But where Muslim souls are involved the situation can be complicated. For example, Muslim converts to Christianity (including a few Malays) not only invite trouble to themselves but to the churches involved in their baptism as well. A few high profile cases brought to the courts in recent years have highlighted the complications especially since religious matters pertaining to Muslims are adjudicated by the parallel Shari'ah courts while non-Muslims abide by only the decisions of civil courts. There is yet another law which allows for the prosecution of the organizers of non-Muslim religious events if Muslims are found present at such gatherings. Again, here is yet another law aimed at protecting Muslims but the practical reality is that the law can have adverse consequences for non-Muslims. This law has resulted in many Christian events, such as evangelization rallies or Christmas concerts, having to display prominently signs which read *For Non-Muslims Only*. Even Christian propagation tools, such as videos and tracts, have to carry the disclaimer. Doing so, of course, seems to suggest that Christians have no qualms proselytizing members of other religions (Buddhists, Hindus, Sikhs, etc.) just because there are no laws forbidding them to.

As can be seen, Muslim-Christian relations in Malaysia continue to be uneasy on account of governmental policies and the Islamization process. This has impacted the churches' relationship amongst themselves as well as with other religions. It is against this backdrop that ecumenism (used broadly here to refer to inter-church as well as inter-religious relations) in Malaysia has to be understood.

The Challenge of Ecumenism

The story of inter-church relations in Malaysia and Singapore is often traced to the establishment of the Malayan Christian Council (MCC) in 1948. The founding churches included mainline Protestant denominations such as the Methodist, Anglican, Presbyterian, Mar Thoma, Syrian Orthodox, Lutheran, Salvation Army, and Brethren, as well as interdenominational organizations such as the YWCA, YMCA, and the Bible Society. In 1961 the MCC was renamed the Council of Churches in Malaysia and Singapore and in 1974 it became two separate Councils, the Council of Churches of Malaysia (CCM) and the National Council of Churches of Singapore (NCCS).

During this period, the more evangelically oriented churches continued to function independently. It was not until 1983 that many of these independent churches came together to establish the National Evangelical Christian Fellowship (NECF) of Malaysia. In 1986 the CCM, the NECF, and the Roman Catholic Church came together to establish the Christian Federation of Malaysia (CFM). A few years earlier, in 1982, some Christian groups had already come together with persons of other religions to inaugurate the Malaysian Consultative Council for Buddhism, Christianity, Hinduism, and Sikhism (MCCBCHS). The Taoist community recently joined the council. This body is now acknowledged as the institution which speaks on behalf of all the non-Muslims in the country.

The formation of both the CFM and the MCCBCHS were by no means motivated primarily by the greater desire for ecumenical dialogue or inter-religious collaboration. Instead, both were established in response to the

Islamization process. The CFM provides a united forum for Christians to speak out against any anti-Christian policy as well as to make representations on behalf of the member churches. Likewise, the MCCBCHS was brought into being to serve as watchdog of government policies affecting non-Muslims as a whole. While the council purports to promote interreligious dialogue the absence of Muslims in the council raises critical questions about the nature and dynamics of such dialogues. Nevertheless, such a body is necessary even if they serve primarily as fronts for non-Muslims to fight for their rights or to bargain for concessions.

The above efforts are but just one part of the ecumenical story. The more significant and undocumented ecumenical ventures are actually those which happen on a daily basis amongst the ordinary people. Schools, hospitals, shopping malls, and night markets are where the real ecumenical dialogues take place. Most Malaysians are always and everywhere interacting harmoniously with persons of other religions. Christians have healthy relationships with their neighbors who are Buddhists, Hindus, Muslims, etc. Christian mission schools and hospitals exemplify this in that they not only cater to a clientele which is in the main non-Christian but are also administered and served by principals, teachers, doctors, and nurses who are Muslims, Confucianists, Sikhs, etc. It comes as no surprise then that the majority of Christians intermarry with persons of other religions, including Muslims. Likewise, Christian conversion to Islam is by no means an exception. In short, there is a relative degree of ecumenical (inter-church as well as inter-religious) peace and harmony present in the lives of the ordinary Christian. But this can very quickly melt away when subject to the mercies of race and religious politics.

In this regard there are groups, especially non-governmental organizations (NGOs), which are speaking out against the instrumentalization of race and religion for political ends. Many are led by Muslim intellectuals and social activists. A great number of Christians are also at the forefront of these NGOs. Unfortunately, many have to do so in their own personal capacities and not as representatives of their churches. In fact, most churches would not dare associate themselves with activities in favor of human rights, in particular those critical of the state's abuse of power, for fear of incurring the wrath of the government. This is so in Malaysia but, as we shall see below, even more pronounced in Singapore.

The Challenge of Church-State Relations

One of the greatest challenges confronting Christianity in Malaysia and Singapore is that as a minority religion its preoccupation is with survival, hence curtailing its prophetic function. This is especially so when the government of the day is unabashed about using its powers to suppress criticism and voices of dissent. Analysts suggest that the state of Singapore fits this profile. Governed by what amounts to a singular political party with a token opposition, Singapore has emerged as one of the wealthiest nation in the world in a span of just a little over 40 years. No mean feat for a country with almost no natural resources and a scarcity of land.

In exchange Singapore's government rules almost by decree, earning a reputation for being an illiberal or procedural democracy. Thus, over the years, Singapore has had legislations controlling practically every aspect of the citizen's life. There was at one time a "stop at two" policy for child-bearing but when this resulted in overly low birthrates it was amended to "three if you can." The latter meant that graduates and educated professionals could have more but poor people would still be penalized for having more than their share of children. The Sterilization and Abortion on Demand Bills were passed to assist in controlling its population growth. It is only in Singapore that one can be fined for possessing chewing gum, a policy enacted when the city-state discovered the menace of chewing gum litter. Its government is so efficient in fining people for practically everything that Singapore is often called the "fine city." One might also recall that an American teenager was sentenced to caning by the *rotan* for graffiti vandalism.

Singapore's political leaders have sought to justify such authoritarian rule by alluding to "Asian values" (read: Confucian submission to authority) which is not only integral to Singapore's predominant Chinese culture but also necessary for a state which is still young and thus in need of a firm parental hand. A by-product of this is that political activism is stifled and political opponents are imprisoned. Chia Thye Poh is the most famous of them, having been detained without trial for 32 years under Singapore's Internal Security Act (ISA) – a draconian law remnant from British colonial days in Malaya.

But it was the ISA campaign of 1987, called *Operation Spectrum*, which was most consequential for Christians in Singapore. It rounded up about two dozen Singaporeans, mostly Roman Catholic social activists, detaining them without trial for extended periods. They were accused of a Marxist con-spiracy with plans for armed struggle. They included the outspoken priest-editor of a Catholic newspaper, a number of other priests, church workers, lawyers, and other professionals. The alleged master-mind was Vincent Cheng, an ex-seminarian who worked with organizations such as Christian Student Societies, Young Christian Workers' Movement, and Justice and Peace Commissions. Some suggest that their real crime was in highlighting oppressive measures by multinational corporations and abuse of power by government machineries. They were not the only victims as the Christian Conference of Asia, a mainstream Protestant international organization actively involved in human rights issues, was expelled from Singapore at the end of that same year. Incidentally, the same ploy was used by the Malaysian government a year later when in the midst of a major political challenge it launched a nation-wide ISA arrest, called *Operasi Lallang,* to silence government critics. Hauled in were a number of Christians including church workers, pastors, university professors, as well as opposition leaders and human rights activists.

Through all of these social engineering and political control, church leaders in Singapore, as in Malaysia, are usually silent and compliant. As leaders of institutions they find themselves having to choose between confronting the power of the state and the survival of their churches. It is in view of this that Christians in Singapore and Malaysia have learned that it is safer if their churches take on a more pro-government stance or remain apolitical and take on more parochial characteristics.

Thus, churches have generally been more preoccupied with intra-church issues such as spirituality, membership, growth, and the nurturing of their own Christian communities. They also reinforce the traditional forms of religious expressions such as devotions to saints (the St. Anne's feast celebration in Penang attracts hundreds of thousands of pilgrims each year) and novenas to Mary, the Mother of Jesus (the weekly Saturday novena liturgies in Singapore are more popular than Sunday liturgies). Aside from this, new forms of religious expressions, but which are also apolitical and stress personal piety and the I-God relationship, have also been on the rise in various parts of Malaysia and Singapore. This is especially evidenced in the genre of the new churches mushrooming throughout the two countries.

The New and Growing Churches

Despite the challenges confronting Christianity in Malaysia and Singapore, statistics reveal that its membership continues to grow. Churches which have grown exponentially, however, are mostly the new, independent, and non-denominational churches. Most of these are thoroughly homegrown: founded, led, propagated, and funded by local Christians. The members are predominantly younger, more educated, and from the middle classes. Many join the churches through university and campus ministries (which are generally domesticated and non-prophetic in orientation) and remain active through their professional lives.

Even if nondenominational, these churches are usually oriented toward Pentecostalism and Evangelicalism, and espouse elements of Calvinist spirituality. This highlights God's rule, grace, and mercy, on the one hand, and human sinfulness and depravity, on the other. Through the Doctrine of Election these Christians believe that some have been chosen for

God's salvation and a clear sign of this is their material blessings. The Gospel of Prosperity feeds well into such theological systems, which in turn feeds into the global capitalist free-market economic structures. The focus is primarily on personal piety and salvation, traditional morality and individual social behavior, with little or no concern for political involvement.

Prime examples of these new churches are the City Harvest Church, the Evangelical Free Church, the Latter Rain Church, and the Full Gospel Assemblies. Began through the efforts of individuals and charismatic leaders, often educated or with ties to America or Europe, they have slowly grown in size and in outreach. Some have even become mega-churches. Many came into ascendancy after the 1960s and especially in the last 20 years, following the rapid pace of industrialization and urbanization in both Malaysia and Singapore. Their growth is attributed to a variety of factors: (1) they have more flexible structures and thus can adjust easily to societal changes; (2) they have less stress on social involvement and so can focus on personal piety and internal church nourishment; (3) they are more emphatic about evangelism and the recruitment of non-Christians as well as other Christians; (4) they are less dependent on professional clergy and foreign missionaries; and (5) they encourage lay participation and maximize membership involvement through cell-group meetings and other such events. In short, these churches are in touch with the people, rooted in their communities, and reaching out to others.

It is no wonder that they are growing, often times at the expense of the more established and traditional churches. But their long-term impact on Christianity in Malaysia and Singapore is yet to be known. Indications are there that they are here to stay. They may well spell the future of Christianity in the region, a future which, unfortunately, is more dependent on the race and religious politics of the day than on the will and power of God's Holy Spirit.

Timeline	
1400	Beginning of Melaka Sultanate.
1511	Portuguese conquest of Melaka. Arrival of Roman Catholicism.
1545	Francis Xavier's mission to Melaka.
1641	Dutch conquest of Melaka. Arrival of Protestantism.
1662	The first New Testament in *Bahasa Melayu*.

1786	British occupation of Penang.
1809	Beginning of Anglican mission.
1810	Roman Catholic seminary, College General, established in Penang.
1815	London Missionary Society establishes base in Melaka.
1823	First translation of the Bible into Chinese produced in Malaya.
1847	Beginning of Borneo Church Mission in Sarawak.
1859	Beginning of Open Brethren mission.
1874	Pangkor Treaty signed. Beginning of British expansion in Malay states.
1881	Beginning of Presbyterian Church.
1882	Beginning of Basel Christian Church.
1891	Beginning of Methodist Church.
1907	Beginning of Evangelical Lutheran Church.
1911	Beginning of Seventh Day Adventist.
1926	Beginning of Mar Thoma Church.
1927	Beginning of True Jesus Church.
1928	Beginning of Borneo Evangelical Mission.
1932	Beginning of Orthodox Syrian Church in Malaysia.
1932	Beginning of Jehovah's Witnesses.
1935	Beginning of Assemblies of God.
1936	Beginning of Pentecostal Church of Malaya.
1941–1945	Japanese Occupation of Malaya.

1948–1960	Emergency and Communist Insurrection.
1948	Malayan Christian Council established.
1951	Christian National Evangelical Commission established.
1953	Beginning of Lutheran Church in Malaysia.
1953	Malaysian Baptist Convention established.
1957	Independence of Malaya from British.
1960	Bible Institute of Malaya established by the AOG.
1963	Formation of the Federation of Malaysia.
1965	Singapore expelled from Malaysia, establishes independent republic.
1979	Seminari Theologi Malaysia established.
1982	Malaysian Consultative Council for Buddhism, Christianity, Hinduism, and Sikhism instituted.
1983	National Evangelical Christian Fellowship established.
1986	Christian Federation of Malaysia established.

Notes

1. Williams, K. The Church in West Malaysia and Singapore: A study of the Catholic Church in West Malaysia and Singapore Regarding her Situation as an Indigenous Church, Doctoral dissertation, Katholieke Universiteit Te Leuven, 1976, pp. 90–92.

Further Reading

Abraham, C. *Divide and Rule: The Roots of Race Relations in Malaysia*, Petaling Jaya: INSAN, 1997.

Batumalai, S. *A Malaysian Theology of Muhibbah: A Theology for a Christian Witnessing in Malaysia*, Kuala Lumpur: Seminari Theoloji Malaysia, 1990.

Chew, M. *The Journey of the Catholic Church in Malaysia, 1511–1996*, Kuala Lumpur: Catholic Research Centre, 2000.

Chia, E. and Shastri, H. "Christianity," "History of Christianity," and "Christian Denominations in Malaysia," in Hassan, K. and Basri, G. (eds.) *The Encyclopedia of Malaysia: Religions and Beliefs*, Kuala Lumpur: Editios Didier Millet, 2005, pp. 100–105.

Hunt, R., Lee, K.-H., and Roxborogh, J. (eds.) *Christianity in Malaysia: A Denominational History*, Petaling Jaya: Pelanduk Publications, 1992.

Moey, M., Kwan, Y.-L., and Goh, K.-P. (eds.) *The Christian and Race Relations in Malaysia*, Petaling Jaya: Graduates Christian Fellowship, 1986.

Rooney, J. *Khabor Gembira: A History of the Catholic Church in East Malaysia & Brunei, 1880–1976*, London: Burns & Oates, 1981.

Wong, J.Y.K. *Singapore: The Church in the Midst of Social Change*, Fort Canning Road, Singapore: Church Growth Study Centre, 1973.

Yap, K.-H., Church Structure Issues in Asian Ecumenical Thought with Particular Reference to Malaysia and Singapore, ThD dissertation, Boston University School of Theology, 1969.

6

The Philippines

José Mario C. Francisco, S.J.

International media typically highlights two clusters of images related to Filipino Christianity. The first, shot every Holy Week in humid Central Luzon towns, shows practices meant to recall and imitate Christ's suffering – the most graphic and grotesque to some being the actual crucifixion of some devotees amidst a throng of locals and tourists alike. The second shows scenes with priests, nuns, and lay people brandishing rosaries and holy images at protest rallies. Best known among them are the people-power revolutions called EDSA 1 and 2 for Epifanio de los Santos Avenue, setting of massive rallies decisive for the ousting of Presidents Ferdinand E. Marcos in 1986 and Joseph Estrada in 2001.

These popular images show the prominent place Christianity occupies in Philippine history and society. Latest available data (2004) count Christians at 91% of a population of 86 million – 83% Catholic and others of various Protestant mainline and evangelical groups. Other religious traditions account for the rest, with Muslims from regions that resisted Spanish colonial rule being the most significant at 5%. Moreover, behind these popular images lie the two issues which have defined Filipino Christianity throughout its history: its dynamic relation to context and its complex role in civil society.

First, images of Filipinos flagellating themselves or carrying crosses, even being nailed to them, indicate the relationship between Christianity and the Philippine context. Though these rituals take place only in certain localities and vary according to ethnic and regional factors, their fundamental impulse to re-live the Christ story in both personal and social situations informs much of native Christian thought and practice. This impulse has emerged out of the long encounter between Christianity in its different historical forms and the changing local cultural context. For more than three centuries of Spanish colonization, late medieval post-Reformation Spanish Catholicism interacted with a traditional Malay culture with Chinese and South Asian influences. Early-twentieth-century American Protestantism faced a changed context characterized by the religious and cultural legacy of this earlier interaction as well as nationalist sentiments among Filipinos then. As a result of this shared history, Christianity and the Philippine cultural landscape have shaped each other profoundly.

Second, images of Christians in political rallies raise another issue defining Filipino Christianity – its involvement in civil society. This involvement is manifested by the continuing and extensive work of Christian individuals, institutions, and churches in social services and education. Moreover, though the voice of Filipino Christianity in civil society has never been monolithic and though it has not always been heeded because of its occasionally close links with those in power, the role of Christian social involvement has been significant at crucial instances such as the nineteenth-century nationalist movement against Spain or the 1986 overthrow of President Marcos' martial law regime. Not surprisingly, Christian leaders and churches often receive trust ratings in surveys higher than other social institutions despite periodic allegations of political interference, sexual misconduct, and financial irregularities.

Because of how it has been defined by these issues, Filipino Christianity has been perceived as too closely tied to culture and politics. On account of its relations to culture, it has been labeled as cultural Christianity without religious value – with Christianity and Philippine culture in a syncretic mixture that leads to split-level or schizophenic behavior. Due to its social involvement, it has been accused of being too political. Though this label often comes from those with their own political agenda, it considers Filipino Christianity only in terms of its role in civil society.

This chapter aims to answer these perceptions of Filipino Christianity by looking at how Filipino Christianity has faced the issues that have defined it throughout its history. One discovers the dynamism of Christianity's relation to the Philippine context and the complexity of its social role. These issues have emerged from its long, even tortuous, history and, at the same time, indicate its greatest resources in facing contemporary challenges in a global and pluralistic world.

Transplanting Spanish Catholicism

The issues that would define Filipino Christianity emerged with the 1521 arrival of Ferdinand Magellan's Spanish fleet in Cebu and the subsequent decision to establish settlements in the archipelago. With Spain's rise as an imperial power and recent conquest of the American mainland, the missionary aim to spread Christianity converged more than ever with the colonial aim to expand and to increase trade as far as China and Japan.[1] This so-called "conquest by the sword and the cross" found its moral and juridical basis in the *Patronato Real de las Indias* – the agreement between the Spanish King and the Papacy that in the colonies, the King served as the effective head of the Church and the Church as "the King's conscience." Thus evangelization and colonization with their respective institutions, church and state, were difficult to dissociate in theory and in practice, though legal and bureaucratic ambiguities as well as animosities between particular officials led to some bitter conflicts.

Within this framework, the colonial church and state sought to create a civilization in its image and to transplant Spanish Catholicism in the islands' tropical landscape. They thereby employed twin strategies of establishing towns and using vernacular languages, both of which would redefine this geographical and social landscape, and facilitate Christianity's social role within it.

In the first place, early colonial and church authorities transformed native space because the accomplishment of Spanish aims was made difficult by the insular geography and pattern of small linear settlements (*barangays*).[2] They adapted their New World strategy of "*reduccion*", creating towns in the Spanish grid pattern with a central plaza where church, civil buildings, and residences of the prominent were contiguous to each other. This strategy was undertaken with such vigor that, for instance, Augustinian missionaries alone founded over 100 towns by the mid-seventeenth century.[3] Even after centuries of haphazard construction and expansion, one can still discern this pattern today in what remains of colonial capital Intramuros and in many places like the then missionary outpost Tagbilaran, Bohol.

Native territories were further divided among different religious orders in accordance with the 1594 royal directive, and became subject to colonial measures based on latitude and longitude as in navigation. Furthermore with the subsequent emergence of agriculture and trade in the eighteenth century, native space was fully redefined under an integrated system of political administration, religion, and commerce under Spanish control.

Accompanying this redefinition of space, buildings had to be constructed and, thanks to endemic earthquakes and other calamities, continually repaired and even rebuilt. Religious orders put to task members knowledgeable in architecture or art. For example, Jesuit priest Antonio Sedeño (d. 1595) built churches in Sta. Ana, Manila and the Visayan missions, and Augustinian priest Juan de Albarrán offered advice to other missionaries in his *Modo de construir iglesias y conventos en las islas Filipinas* (1711).[4] These missionaries constructed churches and mission compounds, drawing from Spanish or New

World designs, and preferring the baroque as a general style because of its adaptability.

Though Spanish in conception, their church designs adapted according to local needs and available materials. Some churches like that of Boljoon, Cebu built by Augustinian priest Julian Bermejo in the early 1800s had to be fortresses as well because of intermittent Muslim raids. Common local materials were used: volcanic tuff (*adobe*) in Luzon, brick and stone in Ilocos, and coral-stone in Cebu and Panay. Moreover, native artisans used their creativity in the ornamentation of the façade or the main backdrop of the altar (*retablo*) and in making images of saints in many churches.

The convergence of these factors resulted in neither Spanish copies nor original designs, and led some to name their style, albeit not too accurately, as "squat baroque" – baroque in general conception but tied to the earth rather than lofty because of local exigencies. But it produced works of outstanding historical and esthetic interest. Ilocos churches are known for their façades which, though massive, appear light because of elaborate curves and ornamentation. Chinese fu dogs in granite guard Intramuros' San Agustin Church, the carved doors of which show luxuriant local flora. Similar ornamentation is characteristic of the Visayan churches in Panay and Iloilo.[5]

For its second strategy, the colonial church decided at the 1582 Synod of Manila to use local languages rather than Castilian Spanish for preaching the Christian message. This linguistic strategy for winning native hearts and minds more easily involved complex components and had far-reaching consequences for the encounter between Christianity and native culture.

The native syllabary of 3 vowels and 12 consonants was first transposed into the Roman alphabet. Vernacular discourse until then was exclusively among natives and primarily oral, save for short carved messages on bamboo or palm leaves. But this transposition brought to it the world of writing and the accompanying technology of printing, and opened these languages to non-native others.

This radical change in the nature and use of the vernaculars produced countless manuscripts and publications. Early missionaries learned the new languages and produced the necessary linguistic tools for evangelization. Twenty-four Tagalog books would be published five decades since the first Tagalog book, *Doctrina Cristiana* (1593) where the "Our Father" appeared in Roman and native scripts. Among them were grammars codifying rules for oral and written Tagalog such as *Arte y regla de la lengua tagala* (1610) by Dominican Francisco Blancas de San Jose, known as the local Demosthenes for mastering Tagalog and Chinese, and *Compendio de la lengua tagala* (1703) by Gaspar de'San Agustin.[6]

Dictionaries were painstakingly accomplished, an early example being Franciscan Pedro de San Buenaventura's 707-page volume (1613) with a Tagalog-Spanish finder list for natives learning Spanish.[7] The care with which these dictionaries were complied is evident in the history of the best known, *Vocabulario de la lengua tagala* (1754). This work was begun by Dominicans – first, Francisco Blancas de San Jose, and later Tomas de los Reyes and Miguel Ruiz for the letters A to D – and then passed on to Jesuits Pablo Clain, Francisco Jansens, and Jose Hernandez. Jesuit Juan de Noceda took over, and after his death, the Spanish-Tagalog mestizo Pedro de Sanlucar completed the work.

Materials needed for evangelization were translated or produced. Prayers and lives of saints were sourced from Europe and the New World; notable was the popular story of St. Filomena, originally in Italian, then translated into French and Spanish, and finally into the local vernacular Cebuano. Augustinian Pedro de Herrera translated Jesuit Francisco de Salazar's *Meditaciones* (1645), and Dominican Antonio Florentino Puansen his fellow Dominican Francisco Gainza's *Milicia de Jesucristo* (1872).[8]

New catechisms were soon produced: Franciscan Juan de Oliver's *Doctrina cristiana* explaining basic Christian prayers (circa 1599), Blancas de San Jose's *Memorial de la vida christiana* (1605) with poems in mixed Spanish and Tagalog, and Franciscan Alonso de Santa Ana's *Explication de la doctrina christiana en lengua tagala* (1628) in question-and-answer form.[9] Sermons of well-known preachers like Blancas de San Jose (d. 1614) were given to new missionaries.[10]

This linguistic and cultural process – began for the Tagalog vernacular of Manila and its environs and replicated for other vernaculars as missionaries settled in new localities – was informed by Spanish attitudes toward the natives and their culture. Despite questions about native rights raised by Juan de Vittoria and Bartolome de las Casas in Spain and the colonies, the Spanish missionaries considered the natives (*indios*) as pagans, and therefore much of their way of life as the work of the devil. Jesuit Francisco Alcina, eighteenth-century chronicler of Visayan life classified the natives according to the hierarchical view of typical of his time: lower than the European Christian and the civilized non-Christian of India and China, but higher than those considered brutes. After his many decades in the Visayas, Alcina described them as childlike, capable of being civilized, and subsequently evangelized.[11]

These two strategies through which the colonial church came to terms with the social and cultural landscape of native society facilitated the dominant presence of the colonial church in social affairs. This presence became initially visible in the person of the parish priest, usually a friar. Given the inadequate number of colonial personnel to administer newly gathered territories, he represented de facto church as well as colonial authority, and took on multiple tasks such building roads or teaching new techniques in agriculture. He also played a crucial role in the colony's social organization: first, by enticing local leaders to teach catechism and lead prayers for the dying in barrios too remote for the priest to attend to and second, by organizing them into sodalities and confraternities like those in Europe and the New World.

But the greater social involvement of the church came through institutions designed to address various social needs. With church organization in place by the seventeenth century, different religious groups offered social services for the young and the sick through orphanages, clinics, and hospitals, some of which like San Juan de Dios Hospital still operate today.

Most significant among these institutions were schools focussed on the young who were more docile to the new faith and also proved to be effective in attracting their parents. This involvement in education began as informal sessions primarily designed for religious instruction but later turned into *seminarios del indios*, boarding schools teaching reading, writing, and music.

More formal educational institutions often started as schools for Spaniards but were eventually opened to natives.[12] In the early seventeenth century, Jesuits founded the Colegio de Manila for those training for the priesthood and the Colegio de San Jose for others, and the Dominicans San Juan de Letran and Colegio de Santo Thomas that became a university by 1611. Colegio de Sta. Isabel for girls was established in 1636. In the nineteenth century, many of these schools including the Ateneo Municipal, newly founded by the Jesuits after their worldwide suppression by the Bourbon dynasty offered higher degrees in many disciplines to the native-born–seminarians and clerics as well children of the emerging elite involved in agriculture and trade. Such profound involvement in education would have far-reaching implications for Christianity as well as colonization and would continue into the present.

The two defining issues of Filipino Christianity then arose out of the intertwined colonial and religious aims of the Spanish enterprise. To fulfill these aims toward transplanting Spanish Catholicism, the colonial church had to confront the local landscape and to be involved in social concerns. Its strategies in redefining native space and using local vernaculars for evangelization, however, brought about unintended consequences as a result of the native response to these aims.

Appropriating Christianity, Resisting Colonial Rule

Natives were initially wary but not hostile to Spanish settlement because of earlier contacts with Muslim, Chinese, and even Portuguese traders. But their long term response to Christianity was shaped by its relation to the native cultural context and its role in social affairs.

Aside from the social services offered by the colonial church, local reception of Christianity was initially facilitated by the defense of the natives by some priests. As early as 1580s, Augustinian missionaries and colonial authorities fought over Spanish treatment of natives. Missionaries alleged that Spaniards who received jurisdiction over land exacted tribute without fulfilling their responsibilities and local leaders who had both judicial and executive functions abused power, and therefore protected the natives from these abuses.[13] These instances plus periodic jurisdictional conflicts between church and government manifested the cracks in the *Patronato* which would facilitate their eventual dissociation in the nineteenth century.

But the most significant sign of the native response to Christianity was the emergence of a Christianity expressed in vernacular terms. This process of reception empowered natives not only to appropriate Christianity but to resist colonial power as well. Both reception and resistance would shed light on the impulses behind the popular images of Filipino Christianity.

Like the development of "squat baroque" in local church architecture, this Christianity was born out of the complex encounter between Spanish Catholicism and native culture. Though missionaries took great care in transplanting Spanish Catholicism with its late medieval trappings and post-Reformation ethos in the local geographical and social landscape, the native asserted itself and similarly shaped this Catholicism.[14] Catechisms had to draw from local experience if they were to be even vaguely understood. Veneration of relics seemed similar but not identical to native belief in amulets.[15] Sermons on Christians being '*alipin ng Dios* (slaves of God]' were heard by natives whose experience of slavery was different from the European practice of chattel.[16]

This encounter between the Spanish Catholic and the native possessed a dynamic beyond missionary aims or native intentions, and is better described as a complex process of translation involving language and culture.[17] This translation of Christian discourse in the vernaculars brought forth a nascent Christianity that was neither a replica of the European model nor a baptism of native practices.[18] Not only were traditional literary forms like folksongs used for prayers to saints, and stories of exemplary Christians told in traditional verse forms, but the vernacular languages themselves carried native meanings and associations into Christian discourse.

Furthermore, these vernacular Christian texts – prayers, catechisms, sermons, and all others – tell the singular story of Christ, now appropriated like a new vernacular epic. This Christ story first appears in full vernacular form in native Gaspar Aquino de Belen's great poem, *Pasiong Mahal* [Sacred Passion] (1704) which presented biblical characters especially Jesus with native sensibilities and drew lessons [*aral*] related to ordinary experience.[19] A century later under the auspices of native priest Mariano Pilapil, it was expanded and modified into what remains the most frequently published local book, *Pasyong Henesis* [*Genesis Passion*], so called because it frames the Christ story within Creation and the Last Judgment.[20]

Like other texts originally produced with church approval, this new magisterial text of the Christ story was perfomed in social contexts like antiphonal group chanting in private homes or stylized dramatization at the town plaza during Holy Week. Such popular practice which then created social space for natives to gather continues today in many provincial towns and even sections of metropolitan Manila.

Through this *Pasyon* text and performance as well as the general Christian ethos in the lowlands, the Christ story entered into native hearts and minds, and the vernaculars became a language of personal and communal redemption.[21]

Missionary accounts speak of how native Christians saw their lives in terms of the Christ story and sought to live in imitation of Jesus. Though direct influence of Pasyon practices might be hard to establish, the witness of these exemplary lives show the influence of the Christ story on Lorenzo Ruiz, martyred with Dominicans on 1637 in Nagasaki, Japan and Ignacia del Espiritu Santo, founder of a community of devoted single women (*beatas*) which has become the first local religious order, Religious of the Virgin Mary (RVM).

Throughout the history of Christianity in the Philippines, this impulse to relive the Christ story in one's life has driven generations of native Christians, including those appearing in the first set of media images typically associated with Filipino Christianity. These individuals who flagellate themselves or are nailed to a cross on account of a solemn promise (*panata*) to show gratitude for favors or repentance for sins undergo these to experience what Jesus experienced. Though such ritual, even literal, imitation of Christ's Passion does not carry official church approval, it expresses for those involved an intimate way of making the Christ story their own.

The second set of media images on Filipino Christianity is similarly rooted in the native appropriation of Christianity and resistance to colonization. These images of Christians – priests, nuns, and lay people – at the forefront of political rallies bring back analogous images from the colonial past when Christians, the native clergy as well as those in the pews, actively participated in the various forms of resistance to colonial power.

Early instances of this resistance were directed against Spanish settlement and redefinition of space. Among those gathered into towns and thereby subject to religious, labor and tribute obligations, some moved away to escape these obligations or to continue their traditional livelihood elsewhere and were thereby called apostates (*remontados*) by colonial authorities. But the more significant resistance to Spanish incursion came from long established Muslim settlements and sultanates of southern Mindanao who defended their territories and, in turn, raided Visayan settlements for slaves throughout the colonial period.[22] Despite occasional truces and treaties for mutual economic or strategic gains, this emnity was fueled by negative cultural attitudes brought about by identifying local Muslims with Moors in Europe then. These attitudes, which were circulated through dramatized metrical romances (*comedia, moro-moro*) in which Muslim characters either converted or remained villains, continue to color Christian-Muslim relations today.

Local revolts directed at abusive parish priests or colonial authorities occurred periodically, indicating the increasing burden of colonization and growing resistance among natives. As early as the 1660s, provincial revolts north of Manila erupted to protest conscript labor. A Jesuit's refusal to give his brother a Christian burial led Francisco Dagohoy of Bohol to lead a revolt in 1744 quelled only decades later.

Some of these local revolts carried religious significations, part-native and part-Christian, best illustrated by the 1842 revolt in Tayabas, Luzon led by Apolinario de la Cruz, a *donado* (lay worker) in San Juan de Dios Hospital barred from any religious order as a native.[23] In 1832, Hermano Pule, as he was called, established the *Cofradia de San Jose* which excluded Spaniards and mestizos along the slopes of Mount Banahaw. Given the cofradia's popularity, its ascetical practices and secret rituals, his confraternity was judged heretical by the local priest and subsequently massacred by government forces who put Hermano Pule's severed head on a stake.

Contemporary accounts of this revolt show the profound influence of the vernacular Christ story on the cofradia's worldview and resolve to resist. Using native imagery and vocabulary, its members saw their experience in the light (*liwanag*) of the Christ story, acting with great interior resolve (*matibay ang loob*) in solidarity (*damay*) with Jesus' life unto death. In his adaptation of a friar's religious poem about heaven, Hermano Pule contrasts earthly inequalities with egalitarian relations in heaven which he ritualized around Mount Banahaw, still considered as the New Jerusalem by similar groups of popular religion.

Later Christian participation in the resistance movement against the wider colonial establishment came with significant social changes in the nineteenth century, particularly the emergence of an educated and landed class. Though it finally led to the birth of the Filipino nation, this movement composed of interweaving nationalist, reformist and revolutionary sentiments was neither formally unified nor unchanging in their views because their members represented distinct political and economic interests.[24] Jose Rizal, Catholic-educated writer of the celebrated novels, *Noli me Tangere* [*Touch Me Not*] (1887) and *El Filibusterismo* [*Subversion*] (1897), was shaped by his family's conflict with Dominican friars over land, his education in Europe and exposure to liberal thought and Masonry. Self-designated *ilustrados* (enlightened) from the elite and lower classes espoused political equality and rationalist ideals. The landed considered the inefficient and inconsistent policies of the often-changing colonial administrators obstacles to economic progress. Thus views about religion among them were similarly mixed: some were anti-clerical and others anti-Catholic, but all united against the friars who symbolically embodied the betrayal of true religion as well as all colonial ills, especially the accumulation of estates by religious orders.

But among those who participated in this resistance without compromising their Christian faith were the native clergy who became increasingly nationalist because of the long-standing issue regarding jurisdiction over and allocation of parishes. In the seventeenth century, the bishop's right to visit parishes under religious orders was disputed. During the 18th, bishops transferred parishes of religious orders to inadequately trained native diocesan clergy. Then an 1826 royal decree ordered the return of parishes temporarily held by the native clergy to the religious orders upon vacancy. This last move showed growing Spanish suspicion of the native clergy and the colonial government's desire to displace them. The native clergy thus aligned themselves with their nationalist school contemporaries. Led by Vicarcapitular Pedro Pelaez of the Manila Archdiocese and Fr. Mariano Gomez of the Cavite clergy, they planned to ask Spain for equal treatment for the native clergy.

Spanish colonial and church authorities feared this growing nationalism and executed Frs. Gomez, Jose Burgos and Jacinto Zamora, collectively known as Gomburza, on false charges of conspiracy in the 1872 Cavite mutiny. Because of this increasingly violent reaction to any desire for reform, much less nationalist aspirations, resistance to colonial rule gained greater support not only from the native clergy but also a wider constituency of natives, mestizos, and creoles.

The Revolution against Spain then was bound to come, even though its 1896 outbreak led by Andres Bonifacio's *Katipunan* (Brotherhood) was unduly precipitated, with uncertain support from other nationalist leaders and on account of Augustinian Fr. Mariano Gil's report to the authorities. This final form of nationalist resistance to colonial rule became the definitive blow that would dissociate Christianity from colonialism.

Christian participation in the Revolution was generally divided along partisan lines.[25] Friars sided with colonial authorities and even became suspicious of those not criticized by nationalist or revolutionary forces. The native clergy's advocacy for equality within the church and despair about reforms under the colonial framework led them to support these forces and be engaged in the Revolution in different ways. Many like Fr. Esteban del Rosario of Ternate for whom it was "a holy war" rallied people, some like Fr. Gregorio Crisostomo of Tanay joined military campaigns and a few like Fr. Pedro Dandan of Cavite participated in local revolutionary councils. Because of this partisanship, some native priests were imprisoned or executed, even without basis, by Spanish officials and civilians the same way that friars suffered under the revolutionary forces in Manila.

Ordinary Christians also participated in the Revolution. Some of the provincial revolutionary forces, especially in central and southern Luzon, ensured that friars were allowed to escape or, if captured, treated with courtesy and even asked to be their parish priest. Moreover, according to contemporary accounts, they participated with great devotion in traditional practices and Masses offered for all revolutionaries and Spaniards who died in battle. Underlying such participation was the influence of the Christ story on those who saw their revolutionary involvement as part of their faith and in terms of their solidarity (*pakikiramay*) with Christ and their desire for *kalayaan* (freedom)[26]

But this religious sentiment would not last with the ascendancy of anti-Catholic leaders like Mabini within the short-lived Philippine Republic proclaimed on 12 June 1898. Influenced by European notions of *independencia* (independence) current then, these leaders sought authority over the church similar to the Patronato's and refused to acknowledge the religious authority of Spanish bishops. There followed fierce debates on proposals regarding constitutional separation of church and state or making Catholicism the state religion.

This heated controversy within the revolutionary government occasioned the birth of the schismatic Philippine Independent Church.[27] Fr. Gregorio Aglipay, Mabini's contemporary in Letran, rose to power as ecclesiastical governor of Nueva Segovia and later as military vicar general. In agreement with revolutionary leaders, he hoped to exercise general jurisdiction over the native clergy independent of existing church authorities. But when the church resisted and eventually excommunicated him, he accepted the leadership of the schismatic *Iglesia Filipina Independiente* (IFI) initiated by nationalist leader Isabelo de los Reyes Sr.

These conflicting sentiments among Filipinos raged even after Admiral George Dewey's victory over the Spanish fleet in Manila Bay on 1 May 1898 and the ceding of the Philippines to America in the Treaty of Paris on 10 December 1898. The native clergy joined the sporadic armed resistance to American occupation because of their nationalist sentiments and suspicion of American attitudes toward religion. Many provided money and intelligence while others like Fr. Jose Natera of Albay joined military attacks. Though native elite factions interested in progress were easily pacified and coopted, resistance continued until 1910 from groups the Americans called 'bandits [*tulisanes*]' and through popular literature heralding socialist Christ figures.

Native response to Spanish Catholicism then paved the way for a Christianity dissociated from colonial control and rooted in native hearts and minds. The missionary strategy to employ the vernaculars for evangelization led to the native appropriation of Christianity especially through the Christ story told in these vernaculars. This story functioned like an epic – providing natives with a narrative within which they could locate their social and personal lives, and moving them to follow in the footsteps of Jesus. Given the historical context then, such an impulse led some of them to resist the oppressive burdens of colonization. Hence the colonial church was divided into those who supported Spanish aims and those who did not. This historical experience that culminated in the birth of the Filipino nation would shape how Filipino Christianity would relate to changing cultural contexts and what role it would play in civil society in the twentieth century.

(Re)Building Mission

With the dissociation of evangelization from Spanish colonization, Christianity faced the same defining issues but now under radically changed circumstances. Its relation to context and role in society had to be defined in view of its colonial legacy – popular Catholic tradition and strong nationalist sentiments – as well as under the new American dispensation and its constitutional separation of church and state. For the Catholic Church, this meant rebuilding from the remains of the tumultuous past, and for the newly arrived Protestants, building a new mission in unfamiliar terrain. These tasks brought them in conflict due to differences in their religious beliefs and views about the local cultural context.

Of course leaders like Methodist Bishop James M. Thoburn, Presbyterian James B. Rodgers, and Baptist Eric Lund had visited earlier, but Protestant missionary work in the islands officially begun with the 1901 Comity Agreement among various Protestant missions.[28] These missions agreed to divide the country as Catholic religious orders did centuries earlier, with the exception of the Seventh-Day Adventists and the Episcopal Church under Bishop Charles Brent, who, in recognition of the Catholic faith of the many, opted to preach to the non-Christian tribes of Northern Luzon and Mindanao.

Protestant American attitudes toward the local cultural context influenced the missionary strategies of these missions.[29] As Protestants of their day, they considered popular religious practice tainted by Spanish Catholicism as superstitious, at best deficient.[30] As Americans aware of their growing imperial power, they regarded Filipinos as inferior like native American Indians. Thus even without any legal links to the American government analogous to the *Patronato*, they agreed with American President William McKinley's benevolent description of the American mandate in the Philippines as being to civilize the Filipinos and Christianize them.[31]

To transform this superstitious and uncivilized people, Protestant missionary strategy had to shift from English and Spanish to the vernaculars, and produce religious materials, especially biblical texts, in them.[32] First disseminated was the 1873 translation of Luke's Gospel into the Pangasinan vernacular which was carried out by Nicolas Manrique Alfonso Lallave, former Spanish Dominican missionary turned Protestant upon returning to Spain, and published by the British and Foreign Bible Society. Early Filipino converts continued this work of biblical translation; Sofronio Calderon, among the first Filipino Methodists, into Tagalog and Braulio Manikan, former Catholic seminarian, into the Visayan vernacular Hiligaynon. Other religious materials in different vernaculars were also produced.

Apart from this shift in language, the question of native leadership in Protestant missions became crucial. From the start, Filipino Protestants devoted themselves to recruitment, using their knowledge of local culture and their own familial ties, and thus contributed much to the growth of the Protestant Churches. Moreover, with their usual background as former Catholics critical of the colonial church in the late nineteenth century, many of them had strong nationalist sentiments and therefore clamored for greater participation in these missions, then solely under American leadership.

Such nationalist clamor led to the 1909 schism among the Methodists headed by Nicolas Zamora, grandnephew of Fr. Zamora of the 1872 Gomburza martyrs and educated in Catholic institutions.[33] Baptized Protestant in 1899, he became the first Filipino deacon the following year. On account of his personal background and the emerging reality of official American attitudes toward Filipino nationalism, he joined forces with other Methodist lay leaders who complained of racial discrimination and condescending paternalism among American missionaries. He sought greater native participation in the missions, and when this appeared unlikely, established the Evangelical Methodist Church of the Philippines.

Native sentiment also played a role in the 1914 founding and subsequent growth of the *Iglesia ni Cristo*.[34] Felix Manalo joined one Protestant denomination after another, and later founded his own, owing to what he claimed was a religious vision. These personal factors notwithstanding, the church he founded promoted a strong native ethos with its extensive use of Tagalog and other vernaculars in preaching and publications. This ethos as well as its cohesive, even centralized, structures account for its continuing social and political influence today, despite its relatively small membership.

Protestant social involvement, like that of the early Spanish missionaries, began with pastoral ministries and developed into social services like schools and hospitals.[35] In 1901, Presbyterians established in the Visayan town of Dumaguete, Negros Oriental, what would become a prominent Protestant educational center, Silliman University. In the same year, the Panay Baptist mission under Lund and Manikan built the first church in Jaro, Iloilo and baptized their first Filipino members by immersion in the river. Opening schools and hospitals followed soon after: Jaro Industrial School (now Central Philippine University) and Baptist Home School (now Filamer

Christian College) in 1905; and Iloilo Mission Hospital with the Presbyterians in 1907. Within a decade, other churches offered pastoral and social ministries throughout Panay island.

Necessary for the success of these ministries was the formation of a supportive ethos different from the dominant Catholic culture. Thus Protestant missionaries organized alternative social activities such as sports, especially popular American games of basketball and softball, through the interdenominational Young Men's Christian Association (YMCA) to counteract what were seen as the typically Filipino Catholic vices of drunkenness and gambling.[36] Schools often had dormitories for boys and girls to provide living conditions aligned with Protestant beliefs and practices.

Seminaries were soon established for the formation of Filipino personnel – Baptist Missionary Training School and the Union Theological Seminary in 1907 and St. Andrew's Theological Seminary for both the Episcopal Church and the Philippine Independent Church in 1947.[37]

Protestant social involvement as well as evangelizing missions achieved significant gains on the regional rather than the national level as a result of differences among Protestants themselves. In the 1920s, for example, the debate about "pure" versus "social" gospel current in the American scene affected local evangelical groups.[38] The 1901 Comity Agreement eventually broke down after the Second World War because of the missionary onslaught by Adventists and other Protestant groups evicted by the 1949 Chinese Communist Revolution. At the same time, there were constant attempts to work together toward unity. In 1929, the Presbyterian Church, the Congregational Church and the United Brethren established the United Evangelical Church, which in 1948 joined the Philippine Methodist Church and Evangelical Church to form the United Church of Christ in the Philippines (UCCP).[39] The National Council of Churches in the Philippines (NCCP), which would become an important national voice for the Protestants, was established in 1963 from the earlier Philippine Federation of Evangelical Churches, but did not include fundamentalist evangelical leaders, who considered the NCCP as "too liberal" and later formed the Philippine Council of Evangelical Churches in 1969.[40]

As the Protestant Churches were building their mission and making inroads in some regions, the Catholic Church was rebuilding its own. Tension and even conflict arose between them because of doctrinal differences. Protestants held public gatherings where preachers contested common views and practices attributed to Catholics. In the early decades of the twentieth century then, the Catholic Church felt under siege from many quarters – these Protestant attacks, the unfamiliar American attitudes toward religion, and the legacy of the nineteenth-century movements.[41] It was ill prepared to face these as the ethos of Catholic leadership remained Hispanic despite the appointment of Filipino bishops: Jorge Barlin for Manila in 1906, Juan Gorordo for Cebu, and Pablo Singzon for Calbayog in 1910.

Moreover, the Catholic Church was confronted by critical and complex issues that had to be resolved urgently to avoid more damaging consequences, and which involved many stakeholders – the American government, native leaders, the IFI and the different Catholic voices from the native clergy, the Spanish friars, and some American church leaders and the Holy See.[42] The first concerned the remaining few friars taking over parishes now under the native clergy. Archbishop Placide Chappelle of Louisiana, the Holy See's Apostolic Delegate, did not support the native clergy's opposition to this move because of his prejudice against and suspicion of Filipinos. The 2nd Philippine Commission under William Howard Taft finally won a compromise – the Holy See publicly refused to bar friars from parishes but privately agreed that they be sent only if the parishes did not object. The second issue involved what to do with the controversial friar estates and church property seized during the Revolution. Negotiations began by the same commission eventually led to the sale of more than 420 000 acres owned by the Augustinians, Dominicans, and Recollects to the U.S. government, only to be taken up by Filipino and American corporations later. Furthermore, legislation was passed giving the Supreme Court jurisdiction over church property taken over by Aglipay's Philippine Independent Church. In 1906, the court ordered the return of such property to the Catholic Church, and in 1909, the return of other assets to their rightful owners.

Education under the new dispensation quickly became another critical issue for the Catholic Church.[43] For the American government and the Protestant Churches, education, especially the establishment of a public school system, was a high priority for both political and religious reasons. And though the American government had no policy to disadvantage Catholics, a lack of Catholic teachers from the USA, the use of American textbooks, and the training of Filipinos in American Protestant universities appeared to subvert the educational work of the Catholic Church.

On the other hand, not enough Catholic personnel were fluent in English. Ateneo Municipal and the University of Santo Tomas continued to use Spanish as a medium of instruction until 1921 and 1923 respectively; the same was true of seminaries run by Jesuits in Manila and Vigan, and by Vincentians in Cebu, Jaro, Naga and Manila.[44]

This Hispanic ethos within the Catholic Church eventually changed with time and with the arrival of new religious congregations with no links to the colonial past. Between 1905 and 1908 came the Irish Redemptorists (CSsR), the Dutch and Belgian Scheut Fathers (CICM), the German Society of Divine Word (SVD), the Dutch Missionaries of the Sacred Heart (MSC) and the Mill Hill Missionaries (MHM). This influx of new religious personnel with

English-speaking members brought not only English-language facility but also new ideas about education and parish life.

Some founded schools from more modern models and with English as medium: Assumption College by Religious of the Assumption (RA), St. Scholastica's College by the Order of St. Benedict (OSB), and De la Salle College by the Christian Brothers (FSC). Religious formation too was increasingly in English; the Vigan seminary switched to English under the Society of Divine Word and the Jesuit novitiate had its first American rector in 1932. The official Catholic Directory listing information about all dioceses, religious orders, and personnel was published in English in 1950 for the first time.

The linguistic shift into English and the entry of religious personnel from other countries together with the increasing influence of American popular culture in the Philippines affected local religious culture. Though official Catholic worship still used Latin, other communal and personal devotions like novenas became increasingly available in English. Though traditional practices such as patronal feasts and processions remained popular in parishes and among the faithful, new devotions were introduced.[45] For example, aside from Friday visits to the Black Nazarene image enshrined by Spanish Augustianian Recollects in the Manila's historic Quiapo church, many would also go on Wednesdays to the Our Lady of Perpetual Help Shrine in Baclaran, Pasay, introduced by the newly arrived Redemptorists. Aside from these additions to the pantheon of saints brought by Spanish Catholicism, new religious associations like the Knights of Columbus and Catholic Women's League were introduced into local parishes.

With the Catholic Church's increasing self-confidence and America's rise as world power, especially after the Second World War, the Philippines was identified as the only Catholic country in the Far East.[46] Promoted by both Philippine civil and religious authorities, this identity pointed to its missionary responsibility to spread Christianity to non-Christian lands in the region, but also carried anti-communist undertones in the context of Cold War geopolitics. Such is evident in the elaborate combination of religious and civic rituals for the 1954 Marian Year celebration and the 1956 Eucharistic Congress in Manila during which Pope Pius XII delivered radio messages.

Christianity's role in society was forged within this new context, and the Catholic Church had the opportunity to recover its voice in civil society.[47] Several factors contributed to this renewed interest in social affairs; among them, the worldwide propagation of Papal social encyclicals, the worsening social situation of peasants in the countryside, and the growing influence of the Communist Party of the Philippines. Thus this resurgence of the Catholic voice had a strong anti-nationalist, anti-socialist, and anti-communist tone in tune with Cold War rhetoric. During the 1950s, for example, the Church protested inclusion of Rizal's novels in the school curriculum and the publication of

Rafael Palma's nationalist biography of Rizal and Teodoro Agoncillo's Marxist history of the Philippines at government expense.

Despite this defensive stance, Catholic involvement managed to create new and eventually effective paths. American Jesuits Joseph Mulry and James Meany founded the Bellarmine Evidence Guild in 1932 and Chesterton Evidence Guild in 1937 respectively, through which students visited the poor, listened to their concerns, and wrote radio plays for the "Catholic Hour," dramatizing social issues from a Catholic perspective. Other efforts included offering Second Sunday Recollections for workers at La Ignaciana Retreat House from 1932.

Though disrupted by the Second World War and the Japanese Occupation, such involvement became more extensive in the following decades. The Catholic hierarchy itself formed Catholic Action of the Philippines (CAP) in 1952 to supervise Church social involvement, and Cardinal Rufino Santos, archbishop of Manila, founded the Asian Social Institute (ASI) in 1962.

The Institute of Social Order (ISO) was founded much earlier in 1947 under the leadership of Jesuit Walter Hogan. Ateneo alumnus Johnny Tan formed the Federation of Free Workers (FFW) in 1950 to provide an alternative between company unions or the Communist-led Congress of Labor Organizations. Another alumnus, Jeremias Montemayor, formed the Federation of Free Farmers (FFF) in 1953. These bodies, influenced by Catholic social teaching introduced by their priest-mentors but independent from the hierarchy, took positions and supported social action that were at times condemned by others in the church. Most controversial was FFW's support for union strikes at the Dominican-owned University of Santo Tomas and the Monte de Piedad Bank that drew condemnation from the hierarchy and CAP, and led to the declaration of Fr. Hogan as *persona non grata* in the Archdiocese of Manila.

Though such differences would increasingly shape Christian social involvement in contemporary Philippine society, they also indicate that Filipino Christianity was no longer imprisoned by its colonial past. The Catholic and Protestant Churches have come to terms with the changed social context brought about by American occupation.

Meeting National Challenges, Engaging the World

From the 1960s onward, rapid and significant social changes have posed serious challenges to Christianity worldwide. Many societies saw the emergence of social movements among those marginalized by the status quo – youth, women, minorities and the poor – and of the mobility of population, services and information due to migration and technology transfer. In dealing with this social upheaval, Christianity could no longer delay its long overdue and fundamental confrontation with modernity, articulated in and symbolized by the call to *aggiornamento* by Second Vatican Council (1964–1968). This historic council offered Catholics and those beyond the Catholic Church with a new paradigm for religion's relation to the world expressed in the banner phrase "reading the signs of the times". Not as dramatic but no less significant have been similar changes in the mainline Protestant Churches under the leadership of the World Council of Churches. These parallel developments among Catholics and Protestants opened avenues for ecumenical dialogue on religious questions and cooperation on common concerns.

Such upheaval and its accompanying change in consciousness helped Filipino Christianity align itself with what was known as "the Third World" then or "the global South" more recently and provided it with a different way of seeing its dire situation of social inequality and its relations with other nations. With this self-identification, Filipino Christianity faced defining issues related to its cultural context and social role in new ways. In the immediate aftermath of Vatican II and during the Marcos years, its response to these issues would focus on cultural identity and social liberation. Since the 1990s, emphasis would fall upon the impact of globalization on Philippine society and Christianity.

The Second Vatican Council's positive regard for culture in general laid the foundations for Filipino Christianity's attitude to the contemporary local context. The resulting vernacularization of worship promoted greater and explicit integration of faith and culture under the rubric of inculturation, but it also divided the worshiping community along geographical and class lines – English usually for the urban, educated and upper classes, and the vernaculars for the rural and poor.

Long suppressed by the colonial past and what some called "Western cultural imperialism" in church and society, native religious creativity found manifold expressions through religious songs in various vernaculars, including English, and in the use of local cultural resources for religious ritual. Jesuit theology professor Eduardo Hontiveros paved the way with liturgical songs composed in local musical idioms and easily rendered by parish communities. The Protestant Asian Institute for Liturgy and Music pioneered in the indigenization of religious ritual, drawing not only from local but also other Asian traditions and thereby identifying the Filipino as Asian. Interest in Zen meditation and other Asian prayer forms became current in the formation of programs for church personnel.

This concern for greater integration between faith and culture was reflected in other areas of Christian life.[48] Local communities of international religious orders became "more Filipino" in food and lifestyle. Though most bishops were Filipinos by the 1970s, nationalization of leadership proved difficult in some religious orders. Other factors notwithstanding, this contributed to divisions into separate ecclesiastical jurisdictions as with the Dominicans or the return of some foreign-born members to their home countries. Theological reflection explored the religious meaning of cultural notions like "*Bahala na*" ("God will provide") and popular images of Christ.[49]

For others influenced by early Latin American liberation theology, "Filipinization" involved transforming unjust social structures more than expressing faith in local cultural terms. Though this tension between contextual and liberationist approaches would characterize internal church life then, the role of Christians in the public arena would tend to be liberationist.

Seeds of this Christian involvement began in the 1960s because of growing awareness about the deterioration of the country's socio-economic conditions. Church agencies initiated development work such as cooperatives and credit unions. Catholic and Protestant educational institutions sent students in exposure programs to poor communities, but some religious women's groups such as the Maryknoll and ICM sisters opted to leave their well-regarded schools in favor of direct work with the poor.

But the limited success of such development initiatives as well as the raging "development debate" worldwide moved such Christian involvement toward Marxist-inspired structural analysis of society and eventually issues of ideology. Even official church pronouncements were influenced by this approach to social analysis in speaking of "social" or "structural sin." Louvain priest-sociologist Francois Houtart introduced this approach to local church leaders in a landmark seminar on religion and development in 1974.[50]

These changes in consciousness were accompanied by new strategies in pastoral practice. Church formation seminars incorporated Marxist tools of social analysis. Though clergy and religious were visible in social involvement, lay men and women took on central roles more than ever. Furthermore influenced by the Latin American experience of *comunidades de base*, dioceses and parishes promoted as the preferred pastoral approach the formation of analogous communities conceived in varying forms.[51] Some were neighborhood-based meetings on Sunday bible readings and their implications for social action; others were organized along class and sector such as workers and peasants. Theological reflection accompanying this social and pastoral involvement has been characterized as a "theology of the struggle" as the way to liberation became clearly protracted.[52]

These developments also brought ideological conflicts raging in Philippine society into the churches.[53] Revitalized by movements among different sectors as well as by the appeal of Marxist social analysis worldwide, the new Communist Party of the Philippines (CPP) and its affiliated national democratic groups, now under the Marxist-Leninist-Maoist line, were attracting sympathy and support from church people. Other groups opposed this under the banner of socialist democratic views. With the greater influence of Arab nations in Southeast Asia from the 1970s, Muslim insurgency fueled by the chronic poverty in Mindanao erupted and took on various ideological strains.[54]

These ideological divisions and the social role of Christianity became critical concerns with President Marcos' 1972 declaration of martial law and establishment of an authoritarian regime under different guises. Both the Marcoses and their allies as well the churches recognized how crucial this role is, but neither foresaw its subsequent impact. First Lady Imelda Marcos, a center of power within government and beyond, cultivated smooth relations with prominent church leaders and attended important traditional devotions.

Catholic and Protestant Churches, then the only institutions of national stature neither under direct government control nor underground like the CPP and therefore a viable avenue of independent information and legitimate criticism, responded to the Marcos regime through their pastoral letters and proclamations. First to condemn it was the Protestant National Council of Churches (NCCP) in 1973.[55] Because of differing ecclesiological and political views among them, the Catholic Bishops' Conference of the Philippines (CBCP) took until 1979 to articulate their stance of "critical collaboration" with government.[56]

Other church agencies and personnel at the forefront of grassroots social involvement opted for outright opposition. Among them was the Association of Major Religious Superiors of the Philippines (AMRSP), especially through its "Signs of the Times" newsletter and Task Force Detainees. Some members of clergy, religious and laity including the charismatic and then SVD priest Edicio de la Torre joined communist or national democratic groups, particularly the ecumenical Christians for National Liberation (CNL). As a result, the shadow of communist infiltration became a constant concern within church groups and religious communities, breeding conflict and even distrust.

Though these ideological divisions raged within the churches, Christian work for the poor and defense of human rights continued. But the government's increasingly direct attacks on Christian groups and individuals widened and intensified religious opposition.[57] Church personnel including priests were detained, tortured, or summarily executed; religious houses and offices were raided. When this repression against churches and other critics of government turned flagrant with the 1983 assassination of opposition leader Benigno Aquino and the manipulation of the 1983 parliamentary and 1986 presidential elections, official church declarations became decidedly critical, best expressed in the 1986 CBCP pastoral letter stating that the Marcos regime had lost all moral legitimacy to rule. Prominent Catholic and Protestant personalities had been privately involved with other civil society groups in seeking alternatives to the Marcos regime. Beginning with the wake and funeral of Aquino which fused political action and traditional religious symbolism, a whole series of protest rallies ensued, leading to the first EDSA

"People Power" revolution and the eventual proclamation of Aquino's widow Corazon as President of the Philippines.

EDSA 1 thrust into the limelight the leadership of Cardinal Jaime Sin, Archbishop of Manila. Though he had been visibly working with religious and civil society leaders against the abuses of authoritarian rule, his call through the Catholic station Radio Veritas on February 22, 1986 proved crucial in bringing millions of Filipinos to surround military camps where Gen. Fidel Ramos and other military officers had withdrawn support from Marcos. Its images of priests and nuns face to face with armed government soldiers and of people clutching rosaries and statues of Mary led to its designation as a "miracle" just like the 1646 Spanish victory over Dutch invaders attributed to Our Lady of La Naval's intercession.

Though this overthrow of the Marcos regime was clearly a complex confluence of many social and political factors as well as different, even some covert, factions, the decisive involvement of Christians cannot be denied. It continued during the succeeding presidential terms of Corazon Aquino (1986–1992) and Fidel Ramos (1992–1998), and focussed on various concerns including strengthening democratic institutions and encouraging active citizenship.[58]

Despite these contributions and continuing involvement, long-standing and fundamental ills of Philippine society were not resolved. Institutionalizing better governance and mature citizenship required more than just enthusiastic goodwill from the restoration of formal democracy. Moreover divisions among EDSA 1 participants, even within Christian groups, soon surfaced because of differing interests and alliances. Despite attempts at reconciliation, communist and Muslim groups who did not support EDSA 1 resumed their insurgent campaigns.

In addition to these social problems, Filipino Christianity had to deal with the fast-changing local context from the 1990s onward. Though still characterized by traditional religious heritage as well as the cultural ethos from American influences, this context turned increasingly globalized and pluralistic because of the accessibilty of information technology and increased Filipino migration to other countries. Thus religious views and practices different from traditional Christianity such as those loosely designated "New Age" circulated among some, particularly the middle class and educated.

Accompanying these changes in context was the rise of charismatic Christianity, perhaps in reaction to what appeared to be the increasingly political role of the churches.[59] This initially urban phenomenon which focused on personal conversion, fellowship and healing began with the arrival in late 1970s of American charismatics–different Protestant Pentecostal groups some of which passed themselves off as ecumenical but eventually tried to convert Catholics, and some Catholic charismatics.

Many of the Protestant Pentecostal groups attracted members through public rallies as well as smaller fellowships. Charismatic groups of Catholics remained within Catholic Church structures because of the Catholic hierarchy's wise handling of the initial tensions brought about by their popularity. Thus though individuals have left Catholic membership and practice as "born again" or "Christian rather than Catholic," the charismatic phenomenon in the Philippines is predominantly Catholic.

Two prominent charismatic groups connected with the Catholic Church deserve mention because of their extensive membership, distinctive characteristics and social involvement. Couples for Christ (CFC) separated from an earlier covenant community in pursuit of church renewal through families rather than individuals and has expanded to approximately 10 000 couples throughout the country and among Filipino communities abroad as a result of a militant evangelical zeal and an effective heirarchical structure based on households of around 8 couples under lay leadership.[60] Though predominantly middle-class and initially conservative in its social involvement like other charismatic groups, CFC participated fully with other Christian and civil society groups in EDSA 2, the January 2001 mass rallies that led to the ousting of President Estrada. It also began *Gawad Kalinga [providing care]* which hopes to build 700 000 homes in 7000 poor communities in seven years and partners with local government, business corporations, schools and overseas volunteers of Filipino and other nationalities. This rapid expansion coupled with personal differences among leaders and conflicting religious views on issues such as the acceptability of partners with non-Catholic practices brought tensions between CFC and GK and eventually led to their separation in 2007.

El Shaddai, the other charismatic group, grew out of a popular radio program in 1981 and counts around ten million followers locally and abroad, especially among the working class.[61] Influenced by American evangelicals like Pat Robertson, founder Mariano "Mike" Velarde combines mass prayer rallies in public spaces and broadcast media to create new forms of religious community. His charismatic popularity, rhetorical style of preaching and focus on forms of prosperity as blessing aroused apprehension among church leaders, but his decision to align with the Catholic Church and his willingness to accept guidance from an officially appointed bishop appeased them while providing El Shaddai legitimate access to the Catholic majority. Reputed to be rich from tithing and prayer requests which include money offerings, El Shaddai provides some assistance to those in need but not a comprehensive and effective social development program. Its involvement in public affairs comes during elections when, like the Iglesia ni Cristo (INC), it is wooed by politicians seeking votes. Unlike other Christian groups like the CFC, it supported President Estrada to the dismay of many Catholic bishops.

The presence of CFC, GK, El Shaddai and even INC communities abroad indicates the impact of global mobility on Filipino Christianity. Whereas earlier Catholic and Protestant missionaries came from other countries, now church personnel from the Philippines serve as missionaries abroad, at times to the same countries of the earlier missionaries. But aside from these priests, religious and lay leaders, millions of Filipino overseas workers likewise bring their faith, along with native religious practices and liturgical songs, to the near-empty churches of Europe or the Christian minorities of Japan or the Middle East. This experience of Christianity in other cultural contexts widens their views of their own as well as other religions.

Moreover, developments in the contemporary world impact the local context and social role of Filipino Christianity. Fall-out from the September 11 attacks on the New York World Trade Center put the local Muslim insurgency in a global context, and despite efforts at dialogue like the Bishops-Ulama Conference, relations between Filipino Moslems and Christians can no longer be addressed simply on the local level.

At the same time, Filipino Christianity has taken a significant role within Christianity in Asia. This role has emerged as a result of the active participation and leadership of Filipino Christians in international bodies like the World Council of Churches and various Catholic meetings as well as of much publicized visits of the late Pope John Paul II. For example, initial steps toward the formation of the influential Federation of Asian Bishops' Conferences (FABC) took place in Manila.[62] Pastoral centers such as the Asian Social Institute and East Asian Pastoral Institute, though founded in the 1960s, include participants from previously isolated countries Vietnam, Myanmar, and China. Many theological schools and formation houses are no longer exclusively for those from or working in the Philippines, as some international religious congregations have chosen to establish local communities. Such a development does not only develop cross-cultural skills for Filipino Christians but also deepens their understanding of the catholicity of Christianity.

"In But Not Of This World"

The sweeping narrative of Filipino Christianity indicates why it is perceived as being too tied to local culture and politics. Beneath common media images of Filipinos carrying a cross during Holy Week or praying the rosary at political rallies have been the two fundamental and related issues that have defined it throughout its centuries-old history.

Filipino Christianity has been deeply immersed in the local context and is therefore entangled with its culture and politics. The Spanish Christianity which missionaries translated with care took on a vernacular character that spoke to the natives as their own. At the same time, this linguistic and cultural translation of Christianity was accompanied by the transformation of the local geographical and social landscape. Since then, this dynamic between Christianity and the local context has enshrined the vernacular Christ story as the operative epic of lowland Philippine society, empowering individuals to lead lives in imitation of Jesus and amplifying Christian voices in civil society.

Moreover, one finds the interplay of appropriation and resistance within this dynamic between Christianity and the cultural context. On the one hand, the translation of Christianity into native tongues has facilitated its reception by the majority and its involvement in social concerns. Catholic and Protestant contributions to education and social services have become more extensive and effective. Christianity has also marked traditional cultural practices and cultural values as well as familial roles and social institutions. For example, youth in both Christian and public schools are socialized to be "*makaDiyos at makabayan*" (godly and patriotic) – the same qualities candidates for electoral office project in their campaigns. Though all these have made Christianity an interior force in local social dynamics, it risks being equated with cultural and national aspirations or being manipulated by political interests. Thus some have indeed asked whether the local cultural context has domesticated Christianity through continuing negotiations between Christianity and popular practices such as beliefs in folk divinities or use of power-invested amulets.[63]

On the other hand, Filipino Christianity has engendered different forms of resistance within Philippine history and society. This has been exemplified by the role Christian involvement played not only in the dissociation of Christianity from Spanish colonization but also in the recent overthrow of authoritarian government. It has also shown its influence in pushing for reforms and promoting social issues such as protecting marginalized communities and safeguarding the environment on both local and national levels.

This interplay between appropriation and resistance has made Christian social involvement more complex and even ambivalent because Christian beliefs, attitudes, and structures interact with other social forces. Thus the voice of Christian leaders is heeded by various sectors on some issues like population control but not on others like the death penalty. Moreover, Filipino Christianity's response to changes in the local context at times has been defensive like the Catholic Church's initial reaction to the entry of American governance and culture, while at others, it has directly confronted these changes such as those brought about by the social upheaval in the 1960s.

This complex and ambivalent role of Christian social involvement often arises on account of the distinction between the moral and the political as well as the differing status of clergy and laity in the churches. In current official church teaching, Christian social involvement must be based on moral grounds and, at the same time, does take different political forms because concrete political options also entail social analysis and strategies. Action on behalf of these options properly belong to laity rather clergy whose primary role is seen as pastoral. Hence even with the presumption of good faith on the part of all, Christian individuals and groups differ in political terms as seen during the Philippine Revolution or the two EDSA uprisings. Moreover, all this is negotiated within the accepted constitutional framework of a modern secular state.

However in practice, especially during political crises, this subtle distinction is easily lost. Thus in spite of the precision with which official church statements have been formulated, they have often been perceived by sectors within and outside the churches as politically partisan. For example, none except the last CBCP pastoral letters during the Marcos regime ever asked President Marcos to step down, but the profound involvement of Catholics from Cardinal Sin to ordinary churchgoers in the protests against the regime could not but be seen as political support for the opposition. Moreover, some church leaders themselves have been unmindful of their respected cultural status and have not been careful in separating their own political positions from official church teaching. Thus different political groups and movements outside the church have often lobbied for official church support to legitimize their own positions. In such cases, Christian social involvement risks simply becoming one of the many political factions competing in an already contentious society.

Filipino Christianity is indeed linked to local culture and politics because of the two issues that have defined its long history and present stature. It has profoundly shaped the local context and played a significant role in civil society. But these links have also posed clear risks for Filipino Christianity itself, as it could be – and has been – used by some outside and within the churches to legitimate cultural discrimination, social inequity, or political interests.[64]

The shape of its future then depends on how it can harness its profound relation to the local context and its prominent social role to avoid these risks. To escape the clutches of the dominant cultural ethos and the lure of political powers, it must listen more attentively to the stories of those at the margins like Muslim and indigenous Filipinos.[65] It could also discover in mutually enriching conversations with other Asian Christians different ways of engaging culture and society. Listening to all these other voices would help Filipino Christianity become more faithful in living the Christ story in an increasingly global context and in spending its social capital at the service of power not its own.

Notes

1. Schumacher, J.N., S.J. *Readings in Philippine Church History*, 2nd ed., Quezon City: Loyola School of Theology, 1987, pp. 1–21; Phelan, J.L. *The Hispanization of the Philippines: Spanish Aims and Filipino Responses 1565–1700*, Madison and London: University of Wisconsin Press, 1959, pp. 153–61.
2. Rafael, V.L. *Contracting Colonialism: Translation and Christian Conversion in Tagalog Society under Early Spanish Rule*, Quezon City: Ateneo de Manila University Press, 1988, pp. 87–91.
3. Galende, P.G., O.S.A. *Angels in Stone: Architecture of Augustinian Churches in the Philippines*, Metro Manila: G.A. Formoso Publishing, 1987, pp. 10–15.
4. Javellana, R.B., S.J. *Wood and Stone for God's Greater Glory: Jesuit Art and Architecture in the Philippines*, Quezon City: Ateneo de Manila University Press, 1991, pp. 23, 28f.; Galende, P.G, O.S.A. *Angels in Stone*, Manila: G.A. Formoso Publishing, 1987, p. 516.
5. Galende, P.G., O.S.A. and Javellana, R.B., S.J. *Great Churches of the Philippines*, Makati, Metro Manila: Bookmark, 1993.
6. Lumbera, B.L. *Tagalog Poetry 1570–1898: Tradition and Influences in its Development*, Quezon City: Ateneo de Manila University Press, 1986, pp. 22–48.
7. Postma, A. (ed.) *Vocabulario Tagalo: Francisco de San Antonio O.F.M. (d. 1624)* Quezon City: Pulong, Sources for Philippine Studies, 2003, pp. xii–xv.
8. Antonio, L.A. (ed.) *Apat na siglo ng pagsasalin: bibliographiya ng mga pagsasalin sa Filipinas (1593–1998)* Quezon City: Sentro ng Wikang Filipino, Sistemang Unibersidad ng Pilipinas, 1999, pp. 1–15.
9. Lumbera, B.L. *Tagalog Poetry 1570–1898: Tradition and Influences in its Development*, Quezon City: Ateneo de Manila University Press, 1986, pp. 30–48
10. Francisco, J.M.C., S.J. (ed.) *Sermones: Francisco Blancas de San Jose O.P. (d. 1614)*, Quezon City: Pulong, Sources for Philippine Studies, 1994.
11. Javellana R.B., S.J. "The Jesuits and the indigenous peoples of the Philippines" in *The Jesuits: Cultures, Sciences, and the Arts 1540–1773*, O'Malley, J.W., S.J., Bailey, G.A., Harris, S.J., and Kermode, F.T. (eds.) Toronto: University of Toronto Press, 1999, pp. 418–438.
12. Estioko, L.R., S.V.D. *History of Education: A Filipino Perspective*. Querzon City: Logos Publications, 1994, pp. 163–179.
13. Schumacher, J.N., S.J. *Readings in Philippine Church History*, 2nd ed., Quezon City: Loyola School of Theology, 1987, pp. 22–36.
14. Macdonald, C.J.-H. "Folk Catholicism and pre-Spanish religions in the Philippines," *Philippine Studies*, 52:1 (2004), 78–93.

15. Schumacher, J.N., S.J. *Readings in Philippine Church History*, 2nd ed., Quezon City: Loyola School of Theology, 1987, pp. 76–77.

16. Francisco, J.M.C., S.J., "*Alipin ng Dios, alipin ng demonio: translatin slavery as religious symbol*," in *Sermones: Francisco Blancas de San Jose O.P. (d. 1614)*, Quezon City: Pulong, Sources for Philippine Studies, 1994, pp. 370–395.

17. Rafael, V.L. *Contracting Colonialism: Translation and Christian Conversion in Tagalog Society under Early Spanish Rule*, Quezon City: Ateneo de Manila University Press, 1988, pp. 136–209.

18. Francisco, J.M.C., S.J. "Translating Christianity into Asian tongues: Cultural dynamics and theological issues," *Asian Christian Review*, 1:2, 70–84.

19. Javellana, R.B., S.J. (ed.) *Mahal na passion ni Jesu Christong Panginoon natin na tolaI*, Quezon City: Ateneo de Manila University Press, 1990.

20. Javellana, R.B., S.J. (ed. and trans.) *Casaysayan nang pasiong mahal ni Jesucristong Panginoon natin na sucat ipag-alab nang puso nang sinomang babasa*, Quezon City: Ateneo de Manila University Press, 1988.

21. Ileto, R.C. *Pasyon and Revolution: Popular Movements in the Philippines, 1840–1910*, Quezon City: Ateneo de Manila University Press, 1979, pp. 15–28.

22. Abinales, P.N. and Amoroso, D.J. *State and Society in the Philippines* Lanham: Rowman & Littlefield, 2005, pp. 42–52; Schumacher, J.N. *Readings in Philippine Church History*, 2nd ed., Quezon City: Loyola School of Theology, 1987, pp. 93–95, 102–113.

23. Ileto, R.C. *Pasyon and Revolution: Popular Movements in the Philippines, 1840–1910*, Quezon City: Ateneo de Manila University Press, 1979, pp. 37–91.

24. Francisco, J.M.C., S.J. "Christianity as church and story and the birth of the Filipino nation in the nineteenth century," in Gilley, S. and Stanley, B. (eds.) *The Cambridge History of Christianity: World Christianities circa 1815–circa 1914*, Vol. 8, Cambridge: CUP, 2006, pp. 528–541.

25. Schumacher, J.N., S.J. *Revolutionary Clergy: The Filipino Clergy and the Nationalist Movement, 1850–1903* Quezon City: Ateneo de Manila University Press, 1981.

26. Ileto, R.C. *Pasyon and Revolution: Popular Movements in the Philippines, 1840–1910*, Quezon City: Ateneo de Manila University Press, 1979, pp. 107–113, 108, 167.

27. Clifford, M.D., B.V.M., "*Iglesia Filipina Independiente*: The revolutionary church," in Anderson, G.H. (ed.) *Studies in Philippine Church History*, Ithaca and London: Cornell University Press, 1969, pp. 223–255.

28. Clymer, K.J. *Protestant Missionaries in the Philippines, 1898–1916: An Inquiry into the American Colonial Mentality*, Urbana and Chicago: University of Illinois Press, 1986, pp. 32–61.

29. Clymer, K.J. *Protestant Missionaries in the Philippines, 1898–1916: An Inquiry into the American Colonial Mentality*, Urbana and Chicago: University of Illinois Press, 1986, pp. 65–92.

30. Clymer, K.J. *Protestant Missionaries in the Philippines, 1898–1916: An Inquiry into the American Colonial Mentality*, Urbana and Chicago: University of Illinois Press, 1986, pp. 93–123.

31. May, G.A. *Social Engineering in the Philippines: The Aims, Execution, and Impact of American Colonial Policy*, 1900–1913, Westport, CT: Greenwood Press, 1980; Miller, S.C. *"Benevolent assimiliation": The American conquest of the Philippines, 1899–1903*, New Haven: Yale University Press, 1982.

32. Kwantes, A.C."The Bible comes to the Philippines," in Kwantes, A.C. (ed.) *A Century of Bible Christians in the Philippines*, Manila: OMF Literature, 1998, pp. 13–27.

33. Trinidasd, R.B. "Nicolas Zamora and the IEMELIF Church," in Kwantes, A. C. (ed.) *Chapters in Philippine Church History*, Manila: OMF Literature, 2001, pp. 203–221.

34. Harper, A.C. "A Filipino Church at eighty years: The *Iglesia ni Cristo* at the turn of the century," in Kwantes, A.C. (ed.) *Chapters in Philippine Church History*, pp. 429–450; Albert J. Sanders, "An appraisal of the *Iglesia ni Cristo*," in Anderson, G.H. (ed.) *Studies in Philippine Church History*, Ithaca and London: Cornell University Press, 1969, pp. 350–365.

35. Diel, D.J. Jr. "Perspectives in Baptist Church history," in Schumacher, J.N., S. J. *Readings in Philippine Church History*, 2nd ed., Quezon City: Loyola School of Theology, 1987, pp. 229–231; Anne C. Kwantes, *Presbyterian Missionaries in the Philippines: Conduits of Social Change (1899–1909)*, 1989.

36. Clymer, K.J. *Protestant Missionaries in the Philippines*, pp. 77–79, 85–86.

37. Clymer, K.J. *Protestant Missionaries in the Philippines*, p. 36; Reyes, R.R.B., J. "The St. Andrew's Theological Seminary," in *Chapters in Philippine Church History*, pp. 359–368.

38. Diel, D.J. Jr. "Perspectives in Baptist Church History," in Schumacher, J.N., S.J. *Readings in Philippine Church History*, 2nd ed., Quezon City: Loyola School of Theology, 1987, pp. 19–21.

39. Apilado, "The United Church of Christ in the Philippines: Historical location, theological roots, and spiritual commitment," in *Chapters in Philippine Church History*, pp. 335–358.

40. Aragon, A.U. "The Philippine Council of Evangelical Churches," in Kwantes, A.C. (ed.) *Chapters in Philippine Church History*, Manila: OMF Literature, 2001, pp. 368–389.

41. Schumacher, J.N. "A Hispanized clergy in an Americanized country (1910–1970)," in Schumacher, J.N. *Growth and Decline: Essays on Philippine Church History*, Manila: Historical Conservation Society, 1989, pp. 247–262.

42. Francisco, J.M.C. "Christianity as church and story and the birth of the Filipino nation in the nineteenth century," in Gilley, S. and Stanley, B. (eds.) *The Cambridge History of Christianity: World Christianities circa 1815–circa 1914*, Vol. 8, Cambridge: CUP, 2006, pp. 538–540.

43. Clifford, M.D., B.V.M. "Religion and the public schools in the Philippines: 1899–1906," in Anderson, G.H. (ed.) *Studies in Philippine Church History*, Ithaca and London: Cornell University Press, 1969, pp. 301–324.

44. Schumacher, J.N., S.J. "A Hispanized clergy in an Americanized country (1910–1970)," in Schumacher, J.N. *Growth and Decline: Essays on Philippine Church History*, Manila: Historical Conservation Society, 1989, pp. 247–262.

45. Schumacher, J.N., S.J. "A Hispanized clergy in an Americanized country (1910–1970)," in *Growth and Decline: Essays on Philippine Church History*, Manila: Historical Conservation Society, 1989, pp. 247–262.

46. Barry, C. Becoming Asian while remaining Catholic: De-colonizing and indigenizing Philippine Catholicism in Asian guise, unpublished paper.

47. Fabros, W. *The Church and Its Social Involvement in the Philippines, 1930–1972*, Quezon City: Ateneo de Manila University Press, 1988, pp. 31–81.

48. Barry, C. Becoming Asian while remaining Catholic: De-colonizing and indigenizing Philippine Catholicism in Asian guise, unpublished paper.

49. Mesa, J.M. de *And God said, "Bahala na!" The Theme of Providence in the Lowland Filipino Context*, Quezon City: Maryhill School of Theology, 1979; Benigno Beltran, S.V.D. (ed.) *The Filipino Face of Christ*, Manila: Arnoldus Press, 1981.

50. *Religion and Development in Asia: A Sociological Approach with Christian Reflections*, Baguio: Feres Seminar, 1976.

51. Mendoza, G.A. (ed.) *Church of the People: The Basic Christian Communities' Experience in the Philippines* Manila: Bishops-Businessmen's Conference, 1988.

52. Torre, E. de la *Touching Ground, Taking Root: Theological and Political Reflections on the Philippine Struggle*, Quezon City: Socio-Pastoral Institute, 1986, pp. 156–159.

53. Moreno, A.F., S.J. *Church, State and Civil Society in Postauthoritarian Philippines: Narratives of Engaged Citizenship*, Quezon City: Ateneo de Manila University Press, 2006, pp. 42–44.

54. McKenna, T.M. *Muslim Rulers and Rebels*, Berkeley and Los Angeles: University of California Press, 1998.

55. Schwenk, R.L. *Onward, Christians! Protestants in the Philippine Revolution*, Quezon City: New Day Publishers, 1986.

56. Moreno, A.F. *Church, State and Civil Society in Postauthoritarian Philippines: Narratives of Engaged Citizenship*, Quezon City: Ateneo de Manila University Press, 2006, pp. 45–51.

57. Youngblood, R.L. *Marcos against the Church: Economic Development and Political Repression in the Philippines*, Ithaca and London: Cornell University Press, 1990.
58. Moreno, A.F. *Church, State and Civil Society in Postauthoritarian Philippines: Narratives of Engaged Citizenship*, Quezon City: Ateneo de Manila University Press, 2006, pp. 243–262.
59. Kessler, C. "Charismatic Christians: Genuinely religious. Genuinely modern," *Philippine Studies*, 54:4 (2006), 560–584; Kessler, C. and Rueland, J. Give Jesus a hand! Charismatic Christians: Populist Religion in the Philippines, Querzon City: Ateneo de Manila University Press, 2008.
60. *Couples for Christ Ten years in the Lord (1981–1991) Families in the Holy Spirit Renewing the Face of the Earth* (CFC 10th anniversary commemorative book). Most materials on CFC are only available in a CD-Rom format.
61. Wiegele, K.L. *Investing in Miracles: El Shaddai and the Transformation of Popular Catholicism in the Philippines*, Honolulu: University of Hawaii Press, 2005.
62. Rosales, G.B. and Arevalo, C.G. (eds.) *For all Peoples of Asia*, Vol. I: *Federation of Asian Bishops' Conferences Documents from 1970 to 1991*, Quezon City: Claretian Publications, 1992, pp. xv–xxii.
63. Cannell, F. *Power and Intimacy in the Christian Philippines*, Quezon City: Ateneo de Manila University Press, 1999, pp. 227–254; Cannell, F. "Reading as gift and writing as theft," in Cannell, F. (ed.) *The Anthropology of Christianity*, Durham and London: Duke University Press, 2006, pp. 134–162.
64. Friend, T. (ed.), *Religion and Religiosity in the Philippines and Indonesia: Essays on State, Society, and Public Creeds*, Washington DC: School of Advanced International Studies, John Hopkins University, 2006.
65. Bankoff, G. and Weekley, K. *Post-colonial National Identity in the Philippines: Celebrating the Centennial of Independence*, Aldershot: Ashgate, 2002, pp. 177–183.

Further Reading

Anderson, G.H. (ed.) *Studies in Philippine Church History*, Ithaca and London: Cornell University Press, 1969.

Fabros, W. *The Church and its Social Involvement in the Philippines, 1930–1972*, Quezon City: Ateneo de Manila University Press, 1988.

Francisco, J.M.C. "Christianity as church and story and the birth of the Filipino nation in the nineteenth century," in Gilley, S. and Stanley, B. (eds.) *The Cambridge History of Christianity: World Christianities circa 1815–circa 1914*, Vol. 8, Cambridge: CUP, 2006, pp. 528–541.

Ileto, R.C. *Pasyon and Revolution: Popular Movements in the Philippines, 1840–1910*, Quezon City: Ateneo de Manila University Press, 1979.

Kwantes, A.C. (ed.) *Chapters in Philippine Church History*, Manila: OMF Literature, 2001.

Moreno, A.F. *Church, State and Civil Society in Postauthoritarian Philippines: Narratives of Engaged Citizenship*, Quezon City: Ateneo de Manila University Press, 2006.

McKenna, T.M. *Muslim Rulers and Rebels*, Berkeley and Los Angeles: University of California Press, 1998.

Rafael, V.L. *Contracting Colonialism: Translation and Christian Conversion in Tagalog Society under Early Spanish Rule*, Quezon City: Ateneo de Manila University Press, 1988.

Schumacher, J.N. *Readings in Philippine Church History*, 2nd ed., Quezon City: Loyola School of Theology, 1987.

Schumacher, J.N. *Revolutionary Clergy: The Filipino Clergy and the Nationalist Movement, 1850–1903*, Quezon City: Ateneo de Manila University Press, 1981.

Sunquist, S.W. (ed.) *A Dictionary of Asian Christianity* (Grand Rapids, Michigan and Cambridge: William B. Eerdmans Publishing Co., 2001).

Youngblood, R.L. *Marcos Against the Church: Economic Development and Political Repression in the Philippines*, Ithaca and London: Cornell University Press, 1990.

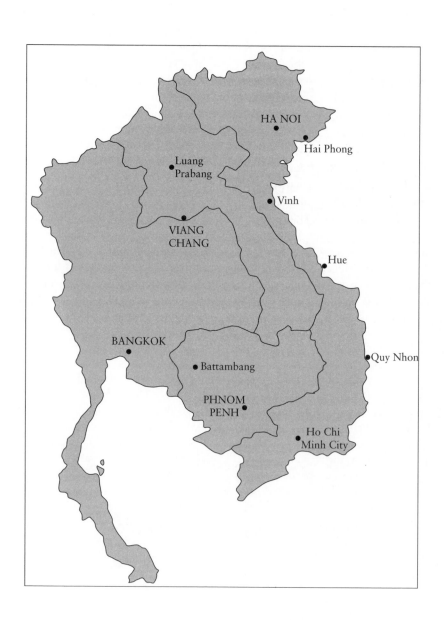

7

Vietnam, Cambodia, Laos, Thailand

Peter C. Phan

In the 1960s and 1970s Vietnam became a household name and even a battle cry in the West, especially in the United States, through the so-called "Vietnam War" – which the Vietnamese themselves dub the "American War." For years the public was bombarded daily with harrowing and haunting images of bombed cities and burning villages, rows upon rows of flag-draped coffins, self-immolated Buddhist monks blazing alive, hundreds of thousands of refugees desperately climbing aboard US warships, and "boat people" escaping to freedom in rickety barks on the high seas. In Washington, D.C., the Vietnam Veterans' Memorial, a shiny, black, V-shaped granite wall, with the names of over 58 000 fallen American soldiers etched into its 140 various-sized panels, has become a sanctuary where pilgrims stroll, heads bowed in silence, fingers achingly caressing the names. The wall also evokes the utter futility of the deaths of more than two million Vietnamese civilians and a million Vietnamese soldiers during the two-decade-long war.[1]

The Vietnam War also engulfed two neighboring countries. To the south-west of Vietnam, the Kingdom of Cambodia (formerly known as Kampuchea) was invaded by the U.S. armed forces. The country was later made infamous by the murderous Khmer Rouge who, led by Pol Pot from 1975 to 1979, killed 1.5 million of their own countrymen in an attempt to enforce a radical form of agrarian communism. Bordered by Vietnam to the east, Cambodia to the south, and Thailand to the west, the landlocked Lao People's Democratic Republic, or Laos, was heavily bombarded along the Ho Chi Minh trail by the U.S. Air Force – more than two million tonnes of bombs were dropped between 1971 and 1973 – to prevent Communist North Vietnamese from infiltrating into South Vietnam and the Communist Pathet Lao from taking over the Royal Laotian government. Of the four countries under study here, Thailand – proudly proclaimed by its citizens as "The Land of the Free" since it has never been colonized by the West –

Christianities in Asia, edited by Peter C. Phan   © 2011 Blackwell Publishing Ltd except for editorial material and organization © 2011 Peter C. Phan

was spared the war but served as the "rest and recreation" paradise of exotic (and erotic) pleasures for American GIs between tours of duty.

Today, three decades after the end of the Vietnam War, Cambodia, Laos, and Vietnam are recovering from the ravages of war and have achieved a measure of political and economic stability. Officially, Vietnam and Laos are among a handful of countries with a Communist government. Cambodia has a constitutional monarchy with a parliamentary representative democracy. Thailand too has a constitutional monarchy with the hereditary monarch as the head of state and an electoral democracy. Economically, except Thailand, the other three countries, despite having achieved a remarkable progress, especially since they embraced, albeit partially, the free market system, still remain among the poorest countries in the world.

Religiously, these four countries share a common religious tradition, namely, Buddhism, which constitutes the great majority of their populations: 95% in Cambodia, 94% in Thailand, 85% in Vietnam, and 65% in Laos. As far as Christianity is concerned, these countries also share a common origin. The Gospel was brought to them by Western missionaries more or less at the same time, in the seventeenth century, with important mission centers in Vietnam and Thailand. Hence, it is appropriate to study Christianity in these countries together. We will first examine Christianity in each country separately and will conclude with an overview of common characteristics and future.

The Socialist Republic of Vietnam

If you are a foreigner touring Vietnam today, chances are your plane will land either in Hanoi – the capital – in the north or in Ho Chi Minh City, formerly Saigon, in the south, once the capital of the now defunct Republic of Vietnam or South Vietnam. There had been, before 1976, two "capitals" in Vietnam – similar to present-day Korea, with Pyongyang in the north and Seoul in the south. After the unification of the country in 1976, the capital of South Vietnam was unceremoniously stripped of its name, and to add insult to injury, the victorious Communist government renamed it after Ho Chi Minh, the founder of the Vietnamese Communist Party.

From colonization to independence to the Socialist Republic of Vietnam

Long before Vietnam was wracked by the 20-year long internecine war between the North and the South (1955–1975), Vietnamese folklore celebrates and promotes national unity. There is the legend that all Vietnamese are descendants of a sea dragon and a mountain goddess. From their union a hundred eggs were hatched, out of whom were born 50 boys, who followed their dragon-father to the sea, and 50 girls, who followed their goddess-mother to the mountain. Mountain and sea – these natural elements describe well the topography of Vietnam, shaped like the capital S, bordered on its eastern side, from north to south, by the South China Sea, and along its western side by tropical mountain ranges.

This myth of a common ancestry served the Vietnamese people well during the millennium-long domination by China, from the Han dynasty to the Ten Kingdoms, from 111 BCE to 938 CE, and again by the Ming dynasty, from 1420 to 1428. In 938 the Vietnamese general Ngo Quyen liberated the country from the Chinese rule and formed the first dynasty. It is this deep sense of ethnic, linguistic, and cultural unity that enabled the Vietnamese to avert a total Sinicization and forged them into a nation-state. Through successive dynasties, from the eleventh to the twentieth century – Ly, Tran, Le, and Nguyen – to name the most important ones, Vietnam developed into an independent country, though still paying tributes to its more powerful northern neighbor and a willing adopter of Chinese culture and religions. From the seventeenth century it began its "Southern March," eventually annexing the Champa kingdom and parts of the Khmer kingdom.

It was under the last dynasty, i.e., the Nguyen (1802–1945), that Vietnam once again lost its independence. France invaded Vietnam in 1858 and in 1883 divided the country into three parts: the north, known as Tonkin; the center, known as Annam; and the south, known as Cochinchina. France turned the south into a colony and the center and the north into protectorates. Later, France colonized Cambodia and Laos as well and made these two countries and Vietnam into what was known as French Indochina.

Vietnam's struggle for national independence was led by various nationalists, of whom the most famous was Ho Chi Minh. In 1941 the Japanese invaded Vietnam and overthrew French rule. After the Japanese surrender in 1945, Ho Chi Minh declared independence, which, however, was short-lived, as France reconquered Vietnam in 1947. From then on, war for independence from France was waged by Ho Chi Minh and his followers, the Viet Minh.

In 1954 France suffered a decisive defeat at the battle of Dien Bien Phu and was forced to withdraw from Vietnam. The Geneva Accords of July 1954 temporarily divided the country into two parts at the 17th parallel, with national elections stipulated for 1956 to determine the political direction of the unified country. Unfortunately, the plebiscite never took place. The division was made permanent, with the Communist-ruled Democratic Republic of Vietnam in the north and the Republic of Vietnam, supported by the United States, in the south. War soon broke out between the two parts of the country, with the ever-wider participation of the United States. In 1960 North Vietnam created the National Liberation Front and its military branch, popularly known as the Viet Cong, to take over South Vietnam. The war dragged on for 20 years, with the United States getting more involved militarily. In early 1968, Washington began looking for a way out of the Vietnam quagmire, and on January 27, 1973, an agreement was signed in Paris to end direct U.S. military involvement in the conflict. The Paris Peace Accords did not, however, end the war itself. On the contrary, fighting grew fiercer and was not ended until April 30, 1975, when the Communist forces of the North captured Saigon, and the South capitulated. In 1976, the two parts of Vietnam were officially reunited as the Socialist Republic of Vietnam.

The decade immediately following the reunification was extremely hard for the Vietnamese people. Political purge through "reeducation camps," forced relocation of city people to "new economic zones," economic embargo by the United States, invasion of Cambodia and border war with China in 1979, rapid population increase, farm collectivization, currency reform, natural disasters – all this brought about widespread famine and misery. Only in 1986 did the living conditions begin to improve when the Communist leadership instituted a more open economic policy called *đoi moi* (renewal) which permitted limited forms of free market economy. The American trade embargo was lifted in February 1994, allowing U.S. trade and investment. In 1995 the United States and Vietnam exchanged full diplomatic ties. In 2001 Vietnam became a member of the Association of Southeast Asian Nations (ASEAN) Free Trade Area and in 2007 it joined the World Trade Organization (WTO).

The early years of Vietnamese Catholic Christianity

If you visit the two largest cathedrals in Vietnam, Saint Joseph in Hanoi and Immaculate Conception in Saigon, the former in Gothic style and completed in 1886, the latter in neo-Romanesque style and completed in 1880, you will no doubt get a vivid sense that Christianity was and perhaps still remains to a significant degree a foreign religion, compared with, for instance, Buddhism, Confucianism, and Daoism, often referred to as the *Tam Giao* (The Three Religions), the other major religious traditions in Vietnam.[2]

Christianity appears to have entered Vietnam for the first time in the third decade of the sixteenth century. According to the *Kham Dinh Viet Su Thong Giam Cuong Muc* [*Vietnamese Imperial Historical Records*] published in 1884, in 1533, under the reign of King Le Trang Ton, there was a rescript proscribing the "*Da-to ta dao*" (the false Christian religion). This new religion is said to have been preached by a certain I-Ni-Khu (Ignatius?) in two villages, Ninh Cuong and Tra Lu, in the province of Nam Dinh, North Vietnam. Between 1550 and 1615, occasional missionaries of the Dominican provinces in the Philippines and Malacca came to Vietnam but their activities left no permanent traces.[3]

Christian mission was consolidated with the arrival from Macao of Jesuit priests Francesco Buzomi and Diego Carvalho and three lay brothers at Cua Han, in Quang Nam in 1615. From 1615 to 1659, the bulk of missionary work was carried out by the Jesuits (mostly Portuguese), of whom the most famous was the French Alexandre de Rhodes (1593–1660). De Rhodes arrived in central Vietnam in December 1624, and after a few months of language study, he was sent to the north (Tonkin) and arrived there on March 19, 1627. After almost four years of highly successful mission, he was expelled from the country, went back to Macao in 1630, remained there for ten years, and in 1640 came back to central Vietnam. For five years, during which he was expelled four times, de Rhodes conducted clandestine missionary activities. On July 3, 1645 de Rhodes was expelled from Vietnam for good.

De Rhodes's accomplishments were extraordinary. Not only did he succeed in bringing about a huge number of conversions (estimated at 10 000), he also produced three long-lasting achievements. First, he set up an organization of lay catechists to assist him in the evangelizing work and to guide the church during the missionaries' absence. Second, after 1645, he went to Rome to lobby for the establishment of a hierarchy in Vietnam. As a result of his tenacious efforts in the face of fierce opposition by the Portuguese crown, in 1658 Pope Alexander VII appointed François Pallu bishop of Tonkin and Pierre Lambert de la Motte bishop of Cochinchina. Third, he was the leading inventor of the modern Vietnamese script, now known as the national script, using the Roman alphabet and diacritical marks to distinguish the various tones of the Vietnamese language, and was the author of the first dictionary and the first catechism in Vietnamese. By the middle of the seventeenth century the Church in Vietnam was growing by leaps and bounds. De Rhodes reported (perhaps with a bit of exaggeration) that in 1650 there were 300 000 Catholics in the north, with a yearly increase of at least 15 000.

The church steeped in blood

Missionary work in the next two centuries, though highly successful, met with grave difficulties. Some of these stemmed from the political situation of the country at the time. A few words on this situation will be helpful to understand the problems facing the missionaries. When Christianity first arrived in Vietnam, the reigning dynasty was the Hau Le (the Later Le dynasty), so named to distinguish it from the Tien Le (the Earlier Le dynasty) of 980–1009. The Later Le dynasty was inaugurated in 1428 by Le Loi, who assumed the name of Le Thai To after liberating the country from the Ming dynasty. It officially ended in 1788 with its last king Le Chieu Thong, but already in 1527, power was wrested from it by the Mac dynasty, which ruled from 1527 to 1592.

In 1532 two clans, the Trinh and the Nguyen, rose up to defend the Later Le dynasty against the Mac dynasty. But the Le kings were little more than puppets; real power was in the hands of the lords of the Trinh and the Nguyen families. Soon bitter rivalries divided the two clans, the former ruling over the north, and the latter over the south (which at the time included only three central provinces, i.e., Quang Binh, Thuan Hoa, and Quang Nam). Military conflicts between the two families erupted in 1627, the very year de Rhodes went to the north, and lasted off and on for 45 years, with altogether seven wars until 1672, without decisive victory for either side. The country was then divided into two parts, with the river Giang as the demarcating line, until it was reunified in 1802 by King Gia Long of the Nguyen clan, who named the country Vietnam.

The rivalry between the north and the south greatly complicated the work of missionaries as each side, especially the Trinh clan, suspected the missionaries to be spies for the other side, and, when convenient, used them as mediators to obtain merchandise and military wares from their countrymen, especially the Portuguese. Though the early missionaries in Vietnam never collaborated with colonial powers, the religion they preached was associated by the Vietnamese, wrongly but perhaps inevitably, with their imperialistic countries.

The second source of severe problems for the mission in Vietnam was the *padroado* system, initiated in 1494 by Pope Alexander VI, whereby it was agreed that the lands discovered by Portugal in Asia and Africa would belong to the Portuguese crown and that no missionary could enter them without its prior permission. At the time, the church of Tonkin belonged to the diocese of Macau in China, and the church of Cochinchina to the diocese of Malacca in Malaysia, both located in Portuguese colonies. After de Rhodes succeeded in having French bishops appointed to the two Vietnamese dioceses and having them placed as "apostolic vicars" under the authority of the *Congregatio de Propagande Fide* (founded in 1622 by Pope Gregory XV), a strain was created between the earlier missionaries, mostly Spanish and Portuguese Jesuits and Dominicans under the Portuguese authority, and the later missionaries, who were mostly French and belonged to the *Missions Étrangères de Paris* (Paris Foreign Mission Society), a society recently founded by Bishop Pallu. The jurisdictional disputes between these two groups did much harm to the missionary enterprise.

The third source of problems was what has been referred to as the Chinese Rites Controversy, which began in China in the early seventeenth century. In the course of this controversy Dominicans, Franciscans, and members of the Paris Foreign Missions succeeded in having the practice of offering sacrifices to Confucius and the ancestors, which the Jesuits allowed, condemned as superstition. In 1710, Pope Clement XI ratified the Holy Office's 1704 decree condemning these practices, and in 1715 enjoined an oath of obedience on all missionaries to Asia. Pope Benedict XIV renewed the condemnation, insisting on the absolute rejection of the Chinese rites in his bull *Ex quo singulari* (1742).

The Chinese Rites Controversy had long-lasting repercussions for Vietnam. Missionaries (mostly Jesuit) who allowed these rites were excommunicated. However, in 1939, *Propaganda Fide* issued, with Pope Pius XII's approval, the instruction *Plane compertum est*, permitting the veneration of ancestors, on the ground that it is merely a "civil and political act." It was only in 1964 that this policy was applied in Vietnam. In the meantime, conversion to Christianity was much hindered by the fact that it was perceived as a religion that forbids the sacred duties of filial piety toward the ancestors.

The last and most severe challenge to the infant Church was the numerous persecutions carried out by various Vietnamese rulers. It is estimated that 30 000 Catholics were killed under the rule of the Trinh clan in the north and under the rule of the Nguyen clan and the Tay Son family in the south during the seventeenth and eighteenth centuries. Another 40 000 Christians were killed under the reign of three emperors of the Nguyen dynasty, i.e., Minh Mang (1820–1840), Thieu Tri (1841–1847), and Tu Duc (1848–1883). In addition, between 1864 and 1885, 60 000 Christians were killed by the Van Than, a royalist movement fighting against the French colonization.

On the way to maturity

In spite of these severe difficulties the church expanded rapidly. In 1802, there were only three dioceses, with 320 000 faithful. In 1889, there were eight dioceses, with 613 435 faithful. In 1933, the first Vietnamese bishop, Nguyen Ba Tong, was consecrated. In 1934, the first Indochinese council was held in Hanoi with the participation of 19 bishops, 5 major religious superiors, and 21 priests. The council issued 426 statutes for pastoral ministry in Indochina.[4]

Unfortunately, the church's enormous growth was soon hampered by the independence war against France. The 1954 Geneva Accords, as mentioned above, divided Vietnam into two parts, the north under the Communist regime and the south under a democratic and pro-Western government. As a result of the partition, 860 000 Vietnamese, of whom 650 000 were Catholic, fled the north, thereby decimating the northern church and dramatically swelling the Catholic population of the south. After this exodus, in the 10 northern dioceses, there were only 7 bishops and 327 priests left to serve some 831 500 Catholics. By contrast, in the south, according to the statistics provided by the *Propaganda Fide*, there were in 1957 1 100 000 Catholics, 67 854 catechumens, 254 seminarians, 1672 catechists, and 1264 priests.

To commemorate the 300th anniversary of the establishment of the first two dioceses in Vietnam (1659–1959) and to mark the growth into maturity of the church, a national Marian Congress was celebrated in Saigon on

February 17, 1959, under the presidency of Cardinal Gregorio Agagianian, Prefect of the *Propaganda Fide*. On December 8, 1960 Pope John XXIII established the Vietnamese hierarchy, dividing the church into three ecclesiastical provinces: Hanoi, Hue, and Saigon, with 20 dioceses. Thus, after 400 years of mission, the Vietnamese Catholic Church became a fully-fledged church with its own hierarchy.

The church in the north since 1954

Cut off from the church in the south and the Church of Rome for almost 21 years (1954–1975), persecuted by the Communist government, devastated by the departure of a large number of clergy and laity in 1954, the church in the north barely survived. With its educational and social institutions confiscated by the government and its clergy practically under house arrest, the northern church limited its activities to sacramental celebrations and popular devotions. It could not benefit from the great reforms instituted by the Second Vatican Council (1962–1965). In the 1990s the government adopted a more open policy toward the church. It allowed one seminary to function in the archdiocese of Hanoi and one for the dioceses of Vinh and Thanh Hoa.

The church in the south until 1975

Compared with the church in the north, the church in the south was in a far more favorable situation. Not only did it benefit from the massive influx of Catholics in 1954, it also enjoyed 20 years of freedom (1955–1975) that fortunately coincided with a period of extensive renewal in the Catholic Church. The southern church was making rapid gains: in 1959, it had 1 226 310 Catholics, 1342 native priests, 715 brothers, and 3776 sisters. In addition, it had a significant influence on the society at large through its numerous first-rate educational, health-care, and social institutions. A Catholic university was founded in 1957 in Da Lat, and a Pontifical Theological Faculty named Pius X was established in 1958 in the same city. Other universities such as Minh Duc, Thanh Nhan, Regina Mundi, and Regina Pacis soon followed. Unfortunately, all these educational institutions were closed after the Communist victory in 1975.

The church under the Socialist regime since 1975

When North Vietnam conquered the South in 1975 and when the country was reunified in the following year, the Catholic Church, like any other religious organization, faced a severe challenge. All its educational and social institutions were confiscated and almost all its religious organizations were disbanded, from the committees of the Vietnamese Episcopal Conference to parish councils. Some 200 priest-chaplains were sent to "reeducation centers." Archbishop Nguyen Van Thuan, who had been appointed coadjutor with rights of succession to the archdiocese of Saigon (Ho Chi Minh City) in 1975, was imprisoned and then placed under house arrest for 13 years, until he was expelled in 1991. Several priests and religious were falsely accused of treason, tried, and sent to prison.

In November 1983, a conference named "National Convention of Vietnamese Catholics for the Building up and Defense of the Country and of Peace" was held in Hanoi, with some 500 Catholics in attendance. The meeting founded an organization called *Uy Ban Doan Ket Cong Giao Yeu Nuoc* [Committee for the Unification of Patriotic Vietnamese Catholics] with 74 members, among whom there were a handful of so-called "state priests" (*linh muc quoc doanh*). It described itself not as a religious entity but as a member organization of the National Front of Vietnam, governed by the constitution and laws of the Socialist Republic of Vietnam. The committee was heavily criticized as a front for establishing a Vietnamese national or patriotic church, in the Chinese model. Had the committee such an intention, which its organizers publicly disavowed, it was never realized, and its subsequent influence on the church was minimal.

Officially, religious freedom is recognized in the national constitution.[5] Regular sacramental celebrations were allowed, but special permission was required for large-crowd religious activities. The number of priestly ordinations was restricted and the appointment of bishops must be approved by the government. Since 1988, however, the Communist government has adopted a more relaxed attitude toward religious institutions. Six seminaries were allowed to reopen. The number of seminarians grew so large that in October 1993, the Vietnamese Episcopal Conference requested the opening of two more seminaries. Besides these official seminaries, there are several underground centers where thousands of seminarians are being trained. The lack of qualified professors is drastic, and the level of academic preparation is far from satisfactory. Recently, the government has permitted a good number of priests and religious to go abroad for higher studies. Bishops too are regularly permitted to do their *ad limina* visits to Rome as well as to travel abroad. There have also been frequent visits by Vatican officials, which have improved significantly relationships between Vietnam and the Holy See, as well as by representatives of the American Catholic Church to Vietnam. Currently there are talks about establishing regular diplomatic relations between Vietnam and the Holy See.

Since the late 1980s, restrictions on the publication of religious works have been eased. Works on the Bible, theology, spirituality, liturgy, and liturgical music have appeared. Deserving the highest praise is a modern translation of the Bible with scholarly introductions and notes, the fruit of 20 years of labor by a team of 14 translators.

Despite external difficulties, the Vietnamese Catholic Church is vibrant and growing rapidly. Currently, Vietnam has the second largest number of Catholics in South-East Asia, after the Philippines. In 2003, it had 25 dioceses, with about six million members, out of the population of 80 million.

Popular devotions

The Catholic Church fosters devotion to the saints, especially Mary.[6] In many countries Marian devotion is often connected with the locations at which Mary is believed to have appeared. Thus, in France, there is Our Lady of Lourdes, and in Portugal, Our Lady of Fatima, just to mention the two most famous sites. Vietnam, too, has its Mary, known as "Our Lady of La Vang." According to tradition, in 1798, during the persecution by King Canh Thinh, a group of Catholics took refuge at La Vang, a forest some 40 miles north-west of Hue, the ancient imperial city. There Mary is said to have appeared to them. Holding the baby Jesus in her arms and with an angel on her sides, Mary promised to protect them and those who would come to this holy ground.

The La Vang apparition has an interesting twist. It is said that the Buddhists in the area thought that the lady who appeared was one of their Buddhas. They built a pagoda to honor her. Later, when they realized that she was Mary of the Catholic Church, they donated the pagoda and the land to the Catholics for their devotion.

In 1885 hundreds of Catholics were martyred at this place. In 1961 the Vietnamese Episcopal Conference chose our Lady of La Vang as the patroness of Vietnam, and the Holy See agreed to their request to elevate the local shrine into a basilica. During the Vietnam War, the basilica was almost totally destroyed, and its reconstruction has been carried out. In 1998, to celebrate the bicentennial of our Lady's apparition, a statue of our Lady of La Vang was commissioned to the Vietnamese sculptor Van Nhan. His work was officially approved by the Vietnamese Episcopal Conference in the same year. An official pilgrimage to La Vang, which is now the national center for Marian devotion, is organized every three years. At first it was opposed by the government, but now it is openly tolerated.

Another popular devotion among Vietnamese Catholics is to the martyrs in Vietnam. In 1988 Pope John Paul II canonized 117 Catholics who bore witness to the faith through their deaths, of whom 96 were Vietnamese (one of them was a woman, Le Thi Thanh).

Vietnamese Protestant Christianity

To complete the picture of Vietnamese Christianity, a brief word on Protestant Christianity in Vietnam is called for. Protestant Christianity is known in

Vietnam as *Giao Hoi Tin Lanh* (Church of the Good News). Protestantism was introduced to Vietnam under the auspices of Christian and Missionary Alliance by Robert A. Jaffrey in 1911. By 1927 it had 4,115 members. That same year saw the establishment of the Evangelical Church of Indochina; in 1950, its name was changed to the Evangelical Church of Vietnam. After 1954, the church's evangelizing activities were aimed at the Vietnamese in the south and at the tribal peoples in the Central Highlands. During the Vietnam War, numerous other Protestant denominations arrived in South Vietnam and expanded the scope of the church's activities to include social and educational projects. By 1974 the Church numbered 45 000 Christians among the tribes.

By 1975, the Evangelical Church of Vietnam had 510 churches with 54 000 members, 276 students at its Bible Institute in Nha Trang, and 900 lay people theologically trained by extension courses. As the result of the Communist takeover of South Vietnam in 1975, most of the tribes churches were closed, 90 pastors were sent to reeducation camps, and 3 were executed in 1978. Despite extreme difficulties, however, the Protestant Churches, like the Catholic Church, are experiencing a healthy revival.

Contributions of Christianity to Vietnam

In comparison with Confucianism, Buddhism, and Daoism, Christianity is a late comer to Vietnam. Yet its contributions to Vietnamese society are many and significant. These must be honestly and publicly recognized in view of the fact that Christianity, in contrast to the other religions, has often been accused of being a "foreign" religion in Vietnam. Worse, Vietnamese Catholics have sometimes been accused of having collaborated with colonial powers, particularly France and the United States, and having done little for the cause of national independence. These charges are by and large unfair.

Concerning national independence, the participation of Catholics (including priests) in the early anti-colonialist parties such as *Viet Nam Quang Phuc Hoi* (Vietnam Restoration Association) and *Viet Nam Quoc Dan Dang* (Vietnamese People's Party) needs to be remembered. In 1945, all the four Vietnamese bishops of the time lobbied publicly for national independence. Among them, Bishop Le Huu Tu (1896–1967) stood out as the fiercest defender of national independence against French colonization. In 1946 he founded *Lien Doan Cong Giao* (Catholic League) to fight for independence and *Viet Nam Cong Giao Cuu Quoc* (Vietnamese Catholic Association To Save the Country) to engage Catholics in political and military services. In fact, Ho Chi Minh made him Supreme Counselor of the State, and it was in this capacity that the bishop protested against Ho Chi Minh after the latter signed a treaty with the French government at Fontainebleau on September 14, 1946 to allow the presence of the French army in North Vietnam. In the struggle against French colonization the legacy of the Catholic Ngo Dinh Diem, the first president of the Republic of Vietnam, is incontrovertible, whatever political opinion one may have about his later political activities and his family.

In terms of culture, mention has been made of the contributions of the seventeenth-century Jesuit missionaries (in particular, Alexandre de Rhodes) to the invention of the national script. To this linguistic achievement must be added the composition by later missionaries of dictionaries (e.g., those by Bishops Pierre Pigneau de Béhaine and Jean-Louis Taberd), grammars, and ethnographic studies (e.g., those by the French priest Léopold Cadière), catechetical and spiritual treatises (e.g., those by the Italian Jesuit Geronimo Maiorica in the *Nom* or demotic script).[7]

Vietnamese Catholics themselves have made contributions of their own in different fields. In language and literature, Petrus Truong Vinh Ky (1837–1898) has left a large body of works in Vietnamese (in both demotic and national scripts) and in French. The poet Han Mac Tu (1912–1940) invented a whole new genre of religious poetry. In linguistics, Paulus Huinh Tinh Cua composed an important dictionary, and Le Van Ly (1913–1992) a path-breaking work on Vietnamese grammar. In social and political reform, Nguyen Truong To (1832–1871) sought to modernize Vietnam with his 14 ground-breaking proposals. In architecture, the cathedral of Phat Diem, built by Father Petrus Tran Luc (1825–1899), popularly known as Cu Sau, is an outstanding achievement. In philosophy, the works of Kim Dinh (1914–1995) laid the foundation for Vietnamese Confucianism.

More than any other religious organization, the Vietnamese Catholic Church has made an enormous and lasting contribution to education and social services. In education, the achievements of male religious, in particular La Salle Christian Brothers, are immense. In medical and social services, the work of women religious is unparalleled. Even during the difficult years since 1975, the Vietnamese Catholic Church continues, quietly and heroically, its ministry of love and service to its people, Catholic and non-Catholic alike. Deserving special notice is its care for the victims of leprosy in more than 30 centers throughout the country.

As with any Asian country, Vietnam is not immune from the political and economic effects of globalization with its twin driving forces, namely, democracy and free market capitalism. In addition to the social upheavals caused by globalization, there are moral and cultural challenges facing Vietnam and Vietnamese Christianity as a whole. If their past is any indication, there is every reason to believe that Vietnamese Christians, both Catholic and Protestant, will be able to meet these challenges successfully.

Cambodia, Laos, Thailand

Christianities in these three countries are studied together not because each of them is not worthy of a separate investigation but because, despite their more than three hundred years of existence, the Christian Churches in these countries still remain a minuscule part of the entire populations.[8]

The kingdom of Cambodia

Cambodia is known to most tourists for its Angkor Wat, a twelfth-century temple. In the twentieth century, its reputation as a gentle and peaceful country was marred by the atrocities carried out by the Khmer Rouge from 1975 to 1978 to impose a socialist regime on the country. Most Cambodians consider themselves descendants of the Khmer Angkor Empire which reached its apogee between the tenth and thirteenth centuries. After the decline of the Khmer Empire, a great part of Cambodia was annexed by the neighboring countries, especially Thailand, the Champa kingdom, and Vietnam. In 1863 the king placed his country under French protection, and in 1887 it constituted, together with Laos and Vietnam, French Indochina until its independence in 1953. As mentioned earlier, Cambodia became engulfed in the Vietnam War. In 1978 it was invaded by Vietnam and was occupied until 1989. Peace returned to the country in 1993 when a constitution was ratified, with the king as chief of state and the prime minister as head of government.

Religiously, of the current population of 14 million, 95% practice Theravada Buddhism. Some 200 000 (the descendants of the Chams) are Sunni Muslims. Christianity first came to Cambodia in the sixteenth century but no substantial presence of Catholics was reached until Cambodia was made part of French Indochina, when missions were entrusted to the Paris Foreign Missions Society. A great number of Vietnamese Catholics settled in Cambodia. In 1970, there were 65 000 Catholics in Cambodia, of whom 60 000 were of Vietnamese descent. During the Khmer Rouge's rule, thousands of Vietnamese-Cambodian Catholics, including most priests and religious, were killed, and the rest expelled. All the churches, except two, were destroyed.

This tragedy proved to be a blessing for the Cambodian Catholic Church since it is now possible for a Khmer to be a Catholic without being associated with being pro-Vietnamese. Today there still are no dioceses as such in Cambodia but only one apostolic vicariate (Phnom Penh) and two apostolic prefectures (Battambamg and Kompong Cham). The apostolic vicariate of Phnom Penh was established in 1850, covering the entire kingdom of Cambodia. In 1870 three provinces of Vietnam, originally parts of Cambodia, namely, Sa Det, Chau Doc, and Soc Trang, were added to the vicariate of Phnom Penh. In 1955, these three provinces were detached from it and in 1968, the vicariate was divided into three parts, the vicariate of Phnom Penh itself and the two prefectures of Battambang and Kompong Cham. A bishop of Battambamg, Paul Tep, was killed by the Khmer Rouge in 1975.

The Christian and Missionary Alliance entered Cambodia in 1923 with David Ellison and his wife. Later, Arthur Hammond came and began translating the Bible into Khmer, a work eventually completed by the United Bible Society. The Overseas Missionary Fellowship began its work in Cambodia in 1973. Protestant missions were completely interrupted two years later by the Khmer Rouge, several missionaries being killed and the rest forced to leave. At that time, there were 14 Cambodian Protestant ministers, and when the Vietnamese defeated the Khmer Rouge in 1978, only three were alive. Today Protestant Churches are multiplying rapidly, with missionaries being Anglican, Methodist, and independent groups, particularly the Evangelicals, from South-East Asia. There is an umbrella group, The Evangelical Fellowship, representing the Evangelicals to the government (75% of Cambodian Protestant churches belong to this group).[9]

The Lao People's Democratic Republic

Laos traces its history back to the kingdom of Lan Xang. Founded in the fourteenth century by Fa Ngum, the kingdom prospered until the eighteenth century when it was divided into three principalities and was dominated by Siam (present-day Thailand). In the nineteenth century it was incorporated into French Indochina. It was not until 1954 that Laos achieved full independence from France and was organized as a constitutional monarchy. As mentioned earlier, Laos was dragged into the Vietnam War, used by North Vietnam as a staging ground and supply route for its war against South Vietnam. In 1975 the communist Pathet Lao overthrew the monarchy and entered into partnership with North Vietnam. Its economy was in a shambles until 1986 when the government of Laos began decentralizing the economy and encouraging private enterprise which produced a spurt of economic growth. The current Laotian population is about 7 million, of which 69% are ethnic Lao.

Christianity entered Laos in 1642 with the coming of the Jesuit Jean de Leria. Nothing is known of the Lao Catholic Church until 200 years later when in 1858 Bishop Jean-Claude Miche, vicar apostolic in Cambodia, entrusted the missionary work in Laos to Fr. Ausoleil and Fr. Triaire, both members of the Paris Foreign Missions Society. The missionary most responsible for the development of the Catholic Church in Laos was no doubt Bishop Jean-Louis Vey (bishop 1875–1909), vicar apostolic of Siam (Thailand), who sent several members of the Paris Foreign Missions Society to Laos. Under Vey's direction, Catholic missions made rapid and spectacular progress so much so that in 1896 Vey proposed to Rome to detach Laos from Siam, which was done the following year. Today there are about 37000 Roman Catholics in Laos (about 0.5% of the population). Like Cambodia, Laos does not have a diocese but four apostolic vicariates (Luang Prabang, Praksé, Savannakhet and Vientiane).

The first Protestant to come to Laos was the Presbyterian Daniel McGilvary. Stationed in Chiang Mai, Thailand, he made several trips to Laos between 1872 and 1898. In 1902 Gabriel Contesse of the Swiss Brethren began work in southern Laos. Mission in northern Laos was begun in 1929 by G. Edward Roffe of the Christian and Missionary Alliance. Seventh-Day Adventists also have churches in Laos. With the coming to power of the Communist Pathet Laos in 1975, all missionaries had to leave the country. Today, the Protestant Churches, organized under the umbrella of the Lao Evangelical Church, have about 35000 members.

The kingdom of Thailand

Known as Siam until June 23, 1936, Thailand had a long history of various kingdoms: Sukhothai (established in 1238–1350), Ayuthhaya (1350–1767), and Chakri (1782 to today, with the capital in Bangkok). Concomitantly, there was also the kingdom of Lan Na, founded in 1296, with its capital in Chiang Mai. It was occupied by Burma from 1558 to 1774. After it ousted the Burmese with the help of King Taksin, the founder of the Chakri kingdom, it gave allegiance to the Chakri kings and in the twentieth century merged into the Thai state. In 1932 a bloodless coup transformed Thailand into a constitutional monarchy, with the prime minster as head of government. Democracy has been fragile since then, with elected governments brought down by numerous coups followed by military rule. A new constitution was approved in a national referendum in 2007 and a new government was formed in 2008. Politically, since 2004 Thailand has been facing a secessionist movement by Muslim Malay separatists in its southern border provinces.

Like Vietnam, Thailand's population is relatively homogeneous, with more than 85% speaking Thai and sharing the same culture. Religiously, it is even more homogeneous, with 94% of the population following Theravada Buddhism. Christianity – Dominican missionaries more precisely – first came to the kingdom of Ayutthaya in 1567, but when Ayutthaya was seized by Burma in 1569, missions came to an end. Franciscan missionaries restarted missions in 1585 and worked until the fall of the Ayutthaya kingdom in 1767. The Jesuits arrived in 1607 and became established in 1655. A seminary was established in 1665 to serve several countries in East Asia. Catholic missions suffered a setback with the end of the Ayutthaya, and Taksin, the founder of the succeeding kingdom, ordered the expulsion of all Catholic missionaries. Subsequently, French missionaries returned to Thailand in 1764, at the invitation of king Rama I. In 1835, about 1,500 Vietnamese Catholics, persecuted in their homeland, took refuge in Thailand thereby increasing the number of Thai Catholics dramatically.

Among foreign missionaries, two bishops stand out. One, Jean-Baptiste Pallegoix (1805–1862, bishop since 1838), is the author of a historical work on the kingdom of Thailand and a dictionary of Thai-Latin-French-English dictionary. The other, already mentioned in connection with Laos, is Jean-Louis Vey, under whose episcopal supervision the Thai Catholic Church enjoyed an extraordinary growth. Today the Catholic Church in Thailand has ten dioceses and 300 000 members, about 0.46% of the total population.

Protestant Christianity arrived in Thailand in 1828 with Jacob Tomlin and Karl Gützlaff of the London Missionary Society. American Baptist missionaries came in 1833 and the American Board of Commissioners for Foreign Missions the following year. Eventually, especially after 1945, most major Protestant denominations are represented. Among the most influential missionaries were Dan Beach Bradley (1804–1873) and Daniel McGilvary. Bradley, a New York medical doctor, together with his wife came to Thailand in 1835. He introduced Western medical practice and printing, and was highly respected by the Thais, including King Mongkut. His daughter Sophia was married to Daniel McGilvary, who was largely responsible for the spreading of Protestantism to northern Thailand, especially in Chiang Mai (where this is the McGilvary Theological Seminary) and in Laos. Currently, there are two major Protestant umbrella organizations: The Church of Christ in Thailand and the Evangelical Fellowship of Thailand. The total number of Thai Protestants is put at 2 to 3% of the Thai population of 65 million.[10]

A Look Into the Future

Christians in Cambodia, Laos, and Thailand, somewhat less so in Vietnam, still are a tiny minority, even after several hundred years of missionary activities. The reasons for the lack of mass conversion to Christianity, which is found in all Asian countries except the Philippines and Timor-Leste, are multiple and complex. One is the fact that Christianity in Asia was linked with Western colonialism and is still, in the eyes of not a few Asians, a religion of the colonizers. This explanation is however not fully satisfactory since, while applicable to Cambodia, Laos, and Vietnam, it is not true of Thailand, which has never been colonized by any Western power. Another possible explanation is that Christianity, while present for many centuries in these countries, has not been, to use a neologism, fully "inculturated" into the cultural and spiritual soil of these places. Its liturgy, theology, and organizational structures – and this true especially of Roman Catholicism – still remain for the most part foreign, like a bonsai planted in a pot and carried from place to place but not yet taken out of its original pot and planted into the indigenous soil and allowed to grow on the local nutrients. Only in this way will Christianity be transformed into something authentically indigenized, quite different from what it was when it was imported.

But even with such an inculturation process firmly in place, mass conversions of Cambodians, Laotians, Thais, and Vietnamese to Christianity do not appear to be likely. The reason is that short of miraculous interventions, religious conversion and the consequent official membership in a religious institution generally occur only when the beliefs and practices of one's religious tradition are no longer perceived as adequate means for coping with the crisis one is undergoing, be it material, physical, intellectual, moral, or spiritual. No one, it seems, would be willing to be "born again," to use a favorite phrase of Evangelicals, if one is fully or fairly satisfied with one's first religious tradition. No Buddhist, for example, will become a Christian as long as Buddhist beliefs and practices are seen as spiritually uplifting and transformative.

It would seem reasonable to say that the future of Christianity in Vietnam, Cambodia, Laos and Thailand, as in any other Asian country, does not lie in its numerical expansion, though of course conversion and baptism into the church should always be offered to all, freely and humbly, as God's invitation to a personal communion with God and with other human beings. Rather the future of Christianity, in these four countries as well as in other Asian countries, appears to depend on its ability to work with the followers of other religions as well as with non-believers to promote peace, justice, ecological well-being, forgiveness, reconciliation, and love.

Such a task can only be achieved, as the Federation of Asian Bishops' Conferences has repeatedly pointed out, through a humble and open dialogue with all peoples. Indeed, it is a fourfold dialogue: dialogue of life, dialogue of action, dialogue of theological exchange, and dialogue of spiritual experiences.[11] This fourfold dialogue does not replace what is referred in missionary circles as the evangelizing mission of the Church or the proclamation of the Good News. It only stresses that dialogue must be the mode in which such mission and proclamation are to be carried out if the Gospel is to gain a favorable hearing from the Asian peoples.

Notes

1. The literature on the Vietnam War is literally endless. For an informative one-volume overview, see Tucker, S.C. (ed.) *The Encyclopedia of the Vietnam War: A Political, Social and Military* History, Oxford: OUP, 1998. A highly

readable account of the Vietnam War is Karnow, S. *Vietnam: A History. The First Complete Account of Vietnam at War,* New York: Viking Press, 1983.

2. For brief introduction to the *tam giao* and the Vietnamese indigenous religions, see Phan, P.C. *Mission and Catechesis: Alexandre de Rhodes and Inculturation in Seventeenth-Century Vietnam.* Maryknoll, New York: Orbis Books, 1998, pp. 13–28.

3. For a general history of Christianity in Vietnam, see Huon, P.P. *History of the Catholic Church in Vietnam,* Vol. 1. *1533–1960,* Los Angeles: Vietnamese Redemptorist Mission, 2002.

4. For an account of Vietnamese Christianity in the nineteenth century, see Phan, P.C. "Christianity in Indochina, 1815–1915," in Gilley, S. and Stanley, B. (eds.) *The Cambridge History of Christianity.* Vol. 8. *World Christianities, circa 1815–1914,* Cambridge: CUP, 2005, pp. 513–527.

5. On the recent history of religious freedom in Vietnam, see Phan, P.C. "The Roman Catholic Church in the Socialist Republic of Vietnam, 1989–2005," in Koschorke, K. (ed.) *Falling Walls: The Year 1989/90 as a Turning Point in the History of World Christianity,* Wiesbaden: Harrassowitz Verlag, 2009, pp. 243–257.

6. On popular devotions in the Catholic Church, see Phan, P.C. (ed.) *Popular Piety and the Liturgy: A Commentary,* Collegeville, Min.: Liturgical Press, 2005.

7. On the works in *Nom* by Geronimo Maiorica, see Ostrowski, B.E. The Nom Works of Geronimo Maiorica, S.J. (1589–1656) and their Christology, Ph.D. dissertation, Cornell University, 2006.

8. For brief information on Christianity in Cambodia, Laos, and Thailand, see the relevant entries in Sunquist, S. (ed.) *A Dictionary of Asian Christianity,* Grand Rapids: Eerdmans, 2001.

9. On Christianity in Cambodia, see Ponchaud, F. *La cathédrale de la rizière: 450 ans d'histoire de l'église au Cambodge [The Cathedral of the Rice Paddy: 450 Years of the History of the Church in Cambodia],* Paris: Fayard, 1990.

10. For a helpful bibliography on Christianity in Thailand, see www.herbswanson.com. The web site is described as "A Resource for the Study of the Thai Church."

11. For a collection of the documents issued by the Federation of Asian Bishops' Conferences and its various offices, see Rosales, G. and Arévalo, C.G. (eds.) *For All The Peoples of Asia: Federation of Asian Bishops' Conferences. Documents from 1970 to 1991,* Vol. 1, New York/Quezon City: Orbis Books/Claretian Publications, 1992), Eilers, F.-J. (ed.) *For All the Peoples of Asia: Federation of Asian Bishops' Conferences. Documents from 1992 to1996,* Vol. 2, Quezon City: Claretian Publications, 1997; Eilers, F.-J. (ed.) *For All The Peoples of Asia: Federation of Asian Bishops' Conferences. Documents from 1997 to 2002,* Vol. 3, Quezon City: Claretian Publications, 2002; and Eilers, F.-J. (ed.) *For All The Peoples of Asia: Federation of Asian*

Bishops' Conferences. Documents from 2002–2006, Vol. 4, Quezon City: Claretian Publications, 2007.

Further Reading

Ho Tai, H.-T. *The Country of Memory: Remaking the Past in Late Socialist Vietnam*, Berkeley: University of California Press, 2001.

Phan, P.C. *Mission and Catechesis: Alexandre de Rhodes and Inculturation in Seventeenth-Century Vietnam*, Maryknoll, New York: Orbis Books, 1998.

Phan, P.C. *Christianity with An Asian Face*, Maryknoll, New York: Orbis, 2003.

Phan, P.C. In *Our Own Tongues: Perspectives from Asia on Mission and Inculturation*, Maryknoll, New York: Orbis Books, 2003.

Phan, P.C. *Being Religious Interreligiously: Asian Perspectives on Interfaith Dialogue*, Maryknoll, New York: Orbis Books, 2004.

Ramsey, J. *Mandarins and Martyrs: The Church and the Nguyen Dynasty in Early Nineteenth-Century Vietnam*, Stanford: Stanford California Press, 2008.

Tana, L. *Nguyen Cochinchina: Southern Vietnam in the Seventeenth and Eighteenth Centuries*, Ithaca, New York: Cornell University Press, 1998.

Tran, N.T. and Reid, A. (eds.) *Viet Nam: Borderless History*, Madison, W.I.: University of Wisconsin Press, 2006.

Wook, C.B. *Southern Vietnam under the Reign of Minh Mang (1820–1841): Central Policies and Local Responses*, Ithaca, N.Y.: Cornell University Press, 2004.

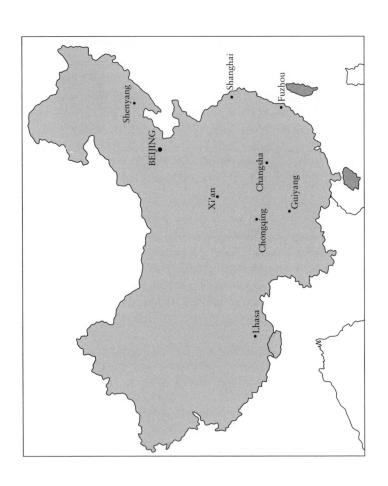

8

Mainland China

Ying Fuk-tsang

A New China

On July 30, 2005, *The Economist* featured an article on China's growing global influence. The article's title, "How China Runs the World Economy," suggested that China's development is not just a powerful driver of internal economic growth; its impact on other economies is also profound and pervasive. In the coming years, inflation and interest rates, wages, profits, oil, and even home prices in developed countries could very well wear the "Made in China" label.

Like it or not, a new China is on the rise, an inescapable fact that was inconceivable even 20 years ago. Roll the clock back to December 1978, when the Chinese Communist Party (CCP) held the third plenary meeting of its 11th Politburo Standing Committee. The CCP was determined to shed the residues of the Cultural Revolution and to promote economic reform, unveiling a new era. During the last three decades, Chinese society has undergone drastic changes in the name of "socialism with Chinese characteristics." These changes have taken China from Deng Xiaoping to Hu Jintao, from planned economy to socialist market economy, from the "initial phrase of socialism" to "three representatives," and from open-door policy to entry into the World Trade Organization. The economic reform that brought about these changes has transformed the Chinese economy. At the same time, it has also brought unprecedented changes in the social, cultural, and religious aspects of Chinese society. Arguably, the last three decades have ushered in the most important epoch in Chinese history since the Cultural Revolution.

Christianities in Asia, edited by Peter C. Phan © 2011 Blackwell Publishing Ltd except for editorial material and organization © 2011 Peter C. Phan

World Christianity and Chinese Christianity

The encounter between Christianity and China

The last three decades have witnessed remarkable changes in the religious domain of Chinese society as well. Christianity in China especially has showed a unique pattern of development.

Compared with some other world religions, Christianity has a short history in China. The earliest mission to China was undertaken by East Syrian Christians (sometimes referred to as "Nestorians") who arrived in China in the seventh century. Christianity, then called *Jinjiao* (Luminous Religion), was given a warm welcome by the Tang dynasty. However, in 845 the emperor Wuzhong implemented the policy of "eradicating Buddhism," which also clamped down on other foreign religions including *Jinjiao*. Subsequently *Jinjiao* disappeared from the Chinese empire. Its history was recorded on the Memorial of the Propagation of *Jinjiao* in China, which had been erected in 781. Buried in Chang'an (present-day Xian), it was not discovered until 1623.

In the thirteenth century, Genghis Khan established his Mongol empire over Europe and Asia. *Jinjiao* and the Roman Catholic Church (the Franciscans) resumed their work in the Chinese empire. However, the mission work of Christianity in China was interrupted again upon dissolution of the Mongol empire. Christianity apparently failed to establish any relationship with the Chinese culture and society until the latter days of the Ming dynasty. With Matteo Ricci's arrival in Beijing in 1601 and his subsequent good relations with the Ming government, the Jesuits turned a new page in the history of Christian missions in China. Unfortunately, the Chinese Rites Controversy later ruptured the relationship between the Catholic Church and the ruling government. In 1717, the emperor Kangxi of the Qing dynasty issued an edict banning Christian missions. Thus the seeds of Gospel planted by Ricci and others were prevented from sprouting. The Catholic Church in China declined, waiting to be reborn at a later date.

In the nineteenth century, Christianity knocked on China's door again, this time in the form of Protestant missions. However, this new arrival only led to new rebuke. Protestant missionaries had arrived in China along with Western colonial expansion, which through military power and unequal treaties forced China to open up its borders for commerce. As a result, Christianity was condemned as a channel for the West's imperialist invasion. Branding Christianity as a "foreign religion" (*yang jiao*), the Chinese rejected it culturally, socially, and politically.

Despite the severe criticism of Christianity and the turbulent sociopolitical conditions of modern China, the number of Chinese Christians has increased steadily. At the outset of the twentieth century, membership in Protestant congregations was more than 100 000. When the Republic of China was proclaimed in 1912, the number reached 200 000. Five years later, another 100 000 were added. Protestants numbered 620,000 in 1936, on the eve of the Sino-Japanese War, and rose to 1 000 000 in 1949. Undoubtedly, the ratio of Protestant Christians to the total Chinese population was still extremely low. However, we should not overlook the enormous growth of the Protestant churches in China during the turbulent first half of the twentieth century. During this time, the number of Protestant Christians grew tenfold.

The development of Christianity in China entered a new phase after the establishment of the People's Republic of China in 1949. Sino-American relations were ruptured by the Korean War. The CCP initiated an all-encompassing anti-imperialism campaign, fueling a strong sense of patriotism all over the country.

In the name of anti-imperialism and patriotism, the Communist government asked Protestant denominations and the Catholic Church to conduct 'self-reformation'. At the same time, Western missionaries, regarded as imperialists or counter-revolutionaries, were expelled from China. As Chinese churches terminated their ties with their Western missionary societies in droves, the Missionary Era in China came to the end. Patriotism became the guiding principle of the development of Christianity in China, and the basis of its survival.

Beginning in the 1950s, due to the "original sin" of being a channel of imperialist invasion, Christian churches in China became a target for political campaigns, which transformed every aspect of the churches' existence, especially in terms of church institution and theology. This culminated in 1966, when Mao Zedong's Cultural Revolution labeled all religions, including Christianity, as evil vestiges of the "old society" and colonialism. Public religious activities were banned. The Red Guards occupied all the churches in cities and villages. Pastors and evangelists were denounced as members of the exploiting class. China seemingly became an "irreligious" nation. Chinese Christianity was engulfed by a revolutionary wave.

Christianity as a Chinese religion

At the end of the Cultural Revolution in 1976, when Chinese society began to rebuild itself from the ruins, Chinese Christianity had to develop within a brand new situation. Since the 1980s, it has enjoyed a striking growth. According to official statistics, there are at the present about 17 000 000 Chinese Protestants, seventeen times the number in 1949 when the Communist government was established. There are 13,000 chapels and more than 30,000 meeting places. On average, six chapels or meeting places resume their religious activities or are under construction every day. The number of Chinese Catholics has also increased: from 3 000 000 in 1949 to 5 000 000 in 2006. Arguably, the weekly number of Christian worshippers in China is far higher than that of Christians in Europe.

While the official statistics are impressive, they do not tell the whole story. It is beyond doubt that the actual number of Chinese Christians far exceeds that put forth by the government. For various reasons, it is impossible to obtain an accurate number. Conservatively, the number of Chinese Protestants in China is estimated to be at least 40 000 000, forty times the number in 1949, and the number of Chinese Catholics to be around 12 000 000. It is noteworthy that the growth of Christianity in China occurred mostly after the 1980s, a period of extraordinary development for China as a whole.

Recent church historians, among whom is notably Philip Jenkins, have been pointing out that Christianity is no longer a "Western" religion. Instead, they note, it is a religion developing across races, regions, and cultures, becoming a global phenomenon. Jenkins believes that the "global South" – that is, Africa, Asia, and Latin America – will be the major home of Christianity in the future.[1]

The development of Chinese Christianity during the last three decades provides an important commentary on the globalization of Christianity. Thanks to its unique historical conditions, especially the policy of self-governance, self-support, and self-propagation advocated by the Chinese government, Chinese Christianity has a peculiar pattern of development, in contrast to Christian communities elsewhere in the world.

Today the number of practicing Chinese Christians is probably no less than that of any other Chinese religion. Christianity has perhaps surpassed any other religion in the number of local organizations. Despite the rather low ratio of Christians to the total population, Christianity is no longer a "foreign religion" but has become one of the Chinese religions.

Regional differences in Chinese Christianity

In a certain sense, "China" as a unified sovereign state is a political construct. Given its vast territory and huge population, China is characterized by multiplicity and heterogeneity. In fact, most of the provinces of China are comparable to a European country in terms of population, geography, and social complexity. To gain a more accurate understanding of China, we should regard it as a complex social community. Behind the entity known as 'One China' stands a country of enormous differences and extreme complexity.

Within this complex that is China, what is "Chinese Christianity"? In terms of regional development, diversity stands out. For example, the distribution of Protestants in China shows a very uneven pattern. Statistics published by the Amity Foundation in late 2004 confirm this point.[2]

Over three quarters of Chinese Protestants come from the Henan, Anhui, Zhejiang, Fujian, Shandong, Yunnan, and Jiangsu provinces. This means that the development of Christianity varies in different regions in China. Christianity does not develop evenly everywhere within a single region. For example, the number of Protestant in Northern Jiangsu far exceeds that in Southern Jiangsu. The development of Christianity in Chaozhou and Santou outranks other regions in Guangdong. The Protestant churches in Wenzhou in Zhejiang have caused the region to be called "Jerusalem in China." Rather than examining the "Chinese" church from the perspective of grand narrative, it will be more useful to know the features of Christianity in different regions and the religious variations between cities and villages in China. Christianity in China can only be properly understood from the perspective of regional studies.

Christianity with Chinese Characteristics

The three traditions of Christianity – Roman Catholicism, Protestantism, and Orthodox Christianity – have had their own special patterns of development in China. The section that follows examines each in turn.

The Vatican and Chinese Catholicism

The contemporary development of Chinese Catholicism is closely related to Sino-Vatican relations. Catholicism emphasizes the catholicity of the church and regards the Holy See as the center of the universal church. As the religious leader of Catholics, the pope appoints bishops of dioceses all around the world. This arrangement has been uniquely complicated for the Catholic Church within the Chinese context.

After 1949, Rome's strident anti-communism resulted in hostility between the Holy See and the newly established, avowedly atheist, Communist government. In the eyes of the Communists, the Vatican was not merely a religious organization. It was also a political agent of imperialism intent on controlling the Chinese Catholic Church. Therefore, the Communist government advocated the so-called Three-Self Movement (self-governance, self-support, and self-propagation) within the Chinese Catholic Church, hoping to mobilize the patriots in the church and to replace the clergymen loyal to the Vatican. However, since the rigorous hierarchy of the Catholic Church effectively defended against political interference by the Communist government, the Three-Self Patriotic Movement in the Chinese Catholic Church met strong resistance. Even as numerous foreign missionaries were charged with engaging in counter-revolutionary activities, the Chinese Catholic Church insisted on boycotting this "three-self" reform. The impact of the political campaign did not sever the relations between the Vatican and the Chinese Catholic Church. From 1949 to 1955, the Vatican appointed 18 Chinese bishops.

In 1955, the Chinese government announced that it had smashed a counter-revolutionary group headed by the Bishop of Shanghai, Kung Pin-mei. Arresting both priests and lay people, the CCP hope to root out all Catholics opposing the "three-self" reform of the church in China. In July 1957, with the support of the government, the National Catholic Conference was held in Beijing, and the Chinese Catholic Patriotic Association (CCPA) was officially established.

The establishment of CCPA was the result of Chinese Catholicism achieving independence in a special political situation. At the time of its inception, CCPA emphasized that it would maintain merely religious relations with the Vatican, obeying the Pope with regard to doctrine and canons in order to preserve the unity and orthodoxy of the Chinese Catholic Church. To ensure that such relations would not harm the interests and dignity of China as an independent state, the CCPA severed any form of political and economic connection with the Vatican and was determined to oppose any interference in the internal affairs of China in the name of religion. An expedient way to achieve religion-state balance, the position of CCPA showed the willingness of the Chinese Catholic Church to compromise politically in order to maintain the catholicity of the Roman Catholic Church.

Despite the establishment of CCPA, relations between the Chinese Catholic Church and the Vatican remained strained. The CCP declared that the Chinese Catholic Church could not have any religious relations with the Vatican, unless the latter changed its anti-communism position and abandoned its relations with the Nationalist government in Taiwan. In other words, the presence of diplomatic relations between the Chinese government and the Vatican are the prerequisite for the religious relations between the Chinese Catholic Church and the Holy See.

This politically charged relationship led to a situation in which many dioceses and apostolic prefectures were without ordinaries or other Vatican-appointed ecclesiastical leadership. In response, the CCPA began to "self-elect" bishops at the instigation of the government. After electing their respective bishops in 1958, in order to legitimize the status of the elected bishops according to the Catholic Church Canon Law, the dioceses of Hankou and Wuchang in Hubei province telegraphed their names to the Congregation for the Propagation of the Faith of the Holy See for the Pope's approval. However, the Congregation turned down their requests because it is the pope's privilege to appoint bishops, which cannot be replaced by election. The dioceses later telegraphed the Congregation a second time, again seeking the pope's approval. The Congregation reiterated that those consecrating bishop without the pope's approval would be excommunicated, together with the bishops consecrated.

In April 1958, the dioceses held their first consecration of self-elected bishops, which led to the schism of the Chinese Catholic Church: all clergies supporting self-election and self-consecration of bishops were obliged to swear to sever their connection with Rome. Those who refused to do so would be arrested.

Self-election and self-consecration of bishops lit the fuse of the split between the Chinese Catholic Church and the universal church. It also became an important historical setting for the schism dividing the Chinese Catholic Church into patriotic and underground segments.

During the Cultural Revolution, Chinese Catholicism came to a standstill. Clerics had to endure public struggle sessions. Some of them were even forced to marry nuns under political pressure. However, political impacts did not entirely take away the Catholics' faith. Upon the implementation of the state policy on religion, Catholic churches in China resumed their activities. In May 1980, the Third Assembly of the CCPA and the first National Catholic Representatives' Congress were held in Beijing, which resulted in the creation of the Chinese Catholic Church Administrative Commission and the Bishops' Conference of Catholic Church in China. The universal Catholic Church regarded the establishment of the Commission and the Bishop's Conference as groundbreaking. The termination of relations with the Vatican and the universal Catholic Church caused great impacts on the institution of the Chinese Catholic Church. Founded in 1957, CCPA was unable to undertake administrative and pastoral work, owing to its unusual political background. Thus, the establishment of the two organizations was to solve the institutional problems of the Chinese Catholic Church. It showed that in the new era of economic reform, the Chinese government expected these two newly established organizations to be responsible for administrative and pastoral affairs, whereas CCPA was designated to implement the principles of patriotic education within the church.

It is well known that there is a segment of the Chinese Catholic Church operating outside of this system of government regulation: the so-called Underground Church operating in the shadow of the officially-recognized Open Church. The formation of the Underground Church could be attributed to the clergy released at the end of the Cultural Revolution. Arrested because of their unwillingness to join CCPA, they laid down a concrete foundation for the development of the Underground Church. Since the 1980s, the Underground Church has experienced flourishing development. The Underground churches form an organic network, which shares the same religious beliefs with the Catholic churches around the world and is in full communion with the Vatican.

The Chinese Catholic Church has been developing in an unusual form for fifty years. Since 1958, the Chinese Catholic Church has self-elected over 170 bishops. In recent years, the Chinese government resumed its contact with the Vatican, negotiating for the normalization of diplomatic relations between the two states. In his letter to the Catholics in China in May 2007, Pope Benedict XVI expressed his wish to have dialogue with the Chinese government. The establishment of Sino-Vatican relations and the unity of the Official Church and the Underground Church, no matter how they are achieved, will be significant for the future development of Chinese Catholicism. It will also inject brand new elements into the development of the universal Catholic Church.

Post-denominational Protestantism

When Protestantism came to China in the nineteenth century, every missionary society belonged to a denomination, save a few interdenominational ones. The churches established by these missionary societies naturally inherited their traditions. Later there were certain indigenous churches, some of which appeared to be non-denominational, for example *Jidutu Juhuichu* (Christian Assembly) and True Jesus Church. However, these non-denominational groups had in fact built up their own theological perspectives and liturgies, making themselves *de facto* denominations. Generally, the multi-denominational situation of Protestantism remained unchanged, though the Ecumenical Movement in the twentieth century did lead to the unity and cooperation of certain missionary societies and denominations. Statistics show that there were more than 120 missionary organizations working in China on the eve of the Communist takeover of the country.

With subsidies from Western missionary organizations ceasing after the Korean War, the relationship between the denominations in China and their parent societies in terms of organization, personnel and finance came to an official end. Under the advocacy of the government, the Three-Self Movement was launched in full force. Following the formation of the Preparatory Committee of the Three-Self Reform Movement in 1951, the Committee of the China Christian Three-Self Patriotic Movement (TSPM) was officially established during the National Christian Conference in 1954.

The objective of TSPM was to create a uniform mechanism to promote the political mission of anti-imperialism and patriotism in the Protestant Church in China comprising numerous denominations. It is noteworthy that the Chinese government instigated the birth of patriotic organization for each major religion, for example, the Buddhist Association of China, the Chinese Taoist Association, and the Islamic Association of China, in order to strengthen the CCP's leadership and control of the religious organizations in China.

There is no doubt that in the era of revolution and class struggle, the highly politicized patriotic religious organizations in China had strong political appeal and enjoyed official status to a certain degree.

Having a Western background, Protestantism and Roman Catholicism were regarded as religions related to the invasion of imperialism. As such, they became the chief targets of the CCP's religious reform. Without a rigorous hierarchy like that of Roman Catholic Church, Protestantism was not able to offer strong opposition from a centralized clerical authority to government-sponsored reforms.

Despite different levels of participation in TSPM among its denominations, the Protestant Church in China on the whole showed its willingness to cooperate with the government to fight against imperialism in exchange for autonomy in the religious domain. Indeed, the objective of TSPM was to advocate "anti-imperialism and patriotism" in the church. Ecclesiastical affairs were not the concern of TSPM. Each denomination's national and regional organizations and local churches continued to hold denominational meetings, ordain pastors, deploy manpower and manage their own financial accounts, showing that they still maintained certain autonomy.

However, as political campaigns intensified, the whole nation emphasized more and more a highly centralized leadership, which inevitably imposed influence on the churches. The function of TSPM soon changed, taking over certain duties of supervision within the denominations. Under such circumstances, many denominational organizations lost their original functions.

The watershed year in the development of the Chinese Protestant Church was 1958

With the implementation of the Great Leap Forward, the battered church sustained a further blow. The form of existence of the Chinese Protestant Church, especially the co-existence of various denominations, resulted in the CCP's adoption of a more radical religion policy. In some regions, such as Wenzhou in Zhejiang province, the government even put forward the experiment of setting up "irreligion" areas, proclaiming officially the ultimate goal of eradicating religion. In the name of changing the situation of China as a semi-colony, TSPM implemented the measure of Unification of Worship all over the country. Congregations had to be united with those of other denominations according to their geographical locations, resulting in the drastic decrease in the number of local churches. For example, there were 208 local churches in Shanghai in 1950. After the implementation of Unification of Worship, the number dropped to 22 and subsequently to 8. In 1958, only 4 local churches were left in Beijing; there had been 65 in 1949.

The ties between local churches and the hierarchical organizations of their denominations, such as general assemblies, synods, or district associations, were severed after the implementation of Unification of Worship, even as these hierarchical organizations on the whole continued to exist in name. Examples were the General Assembly of the Church of Christ in China, the General Synod of Chung Hua Sheng Kung Hui, the General Conference of the Methodist Church of China (Wei Li kung Hui), and the General Conference of the Seventh-day Adventist Church in China.

With the outbreak of the Cultural Revolution in 1966, public religious activities of the Protestant churches all over the country came to a standstill, bringing the official death of the hierarchical organizations of the denominations. Even TSPM organizations at different levels ceased to function during the Cultural Revolution, which was the unprecedented era of darkness in the history of Chinese Protestantism.

After the Cultural Revolution, churches all over the country resumed their meetings and Sunday services. Concerned that the denominations might renew ties with their foreign counterparts, the Chinese government prohibited the reestablishment of denominational organizations, marking the beginning of post-denominational period. To solve the problems arising from the absence of denominational organizations, the China Christian Council (CCC) was established in 1980. Providing theological education, printing Bibles, formulating church order, and ordaining clergymen, the CCC took over all ecclesiastical affairs originally managed by the denominations themselves. Promulgated by CCC and TSPM in 1996, the government document "Regulations on the Protestant Churches in China" was the product of years of discussion, the purpose of which was to set standards for liturgy, clerical ordination, and church management of the Chinese Protestant churches during the post-denominational period.

CCC and TSPM are named collectively as *lianghui* (two associations). While CCC is an ecclesiastical organization in nature, TSPM promotes Chinese Protestantism as a patriotic movement. Strictly speaking, "post-denominational" is not equal to "without denominations". Only under political constraints, denominations previously existing in China did not carry out their ministries in their own names. Denominational organizations at different levels likewise did not resume operations. These denominations joined TSPM under the propositions of patriotism and unity. In other words, CCC is in nature only an administrative organization serving the churches.

Although the Chinese churches are in the post-denominational period, certain former denominations which have strong inclination to restorationism, mainly the Christian Assembly, True Jesus Church, the Seventh-day Adventist Church, still work hard to establish and strengthen their influence as denominations and create more room for development, becoming a very challenge to the post-denominational era.

Moreover, house churches begun after the Cultural Revolution are also a threat to the post-denominational setting. In the contemporary development of Chinese Protestantism, the concept of "house church" is frequently misunderstood. The term generally denotes a Protestant group which is not recognized by the government and has not joined TSPM. The house church phenomenon is often conceived as the counter side of TSPM under a typical framework which regards house churches and TSPM as the two dichotomous blocs in Chinese Protestantism. Indeed, if one is familiar with the development of Chinese Protestantism, such a reductionist viewpoint is not easily maintained. First of all, different from the underground churches of Chinese Catholicism, house churches do not constitute a collective religious movement. Instead, each is independent, closed, regional, and they do not have any ties with one another. They are not monolithic on issues like theological heritage, or the appropriate relationships with the government and TSPM. Secondly, we must distinguish between different types of house churches. Even using a house church's relationship with TSPM as a yardstick, we will find that there are different stances and attitudes among house churches. Surely some leaders of house churches have a strong anti-TSPM stance owing to historical factors. However, to some other house churches, the lack of pastoral care in TSPM churches and their geographical locations are more likely the reasons for their tendency to disunity with TSPM.

Looking into the denominational structure of Protestantism, we can find that the phenomenon of diversification of house church development further manifests the development of the emerging denominations in China. Coming under attack during successive political campaigns, some traditional denominations were dismantled, which provided the ground and space for the gestation of new denominations.

Chinese Orthodox Christianity: an unrecognized church

As the diplomatic relations between Russia and China were established, the Russian Orthodox Church began the propagation of Orthodox Christianity in China at the end of the seventeenth century. The church's first mission to China arrived in Beijing in 1715. Eighteen missions were sent by the church between the eighteenth century and the October Revolution of 1917, after which the Orthodox churches in China severed their subordination to the Moscow Patriarchate and came under jurisdiction of the temporary Synod of Bishops of the Russian Orthodox Church Abroad in Karlovci, Serbia. In 1924, the Spiritual Mission of the Russian Orthodox Church in Beijing was renamed the Orthodox Church in China, whose headquarters in Beijing directed its dioceses of Beijing, Shanghai, Harbin, Xinjiang and Tianjin. In 1946, the Orthodox churches in China came under jurisdiction of Moscow Patriarchate again.

At the dawn of the twentieth century, there were about 30 000 Orthodox Christians in China, most of whom were Russians living in China. An expatriate church, it did not have any Chinese clergymen until 1950, when the Moscow Patriarchate consecrated its first Chinese bishop and more than ten Chinese priests.

Because the CCP adopted a pro-Soviet diplomatic policy after its takeover of China in 1949, the Orthodox Church in China, unlike the Roman Catholic Church and the Protestant Church in China, was exempt from bearing the guilt of assisting the Western imperialist invasion. Russian clergymen still played an important role in church management before 1955. However, after the deterioration of Sino-Soviet relations that year, the Chinese government wanted the Orthodox Church in China to be independent as well, which resulted in the discussion between the church and Moscow Patriarchate on granting autonomy to the former and arranging the Russian clergy's return to their motherland.

In 1956, the autonomous Chinese Orthodox Church was founded. The Archimandrite Vasily was consecrated as archbishop, overseeing its dioceses of Beijing, Tianjing, Shanghai, Harbin and Xinjiang. As the Russian expatriates left for their motherland, the number of Orthodox Christians in China dropped accordingly. During the Cultural Revolution, the work of the Chinese Orthodox Church was brought to a standstill with the dissolution of the remaining framework of the church.

In the 1980s, the Chinese Orthodox Church was permitted to resume its activity in Harbin of Helongjiang Province and Xinjiang Province. The Regulations on Religious Affairs of Helongjiang Province stipulated the legitimacy of the Harbin Chinese Orthodox Church. (Such kind of stipulation is absent from other provinces' Regulations on Religious Affairs.) According to the statistics of the Moscow Patriarchate, there are 13 000 Orthodox Christians in China, of whom about 400 are in Beijing. Among the "Orthodox Remnants" in China, the greatest challenges facing the Chinese Orthodox Church are as follows:

First, there is a lack of church buildings and chapels, since they were taken over by the state during the Cultural Revolution and have yet to be returned for the church's use.

Second, there is a lack of religious professionals in the church, since the remaining Chinese clergy who had received Orthodox theological training died after the Cultural Revolution. Only recently has the Chinese government allowed young Orthodox Christians to receive theological training at the Moscow or St Petersburg Theological Academies.

Finally, there is a lack of legitimacy. Orthodox Christianity is not included in the five religions officially recognized by the Chinese government. Only in certain regions is the church allowed to have religious activities, and only in recent years has the Moscow Patriarchate taken the initiative to negotiate with the Chinese government for the total resumption of the legitimacy of the Orthodox Church in China.

Christianity and Chinese Society

Withdrawal from the public sphere

Christians (including Protestants, Catholics, and Orthodox Christians) account for an insignificant percentage of the total population in China. However, since the modern missionary movement established massive enterprises in China, Christianity became an influential social entity through involvement in education, medical service, and benevolent work.

Take the educational efforts of the Protestant Church as example. In 1949, the Protestant Church ran 13 universities, 247 secondary schools and about 1000 primary schools in China. The church's objective of running schools was mainly to reach students, convert them, and nurture them for the church. Therefore, besides the spread of knowledge, religious education played an important role in both the curricula and academic life of church schools. According to a 1924 survey of church schools in Eastern China, 45% of students of the 42 surveyed schools were Protestants. In a national survey of church secondary schools in 1929, however, Protestants only accounted for 29.2% of the total student population. For church universities, a survey in 1931 showed that 43% of the 4516 surveyed students were Protestants. In view of the huge resources involved, the Protestant Church was obviously dissatisfied with the above figures.

In 1927, the Nationalist government brought into effect a policy of private school registration, under which church schools were incorporated into the private school system and overseen by the government. Known as the Educational Rights Movement, these measures not only required church schools to register at the Ministry of Education, but also implemented the principle of separation of religion and education. Church primary schools were prohibited from offering religious education, performing religious ceremonies, or propagating religion. Compulsory courses on religion in church secondary schools and universities became electives. The schools and universities were not allowed to require students to participate in religious gatherings. As educational rights were regarded as part of national sovereignty, there is no doubt that the movement reflected the tide of nationalism and involved a strong irreligious appeal.

After 1949, church schools were still able to maintain their educational functions within the private school system. Nevertheless, since the new government reiterated the policy of separation of religion and education, the evangelistic function of church schools was further curtailed. The situation became worse since church schools were considered agents of the imperialist cultural invasion. In the midst of the anti-imperialism campaign during the Korean War, church schools endured severe accusations and repudiation. Starting in 1951, the Chinese government put forward the policy of nationalizing education. Church schools at every level were nationalized and officially stepped down from the stage of the Chinese education system.

Like its educational work, Christian medical and charitable work in China also received repudiation and was eventually nationalized. Indeed, Christian auxiliary work relied heavily on Western financial support and failed to achieve the "self-support" required by government religious policies. Upon the termination of overseas subsidies after the Korean War, its survival was under severe threat. Had not the CCP instigated large-scale mass campaigns to condemn it, the enterprise would have inevitably been terminated because of financial difficulties.

The contributions of Christianity by means of educational work, medical service, and charitable work were collectively renounced as evidence of the cultural invasion of imperialism. Finally, when "full transition to Socialism" became the dominant ideology of Chinese society, Christianity could only struggle for its survival.

Christianity's Prospects in China

The myth of the Christian culture fever

Since the recent economic reforms, "Christianity fever" (*jidujiao re*) and 'Christian culture fever' (*jidujiao wenhua re*) have been emerging in China. These so-called fevers expressed themselves mainly in two ways: First, the attitude of Chinese intellectuals towards Christianity has changed from rejection and resistance to appreciation and recognition. Second, a rising number of Chinese are converting to Christianity, mainly to Roman Catholicism and Protestantism.

Some mainland Chinese scholars researching Christianity point out that the recent "hotness" for Christianity is principally relative, comparing with the "coldness" in the past. In other words, during a fairly long period (especially since the CCP's domination), Christianity experienced an abnormal development owing to political and ideological factors. After the Cultural Revolution, when the social conditions became more religiously permissive than before, the popularity of Christianity began to grow.

Christianity is now in vogue. However, reality does not necessarily allow us to be overly optimistic. We must consider the "Christian culture fever" in the context of the "cultural fever" (*wenhua re*) among the Chinese intelligentsia in the 1980s. The so-called cultural fever broadly refers to the phenomenon of cultural issues springing up in the intellectual sphere in China. The central discourse of this fever is determining the relationship of Chinese culture and modernization. Since the 1980s, many intellectuals have hoped to divert the direction of China's development toward democracy and prosperity through cultural reflections.

In the cultural fever discussions, intellectuals have had divergent views on the future of Chinese culture. While some advocated thorough radical anti-traditionalism and total Westernization, others intended to revive Confucianism or traditional culture. There were also intellectuals who hoped to introduce the tradition of liberalism to China. When comparing the merits and demerits of Chinese and Western cultures, some of the intellectuals discovered Christian culture underlying the prosperity of Western civilization. Hence, they strongly believed that whether or not Chinese culture could be modernized would depend on its acceptance of Christianity.

Economic reforms also broke the constraints of the long-held ideological dogmas governing academia. Christian studies has been freed from the fetters of the discourse of "imperialist cultural invasion" and is no longer a "restricted area" of academic research. Under the irreversible wave of academic exchange between China and the West, Christian studies research teams were gradually formed in different domains, especially in Philosophy, History, Literature, and Sociology. During the last decade, research centers for Christian studies have been established in many universities across mainland China. This not only implies that more resources have been put in the field, but also shows that Christian studies is attracting more attention. The group of scholars conducting Christian studies can be generally regarded as Scholars in Mainland China Studying Christianity (SMCSC).

The development of Christian studies shows that it is mainly the cultural form of Christianity for which Chinese academia has high regard. Throughout the last half-century, the China-West dichotomy during the Cold War resulted in hostility to Christianity among the Chinese intelligentsia. Compared with this, the recognition of Christianity from some Chinese intellectuals at present is no doubt a meaningful change of attitude. It is noteworthy, however, that many SMCSC are indifferent to personal confession of or conversion to Christianity. Neither are they concerned with the increase in the number of Christians and the organizational development of the church. What they emphasize, instead, is communication, dialogue, mutual complement and compatibility in the cultural aspects of the faith. They pay attention to the new cultural aura and the enhancement of the quality life in China after introducing the spirit of Christianity in Chinese culture. In other words, the aim of their active promotion of Christian culture is to recognize the immense impact of Christianity in Western countries in terms of cultural inheritance, value norms, moral standards, and social justice.

Of course, it draws more overseas attention that, unlike the community of SMCSC as a whole, individual intellectuals represented by Liu Xiaofeng have shown certain inclination to confession when introducing the spirit of Christianity. However, because such figures keep their distance from established churches, they have a special designation known as Cultural Christians (CC), which shows that they are distinct from the general Christian population.

Undoubtedly, Christian studies has a far stronger development in Chinese academia than does the Chinese Christian Church. One reason for this is that, after the 1950s, the academic tradition of Christianity suffered from the political situation and disintegrated. The nationalization of Christian higher education and the CCP's policy of separation of religion and education markedly forced Christianity to withdraw from academia and the domain of education in China. Moreover, having resumed in the 1980s, theological education in China concentrated on responding to the urgent need for training of pastoral workers, which resulted in the inability to develop academic research work on Christianity at the same time. Such imbalance fostered the above-mentioned situation.

The Chinese Christian Church's failure to foster an environment nurturing for Christian intellectuals has made the church unable to establish its own academic tradition. Therefore, the research and introduction of Christian culture carried out outside the church are indeed a valuable supplement. Nevertheless, if development of the intellectual life of Chinese Christian Church continues to lag behind its academic counterparts, there will be only a widening gap between academia and church in the development of Christian studies in the near future.

Behind the Christianity fever

While the quantity of Christians in China is increasing, we should not overlook the crisis in quality. It is well known that Protestants and Catholics in China are mainly concentrated in rural areas. Rural churches became the mainstream in Chinese Christianity in the 1980s and 1990s. When we analyze the social composition of the members of these churches, we will find that there are "four majorities" (*si duo*) in the church community: rural villagers, illiterates, the elderly, and women.

China has been an agrarian nation since ancient times and her agricultural population has long accounted for 80% of the total population. However, as rural areas have been undergoing rapid social changes brought by the economic reform, the concept of "peasants" in the household register statistics is no longer useful. The rural population is classified into *nongmin* ("peasants" who reside in a village and mainly engage themselves in primary production), *cunliren* ("villagers" who reside in a village but do not engage themselves in primary production) and *cunjichengliren* ("urban people with their household registers in villages" who migrate to cities to work and thus are also called "immigrant workers"). With the recent urbanization of rural areas advocated by the Chinese government, the proportion of the population living in urban areas has increased correspondingly. Yet China will still be a nation of "peasants" in the foreseeable future. The phenomenon of high proportion of farmers in the Chinese Chistian Church is manifested by the fact that almost 80% of Christians come from rural backgrounds. Even though some rural Christians work in cities, they are still identified as "peasants" in their household registers. This has given rise to the emergence of "Christian immigrant workers in the city," who are different from the Christians of urban backgrounds.

The generally low literacy of Christians from rural backgrounds is closely related to the reach of compulsory education. Although China has implemented a nine-year compulsory education, there are still 114 million illiterates in China, according to data gathered in 2005. They are mainly concentrated in poor rural areas, settlements of ethnic minorities and remote areas. With the influx of numerous peasants into cities, the education of the immigrant workers' children has become a major problem facing the governmental departments of education. At the same time, schooling in China has recently developed along the direction of "marketization." The difficulty and high cost of going to school haunt many residents in cities and rural villages.

Moreover, the elderly and women account for the absolute majority of Chinese Christians. According to information published by TSPM/CCC in 1997, 70% of Protestants in China are women. The statistics of Protestantism in Shanghai show that the ratio of women to men among the baptized Protestants from 1980 to 1990 is 4:1. Those aged 60 or above account for 63% of the baptized Protestants whereas those below the age of 40 constitute only 17% of the total. It is believed that the situation in Shanghai is consistent with the nation as a whole.

The phenomenon of "four majorities" explains the "marginality" of the Chinese Christian Church. Drawing primarily on rural, illiterate females, and ageing populations, the churches seem incompatible with the rapid development of Chinese society. Why could the church not attract the better educated youth in cities to become Christians? This is surely a thought-provoking question.

In addition to being beset by the problem of "four majorities," Chinese Christianity is also facing a worrying pastoral problem. Owing to the interference from political campaigns during the 1950s and 1960s, formal theological education suffered greatly, creating a lack of trained ministers from which Chinese Christianity has yet to recover. Since the 1980s, the CCC have established or resumed 18 seminaries and Bible schools. The Catholic Open Church also has 22 convents. However, these theological education institutes are still unable to meet the great demand for pastoral workers. Although at present there are over 1000 ministers ordained and recognized by CCC, 69 bishops and about 1900 priests of the Catholic Open Church, the number of pastoral workers in China is still far from sufficient to answer the pastoral needs of the huge population of believers.

Among Protestant congregations, many rural churches are led by volunteers who lack systematic theological training. Such undereducated leadership has brought to rural Christianity a palpable tendency towards developing itself into a folk religion. Attracted by God's miracles and power, many people there have become converts to Christianity. Yet their belief is mainly based on the efficaciousness of the miracles. Lacking proper Christian teaching for their members, these churches could easily become the roots of various heresies. Such situation urgently needs rectification.

The Chinese Christian Church is now in the rebuilding phrase after going through disasters. Given the various constraints it faces, the church must still overcome a number of obstacles if it hopes to become robust.

Chinese Christianity in the twenty-first century

Tang Yi, a long-time Chinese Christian studies scholar in Beijing, pointed out that there are three possibilities of the future development of Christianity in China.

The first possibility is that with the increasing number of Chinese converted to Christianity, it will enter the mainstream of Chinese culture, changing and renewing the values of the Chinese people. If this prediction proves true, the Christian faith will eventually conquer China and Christianize Chinese culture. The secular, human-centered mentality may eventually be supplanted by the transcendent, Christ-centered spirit through a radical change in the Chinese outlook on history and human nature.

A second possibility is that Christianity may eventually be absorbed by Chinese culture, following the example of Buddhism. It may be adapted to the human-centered mentality and become a sinless religion of the Chinese genre. However, Tang argues that both these situations are impossible.

A third possibility, which Tang believes is the most likely solution to be reached, is that Christianity will retain its basic Western characteristics and settle down to be a sub-cultural minority religion in China. In the end, the public will get more used to it and accept its religious ideals, including its prophetic message, as a complement to Chinese civilization without any fear of jeopardizing the mainstream culture.[3]

What are the prospects Christianity in China? I believe this depends on the following:

1. Political constraints   Although during the period of economic reform, the Chinese Christian Church has a greater room for development than before, we have to admit that the party-state's manipulation and supervision are still an absolute factor. To enjoy the freedom of religious belief granted by the government, the church must have a concrete political foundation. Of course, unlike in the 1950s and 1960s, the center of the CCP's party-line today is economic construction rather than political struggle. Also, the social changes brought by the economic reform in the last three decades, especially the fundamental change of the relationship between state and society, has genuinely provided favorable factors for the development of religions. Nevertheless, the foundations of real protection of religious freedom are the rule of law and social diversity. Thus, the outlook of the development of the political system in China will still impact on the church. Paradoxically, the further realization of religious freedom in China will definitely transform the current Chinese religion market dominated by the so-called "five main religions." How the Christian Church adapts to the opening up of the Chinese religion market is worth our concern.

2. The socio-economic development of China   The economic reform has no doubt brought structural changes to Chinese society. The process of rapid urbanization changes the face of rural society swiftly, posing severe challenges for the survival of the rural churches. Given the influx of rural youths and adults into cities for work, many rural churches encounter the acute problem of losing young believers. At the same time, assorted social problems are derived from the swift pace of urban development. The difference between urban and rural areas in China not only widens the gap between urban and rural churches, but also brings great challenges to the development of Christianity.

3. The self-conditions of the Chinese Church   After suffering through the impact of political campaigns for 40 years, the Chinese Christian Church's vitality has been greatly diminished. Both the "hardware" or "software" of the church are unable to satisfy its current need. With the brisk socio-economic development, can the church undergo a transformation compatible to the current epoch's needs? Can the

constraints on church development, especially those from insufficient theological education and training for full-time and voluntary pastoral workers, be lessened? These issues are worrying.

Perhaps due to the influence of the Christian culture fever, slogans like "Christianity will change and renew Chinese culture" or "Christianity is a force of Chinese modernization" appear among the Chinese intelligentsia. (We cannot deny the possibility of the rising acceptance of Christianity as a cultural and epistemological phenomenon, too.) However, such optimistic opinions sharply contrast with the present situation of the Chinese Church. As early as 1995, when someone asked Chen Zemin, a professor at Nanjing Union Theological Seminary, "What can the church contribute to the realization of modernization?", he replied,

> The church is both young and conservative, foreign, small and backward, in danger of falling apart, not self-supporting, and lacking a theology to gird and equip herself to bear witnesses to the Christian gospel in a modernized China, it is more important and useful to leave this question unanswered, and turn to the second question. How can the church change itself through "self-building" in order to catch up with the whole country and to accommodate the ideas and ideals of modernization? No matter whether one likes it or not, modernization is bound to happen, and it poses the church with threatening challenges.[4]

In twenty-first century China, although Christianity should no longer have to bear the guilt of cultural invasion of imperialism, its development is still greeted with assorted challenges.

Timeline	
635	Beginning of Nestorian Christianity in China.
781	Erection of the Memorial of the Propagation in China of the *Jinjiao* (Nestorian).
845	Implementation of the policy of 'eradicating Buddhism'.
1245	Franciscans arrived China.

1299	First Chapel in Beijing had been found by John of Montecorvino.
1583	Matteo Ricci arrived China.
1601	Matteo Ricci started his work in Beijing.
1610	Matteo Ricci died in Beijing.
1636–1692	The Rites Controversy.
1807	Robert Morrison arrived China.
1839–1842	Opium War and the Opening of China.
1900	Boxer Uprising.
1911–1912	Fall of Manchu and the founding of the Republic of China.
1922–1927	Anti-Christian Movement.
1922	National Christian Conference held at Shanghai.
1937–1945	Sino-Japanese War.
1945–1949	Civil War between KMT and CCP.
1949	People's Republic of China.
1954	Three-Self Patriotic Movement established.
1956	Chinese Orthodox Church established.
1957	Chinese Catholic Patriotic Association established.
1958	Unification of Worship.
1966–1976	Cultural Revolution.
1978	Reform and Opening.
Since 1979	Reopening of Christian churches.

Notes

1. Jenkins, P. *The Next Christendom: The Coming of Global Christianity*, Oxford: OUP, 2002.
2. "How many sheep are there in the Chinese flock?" in *Amity News Services* 2004 11/12. http://www.amitynewsservice.org/page.php?page=529.
3. Tang, Y. "Chinese Christianity in Development," in *China Study Journal* 6:2, 4–8.
4. Chen, Z.M. "Modernization's Challenge to Chinese Christianity," in Wickeric, P.L. and Cole, L. (eds.), *Christianity and Modernization: A Chinese Debate*, Hong Kong: Daga Press, 1995, p. 30.

Further Reading

Bays, D.H. (ed.) *Christianity in China: From the Eighteenth Century to the Present*, Stanford: Stanford University Press, 1996.

Fairbank, J.K. (ed.) *The Missionary Enterprise in China and America*, Cambridge, MA: Harvard University Press, 1974.

Hunter, A. and Chan, K.-k. *Protestantism in Contemporary China*, Cambridge, CUP, 1993.

Kindopp, J. and Hamrin, C.L. *God and Caesar in China: Policy Implications of Church-State Tensions*, Washington, DC: Brookings Institution Press, 2004.

Lambert, Tony. *China's Christian Millions: The Costly Revival*, London: Monarch Books, 2006.

Latourette, K.S. *A History of Christian Missions in China*, Taipei: Cheng Wen Pub. Co., 1975 (Reprint of London: Society for Promoting Christian Knowledge, 1929).

Madsen, R. *China's Catholics: Tragedy and Hope in an Emerging Civil Society*, Berkeley: University of California Press, 1998.

Overmyer, D.L. (ed.) *Religion in China Today*, Cambridge: CUP, 2003.

Tang, E. and Wiest, J.-P. (eds.) *The Catholic Church in Modern China: Perspectives*. Maryknoll, New York: Orbis Books, 1993.

Wickeri, P.L. *Seeking the Common Ground: Protestant Christianity, the Three-Self-Movement and China's United Front*, Maryknoll, New York: Orbis Books, 1988.

9

Taiwan, Hong Kong, Macau

Lo Lung-kwong

These three islands, though very different among themselves in their historical, socio-political, and economic contexts, are similar in three important
respects: (1) they were former colonies of European powers, namely, Dutch
(1624–1662), British (1841–1997) and Portuguese (1557–1999) respectively; (2) more than 90% of their residents are of Chinese origin; and
(3) they are related to The People's Republic of China (PRC), albeit in
different ways. Hong Kong and Macau were reunited with China in 1997 and
1999 respectively, under the policy of "one country, two systems." Taiwan was
separated from the administration of mainland China in1949, after
the Kuomintang (KMT, Nationalist Party) government was defeated by the
Chinese Communist Party (CCP). Taiwan, which is officially known as the
Republic of China (ROC), is claimed by PRC as part of China, eventually to be
reunited with it. Moreover, Taiwan was governed by Japan for 50 years
(1895–1945); Hong Kong was under Japanese occupation for three years and
eight months during the Second World War (1941–1945). Macau kept itself
neutral during the Second World War and was spared Japanese direct rule.

Taiwan, Hong Kong, and Macau share several religious traditions, especially Buddhism and Chinese folk religions. However, their encounters with
Christianity, though closely related to their colonial history, were quite
different. Hence, we will discuss the development of Christianity in these
three places separately.

Taiwan

Taiwan came to the attention of the West when it was discovered by the
Portuguese and Spanish colonial powers in the fifteenth and sixteenth centuries.
It was given the name of Formosa (meaning "beautiful" in Portuguese) since the
Portuguese sailors who first saw the island allegedly cried out "Formosa."

Christianities in Asia, edited by Peter C. Phan   © 2011 Blackwell Publishing Ltd except for
editorial material and organization © 2011 Peter C. Phan

Taiwan is composed of a main island and 14 smaller islands. The main island is located between Japan and the Philippines on the southeastern coast of mainland China. It is a mountainous island with the widest flat land of less than 90 kilometres from the sea, leaving only about a third of its land arable. Taiwan's highest mountain is Yu Shan (Jade Mountain), at 3952 metres (13 114 ft.), one of the tallest mountains in South and North-East Asia. There are also 62 peaks higher than 3000 metres (9750 ft.).

Linguistic and Ethnic Diversity

The history of the earliest settlers of Taiwan is shrouded in obscurity. It is believed that most of the aborigines are Malay-Polynesian; there are strong ethnic and linguistic similarities between them and the Malay peoples in parts of the Philippines, Malaysia, and Indonesia. Although the aborigines are frequently discussed as a single group, there are important differences in culture, customs, language, and ethnicity among the nine major tribes. The aborigines compose only 1.7% of the total population of Taiwan today.

The population of Taiwan was 7.4 million in 1949 and increased to 22.7 million in 2005. The majority of the population are Han Chinese, composed of three ethnic subgroups, whose ancestors migrated to Taiwan from mainland China in different stages. The largest group, more than 72% of the current population, are those whose ancestors migrated from the southern part of Fujian Province which is located just on the opposite side of the Taiwan Strait. Migration was heaviest from the fourteenth to the seventeenth centuries, after the fall of the Ming dynasty in 1644. They have retained much of the culture, religions and lifestyle of their native land, including their language, a dialect known as *Minanyu* (the language of southern Fujian).

The second group is the Hakka people who make up almost 13% of the population. The origin of the Hakka people is uncertain. "Hakka" means "guest people," comparable to Europe's Gypsies. It is believed that about a third of the Hakka people sailed from the Guangdong Province to Taiwan in the later part of the thirteenth century. The last large wave of Hakka migration followed the defeat of the Taiping Uprising in 1864, a major mutiny during the Qing dynasty led by Hung Xiu-quan, a Hakka who was influenced by Christianity. The Hakka are famous for holding firm to their distinctive customs and language despite their long migrations. In contrast to the Fujianese, Hakka women worked in the fields along with men and did not bind their feet. The Hakka seem to have an early association with the aborigines and a comparatively amicable relationship with the recently arrived mainland Chinese, in contrast to the Fujianese.

The third group is the mainland Chinese – called "Mainlanders" or "Outside People" by the native Taiwanese – who came to Taiwan in 1949, after the

Chinese Communists' takeover of mainland China. They make up about 13% of the population. Their main language is Mandarin (Putonghua), which is the official language of China. This group relates closely to the KMT which governed Taiwan from 1945 to 2000. Though a minority, they had power and brought with them an air of superiority. They regarded themselves more educated and more authentically Chinese than the native Taiwanese who in their view had cut themselves off from the heart of the Chinese civilization and furthermore had been tainted by 50 years of Japanese rule.

These groups of Taiwanese are quite distinct in terms of historical origin, language, customs, culture, and political power. A strong "Taiwanese" identity has been formed among the Fujianese group, the biggest group of the population, after more than 100 years of rule by the Japanese colonial government and the Mainlander-dominated KMT government. The Democratic Progress Party (DPP), founded by Taiwan Fujianese in 1986, won the presidential elections in 2000 on the platform of promoting the independence of Taiwan from China. The political atmosphere changed rapidly after 2000 due to the split among the ethnic subgroups and their different political stances. This has caused a major disunity in the country. Ethnic politics has also seriously affected the relationship among Christian churches in Taiwan.

Early Christian Missions: Catholic and Protestant

The history of Christianity in Taiwan can be traced back to the Spanish and Dutch missionaries in the 1620s. The Spanish Catholic Church sent about 40 missionaries to the northern part of Taiwan, especially Keelong, in 1626. They were predominantly Dominicans and Franciscans. In 1642, the Spanish army was defeated by the Dutch and expelled from Taiwan. There were about 4000 Christians at that time.

In 1627 the Dutch Reformed Church, through the Dutch East-India Company (VOC), sent Georgius Candidius as the first missionary to Taiwan. He lived at Sinkang, in the southern part of Taiwan, and tried to learn the language of the aborigines. With the assistance of Robertus Junius, who arrived in 1629, the mission was very successful. According to the record, all the residents of Sinkang, numbered at 1047, were baptized and the first church was built in 1631. However, when the Dutch missionaries required the new converts to abandon their traditional religions, they faced a very strong resistance. Nevertheless, the new converts had to obey the orders of the missionaries and deserted their traditional religions. In 1639, there were 2014 Christians, and in 1659, 6078. Although mission work was terminated in 1662 after the Dutch were expelled by Cheng Chheng-kung (Koxinger), the missionaries had exercised a great influence on the culture of the aborigines. They created a Latinized script (called Sinkang), produced a dictionary, translated the Bible and the catechism and religious tracts, and kept written records of land leases. The Latinized script was in use for at least 150 years, until the early eighteenth century.

The Han Chinese community was established in Taiwan thanks to the Dutch administration. They were recruited by the VOC to work in the sugar plantations in Taiwan. In 1638, there were around 10 000 people, and in the end of the Dutch rule, there were 35 000 to 50 000. This number was greatly expanded after Cheng Chheng-kung's takeover of Taiwan. During the Dutch colonial rule, the Dutch Reformed Church sent 36 ministers to Taiwan. Among them were Daniel Gravius, who published the existing Sinkang Gospel of Matthew in 1661, and the Bible translator Antonius Hambroek, who was beheaded by Cheng Chheng-kung in 1662. After the expulsion of both Spanish and Dutch rulers, these two missions were largely dissipated within a half a century.

The missionary movement began for the second time in the 1860s under the influence of the "Great Missionary Movement" of the West. It was occasioned by the second Opium War (1856–1860), which resulted in the Tianjin Treaty in 1858, ratified by Chinese in 1860. The treaty entailed the opening of several seaports in Taiwan, including Keelong, Tamsui, and Takao (now Kaohsiong), and ensured the freedom of evangelism in those areas. In May 1859, the Dominican fathers Fernando Sainz and Angel Bufurull, along with three Han catechists from Amoy (Xiaman), an important city of Fujian Province, came to Takao and established a church in Ban-Kim-Chng. After more than thirty five years of missionary work, there were about 1300 Catholics in 1895 and 9000 in 1938. Facing antagonism from the Taiwanese people and later competition from Protestant missionaries, the Dominicans adopted a "qualitative" approach to mission until the end of Second World War. They emphasized that undue haste in baptizing half-instructed natives would be a wasted effort since most of them would revert to their former religious practices.

The Protestant missionaries Carstairs Douglas and H. L. Mackenzie of the English Presbyterian mission in Amoy came to northern Taiwan in September 1860. Douglas urged his church to start a new mission in Taiwan, preferably as a medical mission. In May, 1865, James L. Maxwell, a medical doctor, accompanied by Douglas and three Han associates, came to Takao in southern Taiwan, and began a medical mission in Hu-sian (now Tainan). However, local resistance soon forced a return to Takao. In August, 1866, four Han Chinese were baptized by W.S. Swanson, the first fruits of the Protestant missionaries. William Campbell, a church historian, edited a comprehensive Taiwanese dictionary and initiated ministries to Penghu (the Pescadores) and among the blind and the deaf. Thomas Barclay arrived in 1874, founded Tainan Theological College in 1876 and the Taiwan Church Press in 1884, helped organize the first southern presbytery in 1896, and translated the entire Bible into Romanized Taiwanese. In March 1872, George Leslie Mackay (1844–1901) of the Canadian Presbyterian Church, who was married to the Taiwanese woman Chang Tsong-ming, arrived in Tamsui and began his 30-year ministry in northern Taiwan. He single-handedly established the groundwork of the northern Presbyterian mission. He was succeeded by William Gauld, who, with the cooperation of local leaders, built many beautiful churches, helped organize the first northern presbytery in 1914, and fostered the formation of the Taiwan Synod in 1912, the forerunner of the Presbyterian Church in Taiwan (PCT). The result of the early missionary effort was very encouraging: there were around 1000 converts in the first ten years.

Soon however missionaries and local converts suffered persecutions due to native anti-foreigner sentiments, especially in the northern churches, during the Sino-French War in 1884. In response, in order to avoid the massacre, some missionaries, such as Thomas Barclay and Duncan Ferguson, helped the Japanese enter Taiwan and lay siege to Tainan in 1885.

Early Presbyterian missionaries adopted a more contextualized approach to mission, engaging in medical, educational, and social services in addition to evangelism. From 1915 onward, while Taiwan was under the Japanese rule, some local leaders, notably Gou Hi-eng, began to advance the missionary principle of "self-support, self-government, and self-propagation." Missionaries began to ordain native ministers in 1895 in the north and in 1899 in the south. The Taiwanese Church was forced to become autonomous, a process spanning several decades, only when all the Western missionaries were expelled by the Japanese government in the early 1940s.

During the Japanese rule, especially after the outbreak of the Pacific War in the 1940s, the Japanese government in Taiwan began the so-called "royal citizen movement" to Japanize the Taiwanese people and to enforce Shinto-ism as well as emperor worship and military patriotism. Church schools, hospitals, seminaries and many churches were either closed or confiscated up until the end of the war in 1945.

Under the Japanese segregation policy, two missionaries, Mr. Inoye from Japan and N.P. Yates from Canada, began working among the aborigines. Chi-wong, a female aboriginal Christian, who is called the mother of the Taiwanese aboriginal church, together with her co-workers, bravely evangelized among their own people during the Japanese occupation. The rapid growth of the aboriginal churches immediately following the Japanese rule has been hailed as "the miracle of the twentieth century". In 1947, Yu Shan Theological College was established to train aboriginal preachers. Nowadays, more than half of the aboriginal people are Christian.

Until the end of the Second World War, except for some small Japanese churches, the PCT was the only significant Protestant missionary force in Taiwan. The other two small ones were Taiwan Holiness Church (founded in

1928) with Japanese background and True Jesus Church (founded in 1926), a Chinese indigenous church established in Beijing in 1917. In the late 1940s, however, with the defeat of KMT in mainland China, many mainline denominations came to Taiwan, including the Southern Baptists, the Lutherans, the Methodists, and the Anglicans. Numerous smaller denominations also came, such as the Mennonites, the Assemblies of God, the Seventh-Day Adventists; and Chinese indigenous churches, such as the Little Flock founded at Fuzhou in 1920s by Watchman Nee, and other independent churches. By 1955, church denominations had grown to 36. Two hundred and eighty missionaries served in Taiwan, of whom more than 220 were Americans.

In 2003, the Orthodox Church of Taiwan was established by the Orthodox Metropolitanate of Hong Kong and South East Asia, under the spiritual jurisdiction of the Ecumenical Patriarch of Constantinople. However, membership in the Orthodox Church is quite small.

The Changing Face of Taiwanese Christianity

According to diverse sources, there were around 2000 members in Taiwan Holiness Church in 1940; 5050 members in True Jesus Church (one quarter of whom are aborigines) in 1945; 30 429 members (including children) in the PCT in 1949; and 23,579 Roman Catholics in 1953. The Catholic Church grew to 104 779 in 1957 and 265 555 in 1964. The rapid growth of the Roman Catholic Church was due mainly to the influx of Catholic Mainlanders to Taiwan. The Protestant Churches also enjoyed a rapid increase in membership. In 1964, there were 283 225 Protestants, 176 255 in the PCT and 23 183 in True Jesus Church. However, the numerical increase has been slowing down since 1965. In 2005, there were 298 028 Catholics. The Protestants grew to 741 414 in 2005, a better growth than that of the Catholic Church. The PCT had 222 381 members in 2005; it is still the denomination with the largest number of members, but the rate of increase is very slow.

The churches with the fastest increase rate are the independent Christian churches and Little Flock. The development of the Ling Leung Church (Bread of Life Christian Church) has been most impressive since 1977, under the new leadership of Rev. Chou Sheng-chu. It was founded at Taipei in 1954 by Rev. Chao Shi Kwang, who started his ministry in Shanghai and moved to Hong Kong in the late 1940s. Church membership increased dramatically in the last two decades, with a total of 33 132 members in Taiwan in 2005. Another 134 churches have been planted all over the world, including Asia, Africa, Europe, Australia and New Zealand, North and South America. In addition to planting churches, the Ling Leung Church started its own seminary in

1990 to train pastors and church planters. In 2005, the total number of Christians in Taiwan, including Protestants and Catholics, were 1.04 millions, with 3799 churches. Christians in Taiwan form 4.6 % of the total population.

Education, Medical, Social Service and Para-Churches

As elsewhere, in Taiwan missionaries were pioneers in setting up schools, hospitals and social service organizations. Before the Sino-Japanese War (Second World War), among many missionary schools were Cheng Shin Girls' School in Taipei, operated by the Catholic Church; four Protestant schools of which the Chang Jung Boys' School and Chang Jung Girls' School were established by the Overseas Mission of the Presbyterian Church of England in 1885 and 1887 respectively; and Tamsui Boys' School and Sun Ti Girls' School in North Taiwan, founded in 1882. In the 1960s, the Protestants had two universities, Soochow University and Tung Hai University; two registered colleges, Oxford College at Tamsui and Chung Yuan Christian College of Science and Engineering at Chung Lit. The Catholics sponsor one university, Fu Jen Catholic University, at northern Taiwan (1961, originally founded in Beijing in 1925). However, since there are more than a hundred post-secondary colleges and universities in Taiwan, Christian colleges and universities are a minority.

Health and medical services have always been an integral part of the ministry of Church. In Taiwan, as mentioned at above, among the earliest Protestant missionaries, James L. Maxwell and George L. Mackay were medical doctors. The clinics founded by Maxwell were merged into the Sin Lau Hospital in 1900. In 1922 and 1923, curing centres for opium addiction, leprosy and tuberculosis were started. Mackay Memorial Hospital in Taipei was opened in 1912 to commemorate Mackey's great service and it is the best Christian hospital in Taiwan today. The Seventh-Day Adventist Church moved their hospital from Shanghai to Taipei in 1949. The Catholic Church has ten hospitals all over Taiwan, including the Cardinal Tien Hospital at Taipei, a general hospital and a fully accredited regional teaching hospital. In addition to education and health care, the churches' social services focus on orphanages and services for the blind, the elderly and the disabled.

There are very active Christian organizations serving students and the media. Among the Protestants, there were more than 100 publishers in 2005. *The Cosmic Light*, founded in 1973, is a multi-media organization for young people. In recent years it has provided services in the areas of counselling, broadcasting, social service, arts and cultural activities. The Protestants run a newspaper, *The Christian Tribune*, founded in 1965. The PCT has been publishing *Church News* since 1885, the oldest publication in Taiwan. There are also radio broadcasting stations under the aegis of the churches, two run by Catholics and three run by Protestants. In 2001, the PCT established Fund for Mass Media; with this fund the New Eyes Television started its broadcasting in June, 2006.

Theological Education, Theological Issues, Theologians and Church Leaders

Tainan Theological College and Seminary (TTCS) was established in 1876 by Thomas Barclay, 11 years after the arrival of the first British Presbyterian missionaries and Fujianese evangelists, and is the oldest theological school on the island and among the Chinese. The theological education for the PCT in northern Taiwan was started by George Mackay who built the first building of Oxford College in 1882. Since 1945 it has been known as Taiwan Theological College and Seminary. Yu Shan Theological College and Seminary was founded in 1947, the only theological institution for Taiwan's aboriginal people.

There are at least four other main seminaries established by denominations, mission boards, or individual Christians. They are the Central Taiwan Theological Seminary, the Taiwan Baptist Theological Seminary, the Holy Light Theological Seminary, and the China Evangelical Seminary. All these seminaries are members of the Taiwan Association of Theological Seminaries (TATS). Most of their programmes are accredited either by the Asia Theological Association (ATA) with a strong evangelical background or by the Association for Theological Education of South East Asia (ATESEA) with an ecumenical background.

One of the main issues confronting Christianity in Taiwan is that of national identity. Taiwan was governed successively by Spanish (in the north, 1624–1642), Dutch (1624–1662), Qing Chinese (from 1662), Japanese (1895–1945), and the KMT governments. The experience of being dominated by outside powers has aroused a lot of anti-foreigner sentiments among the Taiwanese people. There is a deep division between the "local Taiwanese" and the "Mainlanders". This division is exacerbated by differences in languages (Fujian vs. Mandarin), customs, and socio-political and economic groupings (agricultural and business people versus government and military officials). The ending of the Martial Law by President Chiang Ching-kuo, son of Chiang Kai-shek, in 1987 changed the social and political map dramatically. The demand for justice has developed into a social movement supporting the political agenda of the newly formed Democratic Progressive Party (PPP) in opposition to the ruling KMT. The basic political platform of the DPP is the independent sovereignty of Taiwan.

The division between the local Taiwanese and the Mainlanders is also reflected among Taiwan's Christian churches. The PCT represents the interests of local Taiwanese whereas the churches and denominations which came to Taiwan from mainland China after 1949 represent those of the Mainlanders.

From 1970s onward, the KMT government (ROC) had to face a lot of political difficulties, including democratic movements organized by the local Taiwanese, expulsion from the United Nations, and the breaking of diplomatic relationships with its strongest allies, Japan, Korea and USA. The political future of Taiwan became paramount. The PCT issued a series of three political statements: "Statement on Our National Fate" (1971), "Our Appeal" (1975), and "The Human Rights Declaration" (1977). These statements called for social and political reforms, proclaimed the right of Taiwanese to self-determination, and expressed a hope for establishing a "new and independent country." Most of the churches of the Mainlanders and the Catholic Church, which was then led by Mainlander clergy, did not share the same convictions and criticized the PCT. The conflicting political ideologies and attitudes toward the KMT and the policy toward China have caused deep divisions between the local Taiwanese and Mainlanders in both society and the churches.

This division was deepened after the DPP presidential candidate, Mr. Chen Shui-bian, was elected President in 2000 and re-elected in 2004. However, the serious defeat of the DPP in the elections for the Yuan (Parliament) and for the President in January and March, 2008 respectively, proved that most Taiwanese disapproved of the political platform of the DPP, which was based on a sharp division between the local Taiwanese and the Mainlanders. The people of Taiwan look for reconciliation rather than division among themselves. A search for a new social and political *modus vivendi* and a new identity for Taiwan is afoot.

During the last 50 years, a good number of renowned Taiwanese theologians have emerged. Among the most famous was Hwang Chang-hue (or Ng Chiong-hui, 1914–1988), better known as Shoki Coe in the West. He served as President of TTCS and later Director of the Theological Education Fund of the World Council of Churches (1970–1977). He was especially known for his proposal to replace "indigenization" with "contextualization." Another famous theologian is C.S. Song (1929–) who also served as President of TTCS and as Associate Director of the Secretariat of the Faith and Order Commission, WCC. Given his prolific writings in English, Song is probably the most well-known Taiwanese theologian in the West. Wang Hsien-chih (1941–1996), a student and a close follower of C. S. Song, was an Anglican priest and taught at TTSC for most of his teaching career. He was one of the most important champions for the "Homeland Theology". Huang Po-ho (1951–) is one of the younger Taiwanese theologians well known outside Taiwan. He served as Moderator of the Council for World Mission (CWM) and is President of TTCS. He is one of the major proponents of Chhut-thau-thin theology (Taiwanese pronunciation of the Chinese words for "raising the head above the sky" which mean liberation).

Taiwanese Catholic theologians, as mentioned above, were more influenced by the Mainlanders until the end of the 1970s. Their theological concerns focused more on traditional Chinese culture than on the current socio-political context. One of their main concerns was how to implement the Instruction *Plane Compertum Est* (1939), approved by Pope Pius XII, which permitted Chinese Catholics to take part in ceremonies honouring Confucius and the ancestors. These so-called Chinese rites had been banned by Pope Benedict XIV's decree *Ex quo singulari* (1742) during the Chinese Rites Controversy (see the discussion of this in the section on Macau). Filial piety and inculturation were the main concerns for Roman Catholic theologians. John Wu Ching-hsiung (1899–1986), a lay Catholic, wrote a number of works on the relationship between Christianity and Chinese culture. Cardinal Yu Bin (1901–1978) publicly performed, on the Chinese New Year of 1971, the ritual of ancestor worship in Taipei. The cardinal also promoted dialogue between Christianity and Chinese religions.

In 1979, the Catholic Bishops' Conference of Taiwan published an open letter on the future of Taiwan, addressed to all the bishops, Christians and those "committed to justice" worldwide. This provided an opportunity for theological discussions of Taiwan's contemporary radical economic and socio-political changes as well as the Church's social ministries. By the 1990s, there was a plethora of writings advocating the application of the Christian faith to the socio-political conditions of Taiwan. Fr. Chang Ch'un-shen and Fr. Mark Fang Chi-jung are two well-known Catholic theologians active in this endeavour. Also in recent years there began a notable development in carrying out theology ecumenically, as demonstrated by the series of Joint Study Days and Catholic-Protestant Dialogues held in Taipei.

In addition to theologians, there have been several influential church leaders. The most famous is Chow Lien-hua (1920–). He was born in Shanghai and is a Baptist minister with a strong ecumenical mind. He earned his D.Th. from the Southern Baptist Seminary, Kentucky and has served as the chaplain to the President of ROC since the 1950s. He conducted the funeral services for both President Chiang Kai–shek and his son, President Chiang Ching-kuo, as well as for Madam Chiang Kai-shek. Though he is himself a Mainlander and has close connections with the political leaders of the KMT, he also has close relationships with the PCT leaders and participated in the discussion of the first political statement issued by the PCT, "Our National Fate," in 1971. Among Catholics, Cardinal Yu Bin (1901–1978), Archbishop Stanislaus Lo Kuang (1911–2004) and Cardinal Paul Shan Kuo-shi (1923–) are the most famous leaders.

Future Prospects

The overall growth of the number of Christians in Taiwan has been slowing down since 1964. On the other hand, the PCT has been very active in the democratic movement and has made the Christian presence very visible in the society. Unfortunately, the political split between the local Taiwanese and the Mainlanders has seriously affected the unity of the Church. After the corrupt government of both the KMT (1949–2000) and the DDP (2000–2008), and with the return to power of the KMT in their landslide victories in both the Yuan and the presidential elections, the hope for unity has become the common aspiration of the whole society.

This new social political context also contributes to the unity of the Churches. With this hope and the Churches' activities in social services, education, medical services, and theological formation, Christianity is poised to play a significant role in the improvement of the Taiwanese society and in the search for a new identity for the Taiwanese people.

Hong Kong

In the headlines of many Western newspapers and magazines, the year 1997 was depicted as the endgame for Hong Kong. On July 1 of that year, the last internationally-known prosperous British colony was returned to China, ending 156 years of British rule. Much to the surprise of Western observers, Hong Kong not only survived the change: it also successfully weathered the Asian financial crisis during which the transition took place.

A Social and Political Miracle

Long seen as a tiny place that creates miracles, not only economically, but also socially and even politically, Hong Kong continues to be prosperous today. It is the world's eleventh largest trading economy, the fourth largest financial centre in the world, and home to a major service economy with particularly strong links to mainland China and the rest of the Asia-Pacific region. With a GDP of US $189 billion (2006) and a GDP per capita of US $27 527 (2006), Hong Kong's standard of living is much higher than that of mainland China and most other Asian countries as well.

Located at the south-eastern tip of China, Hong Kong is an international city composed of Hong Kong Island, Lantau Island, the Kowloon Peninsula, and 262 outlying islands known as the New Territories, which account for 80% of the city's land. Between Hong Kong Island and the Kowloon Peninsula lies Victoria Harbour, one of the world's most renowned deep-water harbours, the name of which in Chinese means "fragrant harbour". The total area of Hong Kong is very small; only 1104 square kilometres (about 410 sq. miles), just 1/33 the size of Taiwan. Most of the areas are hilly, with less than 25% of the land developed. The total population was approximately 6.9 million in 2006; the population density at the time was 6350 people per square kilometre, making it one of the most densely populated places in the world.

Hong Kong's population is 95% Chinese, with foreign nationals comprising the remaining 5%. Among the Chinese residents, 89.1% are Cantonese speakers; Mandarin speakers account for only 0.9%, and other Chinese dialect speakers total 5.4%. Though Hong Kong was a British colony for more than 150 years, native English speakers make up just 3.2% of population. Nevertheless, English and Chinese are the two official languages, with English widely used in government, business and professional circles.

To put it mildly, there is very little ethnic variety in Hong Kong. Yet it is not without its diversity. The most important characteristic of the population is that only half of Hong Kong's residents were born in the city. Most of the other half moved from regions throughout mainland China at different times. They came, in large part, as refugees and illegal immigrants, especially after the takeover of mainland China by the Chinese Communist Party (CCP) in 1949. Despite such potentially de-stabilizing events, Hong Kong has been without much social turbulence in the last six decades. Influxes of refugees and immigrants have integrated into the fabric of the society, eventually becoming a human resource essential to the prosperity of the city. This is surely a social miracle.

Today, Hong Kong is a Special Administrative Region (SAR) of the People's Republic of China (PRC). China assumed sovereignty under the principles of "one country, two systems" and "Hong Kong people ruling Hong Kong," which are stipulated in the Sino-British Joint Declaration signed in 1984. According to the declaration, Hong Kong is permitted to manage its social, legal, and economic systems differently than does the PRC. The Hong Kong SAR's constitutional document, the Basic Law, ensures that the current political situation will remain in effect until 2047, fifty years after the transfer. Thus, Hong Kong's economy is characterized by free trade; it remains a typical capitalistic society with low taxation and minimum government intervention under the authority of the world's largest communist government. This is surely a political miracle.

A Strong Christian Presence

Travelers to Hong Kong today will find church buildings in various architectural styles – Gothic, English country church, Chinese temple, and modern – many in prominent locations. There are also hundreds of churches in shopping malls, on the second or third floors of commercial and residential high-rise buildings, and in schools and social service centres. More than 50% of schools and social service agencies are managed by churches, and Christian hospitals as well as Christian post-secondary colleges are found throughout the region. Christianity appears to be a very influential religion in Hong Kong.

This has not always been the case. On 25 January, 1841, the British army landed on Hong Kong Island. The following year it was made into a British colony by the Nanjing Treaty. Before the British landing, there was no Christian and all of its 5450 residents were adherents of Chinese religions. Even today, Christians remain a minority in Hong Kong. According to the 2006 report of the Hong Kong government, the Christian community – mainly Protestants and Roman Catholics – numbers about 663 300 people (including 100 300 Filipino Catholics). Christians thus comprise less than 10% of the population of 6.9 million. Currently, Protestant churches have a membership of 320 000, divided among more than 50 denominations and around 1200 congregations. Most of the major denominations are represented in Hong Kong. There are also hundreds of indigenous independent churches such as True Jesus Church and the Little Flock. Baptists form the biggest group, with more than 100 congregations. There is also a congregation for gays and lesbians.

Most of the congregations have less than 100 members and do not fulfil the requirements for membership in the Hong Kong Chinese Christian Church Union, which was established in 1915. With a current roster of around 300 congregations, the Union has three membership requirements: the congregation must be the owner of the church property; it must be ministered by a full-time ordained pastor; and it must be financially self-supporting. The Union is organized to gain bargaining power in negotiations with the government concerning the administration of old people's homes, Christian cemeteries, and occasional city-wide evangelistic rallies.

In 2006, the Catholic population of Hong Kong numbered about 243 000, served by 289 priests, 72 brothers, and 508 sisters. Religious services are conducted in Cantonese. Three fifths of the parishes also provide services in English and, in some cases, in Tagalog (a Filipino language). Also based in Hong Kong is the Greek Orthodox Metropolitanate of Hong Kong and Southeast Asia, which started its ministry in 1997. The Metropolitanate has less than 100 members, most of whom are non-local residents.

The relationship between Protestant, Catholic, and Orthodox Churches is quite close. An ecumenical organization, The Hong Kong Christian Council (HKCC), is a member of both the World Council of Churches and the Christian Conference of Asia. It is composed of mainline denominations, ecumenical service agencies, and the Orthodox Metropolitanate of Hong Kong and Southeast Asia. Since its formation in 1954, HKCC has been committed not only to facilitating cooperative work among the Protestant churches, but also to building a closer relationship among all the churches, and between the churches and other religions. HKCC has organized mission conferences, creating an ongoing opportunity to draw leaders of different Christian traditions together to discuss the common mission of the church in Hong Kong. HKCC also organizes an annual ecumenical Holy Communion service, in which priests and ministers from Protestant, Catholic, and Orthodox churches participate. The Council serves also as the secretariat for the Round Table of Six Religions, whose membership also includes the Buddhist Association, the Daoist Association, the Islamic Association, the Confucius Association, and the Catholic Diocese. Since its establishment in 1957 the Christian Study Centre for Chinese Culture and Religions has been a devoted advocate of inter-religious dialogue

Though the Christian community makes up less than 10% of the population, Protestants and Catholics enjoy a disproportionate degree of influence in Hong Kong. The extent of their influence is most obvious when compared with that of the Buddhist and Daoist communities, which compose more than 80% of the population but run less than 20% of Hong Kong's schools and social service agencies.

The Protestant community runs three post-secondary institutions: the Chung Chi College of the Chinese University of Hong Kong, Hong Kong Baptist University, and Lingnan University. In addition, St. John's College is a student hostel of Hong Kong University managed by the Anglican Church. Protestant churches run more than 630 schools, 116 nurseries, and more than 20 theological seminaries and Bible schools.

Protestant influence does not stop at schools. There are 30 Christian publishing houses and seventy Christian bookstores. There are two Christian weekly newspapers, the Christian Times and Christian Weekly, as well as half a dozen Christian media agencies that broadcast Christian TV programmes regularly. There are four weekly Christian radio programmes on Radio Television Hong Kong (RTHK) owned by the government. Furthermore, more than 250 para-church agencies and Christian action groups attend to the needs and aspirations of the Protestant population. These include student ministries, industrial worker ministries, mass media, evangelistic ministries, support emergency relief and development projects in mainland China and developing countries. The Protestant community also runs seven hospitals and eighteen clinics. Sixty social welfare organizations provide a wide range of services in more than 250 communities, including children's homes, youth centres, family services, homes for the elderly, and centres dedicated to mental and physical disabilities and drug rehabilitation. Protestants also provide chaplaincy services for prisons, hospitals, and the airport, as well as fifteen campsites and six international hotel-style guesthouses.

Catholic influence in Hong Kong is less far reaching, but still significant. In 2006, the Catholic Diocese administered 309 schools and kindergartens, catering to about 250 000 pupils. While there are no Catholic institutes of higher learning, Hong Kong University does have a student hostel, Ricci Hall, managed by the Jesuits. Medical and social services are provided by the diocese to at least six hospitals, fourteen clinics, thirty social and family service centres, eighteen hostels, thirteen homes for the aged, twenty rehabilitation service centres, and several self-help clubs and associations. Many of these institutions are overseen by Caritas, the official social welfare arm of the Catholic Diocese of Hong Kong. These services are offered to everyone and, indeed, 95% of those who have benefited from them are not Catholics. The diocese publishes two weekly newspapers – Kung Kao Po and the Sunday Examiner (English). It also produces cultural and educational programmes for television broadcast and for use on instructional DVDs.

Clearly, Christianity in Hong Kong is vibrant and influential. Part of its influence is closely related to the colonial history of Hong Kong. According to Christian sources, within days of the British landing, a party of missionaries came from Macau, which is only 64 kilometres away and was then a Portuguese colony dominated by Catholics since the sixteenth century. These missionaries came to look over the island to determine if Hong Kong would be a better place for their work. In February 1842, the Rev. Issacher J. Roberts, a Baptist, became the first missionary to move from Macau to take up permanent residence in Hong Kong. In the following forty years, missionaries from the London Missionary Society, the Anglican Church Missionary Society, the Basel, Rhenish, and Berlin Missionary Societies, the American Congregational Church, and the British Methodist Church arrived in Hong Kong. The Roman Catholic Church was established as a mission prefecture in 1841; the prefecture became a vicariate apostolic in 1874, and a diocese in 1946. Jesuits, Canossians, Salesians, Sacred Heart religious, and others arrived at different times to start their missions. Before the communist takeover of China, the churches in Hong Kong had two main functions: (1) running schools and providing medical as well as social welfare services with the financial support of the British colonial government, and (2) using Hong Kong as a stepping stone for entering China to do missionary work with the strong support of Western churches.   Christian churches in Hong Kong had abundant resources to support a long tradition of educational and social ministry and to maintain a close relationship with the churches in China.

Growing into a Local Christianity

The influx of refugees from mainland China during the civil war (1946–1949) and the defeat of the KMT by the CCP in 1949 drastically changed Hong Kong and its Christianity. Its population at the time of its surrender of the

Japanese army – August 30, 1945 – was around 600 000. By 1949, it had increased to 1 600 000. In 1985 it was 5 400 000. After 1949 western missionaries working in different parts of China were expelled by the CCP government and came to Hong Kong with numerous Chinese Christians. Most of these missionaries, assisted by Western churches, worked to bring relief efforts to the refugees, and started new churches and social service agencies. This turned Hong Kong into a supermarket of denominations.

During most of its 160-year history, Christianity in Hong Kong has not only acted as a partner of the colonial government to provide educational, social, and medical services, it has also expressed concern over social issues and put pressure on the colonial government to remedy them. These issues concerned hygiene in 1894, the sale of opium in the early years of the twentieth century, and the anti-*mui-tsai* behaviour (Chinese term for female child-servant in some rich families) in 1921–1938. Christians were silent about social problems during the Japanese occupation and in the period when refugees flooded in from China in the 1950s. However, as social problems became more serious, as when the refugees had to stay in Hong Kong rather than returning to mainland China, the church became very responsive.

Beginning in 1948, a full six years before the government took similar actions, Bishop Ronald Hall of the Anglican Church pioneered various housing schemes, which were followed by other denominations. After the riots caused by young people and leftist trade unions (in 1966 and 1967, respectively), the Christian Industrial Committee was established under the auspices of the Hong Kong Christian Council in 1968 to defend the workers' rights. It eventually became a pioneer organization for social movements of Hong Kong. The city's rapid economic growth enabled most of the mainline churches to become financially independent from their Western mother churches. Young Christians who were born or grew up in Hong Kong after 1949 became more and more active in church ministries, especially regarding social issues such as support for low-income people, the rights of blind workers, corruption, and the expansion of gambling and pornography in media.

Various social-concern groups were organized such as the Justice and Peace Commission of the Hong Kong Catholic Diocese, Christians for Hong Kong Society, and the Hong Kong Christian Institute. In 1980, under the leadership of HKCC a coalition against a bus fare increase became a city-wide social movement joined by Protestants and Catholics as well as by left wing trade unions and non-Christian organizations. A campaign for building a hospital in the Hong Kong Island East was led by priests and members of local Catholic, Methodist and Baptist and independent churches. During the Sino-British negotiations on the future of Hong Kong (1981–1984), three public documents offering Christian views on the future of Hong Kong were released in 1984.[1] During the student demonstration in Tiananmen Square in the spring of 1989, the Hong Kong Christian Patriotic Democratic Movement was founded to support the development of democracy in Hong Kong and China. Christians and the churches of Hong Kong have developed their own pattern of social concern in response to different situations at different critical times. Christians in Hong Kong not only provide diverse institutional social and educational services in partnership with the government, they also initiate social actions to influence government policies for the betterment of society.

Prospects for Hong Kong Christianity

Hong Kong has created economic, social, and political miracles and has made a great impact on the modernization of China. Concomitantly, Christianity in Hong Kong has undergone a process of contextualization which on the one hand maintains the various denominational western traditions and on the other, creates a unique ecumenical spirit under the leadership of local Christians. The future of Christianity in Hong Kong will be linked to Christianity in mainland China, which claims to be a post-denominational Christianity. Although denominationalism is a bad thing, it would be difficult for a healthy church to deny its traditions. Thus, the denominational traditions inherited by the churches in Hong Kong without an emphasis on denominationalism could be resources for a healthy development of Christianity in China.

Furthermore, there are more than twenty theological seminaries and Bible schools in Hong Kong, including the Catholic Holy Spirit Seminary and the Divinity School of Chung Chi College, which is the only theological educational institute located in a Chinese public university. These schools could be important resources for the development of theological education not just in Hong Kong, but in China as a whole. In addition, the experiences of searching for a Chinese Christian identity in a land governed by the "one country, two systems" principle could offer a unique direction to the search for Christian identity.

Macau

In the Cross of Christ I glory, Towering o'er the wrecks of time; All the light of sacred story, Gathers round its head sublime.

This famous hymn by John Bowring (1792–1872) is purportedly inspired by the sight of the towering cross on the top of the massive facade of St. Paul Cathedral in Macau. The church was built in 1580, consecrated in 1603, and destroyed by a fire in 1835. Although Bowring had likely visited the ruined cathedral after he became the British Consul at Canton in 1849 and the Governor of Hong Kong in 1854, the hymn was included in his *Hymns, as a Sequel to the Matins, 1825,* 24 years before he came to China. The facade of

St. Paul Cathedral and the magnificent flight of steps leading up to it remain as the symbol of Macau, which, along with other eight baroque-style church buildings, were declared by UNESCO in 2005 as World Cultural Heritage.

With an area of only 29.2 square kilometres (one fortieth of Hong Kong) and 29 huge casinos, Macau is billed as the "Monte Carlo of the Orient" or "Asia Las Vegas." Historically, Macau had a very important position in China's foreign relations and in Christian mission. Unfortunately, after 400 years of missionary effort, the number of Christians in Macau is very small. They constitute 5% of the population, with 24 000 Catholics and 4000 Protestants among 540 000 residents.

Catholic Missions

In 1553, Portuguese traders and priests arrived in Macau to establish their first settlement there. They expected it to become a bastion of Christianity as well as an important trading port for the Far East. They named it the "City of the Name of God." Macau was just a little dot in the big map of ancient China. The Portuguese claimed that their suppression of piracy had earned them the right to settle there. The Chinese disputed this claim but agreed to allow Macau to be used by the Portuguese in order to control the entry of westerners, especially traders, into mainland China. Since 1557 Macau remained the sole entry point into China for westerners until Hong Kong became a British colony in 1842. Until its reunion with China in December 1999, Macau had been a Portuguese colony for more than 440 years.

The first Catholic to come near to Macau was Francis Xavier, a Jesuit missionary to Japan. In 1552 he attempted to enter China but died on Shangchuan Island, just south of Macau. In the 1560s, more Jesuit missionaries from Goa and Malacca tried to fulfill Francis's dream. The Diocese of Macau was established in 1576, covering the whole of the Far East, including Indochina, China, Mongolia, Japan and Korea. The first bishop was Belchior Carneiro Leitao, S.J. There were then about 5000 Catholics, most if not all were Portuguese. In 1584, under the directives of Alessandro Valignano (1538–1606), the famous Jesuit Matteo Ricci (1552–1610) and Michele Ruggieri (1545–1607) succeeded in entering China via Macau. In 1588, with the establishment of the Diocese of Funai, Japan was separated from Macau. Due to the political conflicts resulting from the union of Portugal and Spain in 1633, the See of Macau was vacant for 57 years. With the arrival of Bishop Joao de Casal in 1692, the ecclesiastical situation became stable. However, with the establishment of two new vicariates covering China, Mongolia, Korea, Vietnam and Indonesia, the original territory of the Diocese of Macau was drastically reduced.

During the early days of Catholic missions work in charity and education flourished. In 1569, the first bishop of Macau established the Santa Casa da

Misericordia (Holy House of Mercy) and a hospital for the poor, later known as St. Raphael's Hospital, and the Leper Asylum of St. Lazarus. In 1565, the Jesuits opened the Mother of God (or St. Paul's) public school, which was made into a university college (the first in Asia) in 1594. In 1580, the construction of St. Paul Cathedral was started. In 1728 St. Joseph's Seminary-College was founded by the Jesuits for the training of missionaries for China and local students.

Unfortunately, the so-called Chinese Rites Controversy changed the whole situation of Catholic missions in China and Macau. The question was raised among different Catholic orders, especially between Jesuits on the one hand and Dominicans and Franciscans on the other, whether the "Chinese rites," that is, the cult of ancestors, which was central to the Chinese family and clan system, and the veneration of Confucius in the temples dedicated to his name, would be permitted to Christian converts. In a decree of 1704, reinforced by the bull *Ex illa die* of 1715, Pope Clement XI banned the rites, which were supported by Matteo Ricci and many other Jesuits. In 1742, Pope Benedict XIV ruled against the rites and imposed an oath on all Catholic missionaries to China to obey his decision. As a consequence, Catholic missionaries were expelled from China and an imperial edict to ban Christianity was issued. Prohibition of mission to the Chinese was enforced in 1746. In 1762, even the Jesuits were banned from Macau. St. Paul's College was closed, and in 1784 the responsibility for St. Joseph's Seminary was taken over by the Lazarists. The golden age of the inculturation of Christianity into the Chinese soil was gone. In 1834, all religious orders were banned in Portugal and its colonies, resulting in Macau's complete loss of control over the China mission. It was only in 1981 that the Diocese of Macau handed to the local hierarchies the parishes it had in Singapore and Malacca. This once powerful diocese now administers the small area of Macau alone.

Protestant Missions

While Catholics experienced a serious set-back because of the Rites Controversy and the political conflicts in Portugal, the first Protestant missionary to China, Robert Morrison (1782–1834), of the London Missionary Society, arrived in Macau in 1807. He served in China for 27 years (1807–1834) and was buried in Macau.

Morrison entered Guangzhou on 7 September, 1807, only three days after his arrival in Macau. Unfortunately, the prohibition against Christian missions made Morrison's missionary plan impossible. To be permitted to live in Guangzhou he had to work as a translator for the British East India Company. In 1815 he published in Macau *A Dictionary of the Chinese Language, Part I* (grammar), the first English-Chinese dictionary. With the help of Rev. William Milne (1785–1822) and many Chinese language teachers, including two Chinese Roman Catholics, he successfully translated the entire Bible into Chinese and published it in Malacca in 1823. In Macau, he baptized the first Chinese convert, Mr. Tsae A-Ko, in 1814, and in 1824 he ordained the first Chinese evangelist, Liang Fa, in Guangzhou. In 1818, he created the first modern Chinese school, Ying Wah College, in Malacca, which was moved to Hong Kong in 1842. In 1820, with a Chinese medical doctor Morrison established a clinic. Morrison carried out most of his missionary work in Macau, making the island the birthplace of Protestant Christianity in China.

Chi Tao Church is probably the first Chinese Protestant Church in Macau. It was started in 1898 by the Hop Yat Church in Hong Kong, the first Chinese independent church in Hong Kong, previously called To Tsai Church. The first woman to be ordained an Anglican priest was Florence Li Tim Oi. She was ordained by Bishop Ronald Hall in 1944 at Shauqing, China, so that she could conduct Holy Communion in Macau. Though her ordination had not secured the permission of the Archbishop of Canterbury, it is seen as the starting point for the movement of women's ordination in the worldwide Anglican community.

Christianity in Modern Macau

The development of Christianity in Macau was fraught with difficulties. In its early days, the political instability of Portugal and later the Chinese Rites Controversy caused a serious debacle. In the 1950s, after the Communists' takeover of mainland China, there was an influx of many religious societies and Christians. In 1976, after both the victory of the Socialist Party in Portugal and the ending of the Cultural Revolution, a large number of illegal immigrants came to Macau from mainland China. In order to provide for their spiritual and physical needs, more religious orders and associations joined forces with earlier missionaries. The Catholic Church continues to pour resources to secure the well-being of Macau residents.

Today, after 450 years of Catholic missions and 200 years of Protestant missionary work, the number of Christians in Macau, as pointed out above, remains small. The process of indigenization in the Catholic Church in the island has been very slow. The first Chinese bishop, Domingo Lam Ka Tseung, was installed only in 1988, the year after the completion of the negotiations between China and Portugal regarding the future of Macau.

The development of the Protestant churches in Macau has been very slow too. Although the mainline churches such as the Anglican Church, the Baptists and The Church of Christ in China started their work in Macau over a century ago, the fruits are few. However, a conservative independent church, The Evangelical Church (Christian Shuen Tao Church of Macau), which is supported mostly by local members, has seen great development in recent years. It started in 1950 and has been operating according to the three principles of self-support, self-government, and self-propagation. More than half of the Protestants in Macau are members of this Church, with more than ten local congregations.

Future of Christianity in Macau

The history of Christianity in Macau is unique. It has been called the Rome of the Far East and the Mother of Missions in Asia. In spite of its glorious past, the future of Christianity in Macau is uncertain. Since the majority of its members are illegal immigrants, its membership is unstable. Furthermore, since the economy of Macau depends mainly on gambling, its ethos and its value system are in tension with the Christian faith. Many of its youth prefer to work in the casinos than in other careers. It is very difficult for the Church to attract the young. Nevertheless, many devoted missionaries and local Christians continue to proclaim the gospel in this land.

Notes

1. All three documents (in Chinese; English translation is available) were released in 1984, just before the conclusion of the Sino-British negotiation on the future of Hong Kong in September of 1984. They are: "A Manifesto of the Protestant Churches on the Religious Freedom," "The Conviction Held by Christians in Hong Kong in the Midst of Contemporary Social and Political Change," and "A Position Paper on the Future of Hong Kong by the Delegation of Christian Leaders Visiting Beijing."

Further Reading

England, J.C. (ed.) *Asian Christian Theologies: A Research Guide to Authors, Movement, Sources*, 3 vols, Maryknoll, New York: Orbis Books, 2004.

Latourette, K.S. *A History of Christian Missions in China*, New York: Macmillan, 1929.

Li, G.(李桂玲) *General Situations of Religions in Taiwan, Hong Kong and Macau*(in Chinese: 台港澳宗教概况), Beijing: Oriental Press, 1996.

Moffet, S.H. *A History of Christianity in Asia*, Vol. 2. *1500-1900*, Maryknoll, New York: Orbis Books, 2005.

Sunquist, S.W. et al. (ed.) *A Dictionary of Asian Christianity*, Grand Rapids: Eerdmans, 2001.

Taiwan

Chou, W.Y. *Pictorial History of Taiwan: From Pre-historical to 1945* (in Chinese: 台灣歷史圖說(史前至一九四五年)), Taipei: Luen Ching Press, 1998.

Huang, C.H. *Joint Action for Mission in Formosa*, New York: Friendship Press, 1968.

Johnson, J. *China and Formosa: The Story of the Mission of the Presbyterian Church of England*, New York: Friendship Press, 1987.

Lin, J. (ed.) *Taiwan Jidujiaoshi* (in Chinese: 台灣基督教史), Beijing: Jiuzhou Press, 2003.

Olivier, L., Chan, C.-H. and Sun, T.-C. *Church Alive: The Catholic Church among the Aboriginal Peoples of Taiwan Past, Present and Future* (in Chinese: 活力教會-天主教在台灣原住民世界的過去現在未來), Taipei: Kuangchi Cultural Group, 2005.

The Presbyterian Church in Tawain *Public Statements*, Taipei: The General Assembly, The Presbyterian Church in Taiwan, 1993.

Roy, D. *Taiwan: A Political History*, Ithaca: Cornell University Press, 2003.

Swanson, A.J. *Perspectives on Church in Taiwan: A Retrospect and Looking Forward from 1980* (in Chinese: 台灣教會面面觀-1980的回顧與前瞻, 基督教在台灣的發展), Taipei: Association for Church Growth in Taiwan, 1981.

Tong, H., *The Development of Christianity in Taiwan* (in Chinese: 基督教在台灣的發展), Taipei: Self-publication, 1962, reprinted in 1970.

Wu, S.-M. *From Dependence to Autonomous: A Study of the PCT at the South before the End of World War II* (in Chinese: 從依賴到自立-終戰前台灣南部基督教長老教會研究), Tainan: Ren Kuang, 2003.

Hong Kong

Endacott, G.B. and She, D.E. *The Diocese of Victoria, Hong Kong: A Hundred Years Church History, 1849-1949*, Hong Kong: Kelly & Walsh, 1949.

Hong Kong Catholic Diocese, *Hong Kong Catholic Church Directory* (in Chinese: 香港天主教教區概覽), Hong Kong: Communication Department of Catholic Church, 2007.

Hong Kong Chinese Christian Church Union *The Special Journal for 90th Anniversary of the Hong Kong Chinese Church Union* (in Chinese: 香港華人基督教聯會九十週年紀念特刊), Hong Kong: Hong Kong Chinese Christian Church Union, 2006.

Lau, S.-L. *The Foundation of Chinese Churches in Hong Kong: 1842-1866* (in Chinese: 香港華人教會的開基: 1842-1866), Hong Kong: China Graduate School of Theology, 2003.

Lau, Y.-S. *Church History of Hong Kong* (in Chinese: 香港教會史), Hong Kong: Hong Kong Baptist Church, 1941, expanded in1996.

Lee, C.-K. *Studies of Hong Kong Church History* (in Chinese: 香港教會史研究), Hong Kong: Tao Shing, 1987.

Lo, L.-K. "The Future of the Church in Hong Kong," *in Word & World: Theology for Christian Ministry*, vol. XVII, no. 2, spring 1997, pp. 203–211.

Lo, L.-K. "A Historical Review and Reflection on the Mission of the Church in Hong Kong," (in Chinese: 香港教會宣教的歷史回顧與反思) revised ed., in Lo, L.-K. and Yeung, K.-K. (eds.) *Search for Identity of the Hong Kong Christianity* (in Chinese: 香港基督教身分的尋索), Hong Kong: Christian Study Centre for Chinese Culture and Religions, 2002.

Smith, C.T. *Chinese Christians: Élites, Middlemen, and the Church in Hong Kong*, Hong Kong: OUP, 1985.

Ying, F.-T. *Introduction to Christian Church History of Hong Kong* (in Chinese: 香港基督教教會史導論), Hong Kong: Alliance Bible Seminary, 2004.

Macau

Diocese of Macau (ed.) *Directorio Catolico de Macau 2005* (in Chinese: 二〇〇五年澳門天主教手冊), Macau: Publicado pela Câmara Eclesiástica, 2005.

Instituto Cultural de Macau (ed.) *Churches of Macau*, Macau: Instituto Cultural de Macau, 1993.

Lee, C.-K. *Protestant Christianity in Macau* (in Chinese: 澳門基督教), Macau: Macau Christian Literacy Association, 2003.

Lim, K.C. *An Introduction to the Bishops of Macau* (in Chinese: 天主教澳門教區歷任主教簡介), Macau: Bishop Office, 2004.

Macau Diocesan Social Communication Centre (ed.) *25th Anniversary of Macau Diocesan Social Communications Centre*, Macau: Macau Diocesan Social Communication Centre, 2000.

Secretary of Culture (ed.) *Magazine on Culture, Vol. 21 (second series), Special Issue for Papers on 400th Anniversary of St. Paul College of Macau: 1594–1994*(in Chinese: 文化雜誌: 1594-1994 澳門聖保祿學院四百周年論文特輯，中文版第二十一期 (第二系列)), Macau: Secretary of Culture, 1994.

Shipp, S. *Macau, China: A Political History of the Portuguese Colony's Transition to Chinese Rule*, Jefferson, N.C.: McFarland, 1997.

10

Japan

Mark R. Mullins

Introduction

The archipelago that comprises Japan includes several thousand islands, but the population of 127 million is concentrated on the four main islands of Honshu, Kyushu, Shikoku, and Hokkaido. The country is roughly the size of the state of California, but with three quarters of the land being mountainous, most people live in densely populated urban centers, such as Tokyo, Yokohama, Nagoya, and Osaka. Today Japan is widely recognized as a successful case of modernization in Asia and often looked to as a model by many other nations that are eagerly pursuing their own development. The country boasts a literacy rate of 99%, and the rapid improvement of health, education, and living standards over the past century has produced the highest life expectancy rates in the world – 85.49 years for women and 78.53 for men.

A traveler arriving in Japan from nearby South Korea, where at least a quarter of the population is Christian, would immediately be struck by the general absence of neon crosses and other visible expressions of a Christian presence. Although a relative latecomer to the Japanese religious world and often regarded as an intrusive "foreign" influence or "outsider" from the West, Christianity is not the only foreign-born religious tradition in Japan. The history of Japanese religion, in fact, is the story of an ongoing process of absorption and cultural reshaping of traditions from abroad – Buddhism and Confucianism transmitted from China and Korea from the sixth century and Christianity from Europe beginning in the sixteenth century. Shinto, the native religion of Japan, developed into various forms – folk Shinto, shrine Shinto, and State Shinto – over centuries of interaction with these imported traditions.

During the past several decades, survey research has consistently discovered that only 30 to 33% of the Japanese population claim to have a "personal

Christianities in Asia, edited by Peter C. Phan © 2011 Blackwell Publishing Ltd except for editorial material and organization © 2011 Peter C. Phan

faith." Although the large majority profess to be "without religion" (*mushūkyō*), what this actually means for most Japanese is that they are without an exclusive commitment to one particular organized religion. The vast majority of Japanese continue to participate in religious life, including rituals over the course of the life cycle (birth, marriage, and death), ceremonies related to household and communal obligations, and in annual festivals and celebrations connected to Shinto shrines and Buddhist temples. As far as those claiming to have a personal faith are concerned, Buddhism, with 27%, claims the allegiance of the largest number of Japanese, followed by Shinto (3%) and Christianity (2%).

The combined membership of all Christian denominations and churches in the modern period has never reached 1% of the population, which means there are some "hidden Christians" who remain outside of and unaffiliated with any Christian church. Since the early postwar period (1948), the total Christian membership has increased from 331 087 (0.423% of the population) to 1 138 712, or 0.891% of the population (2007). This latest figure breaks down as follows: 481 546 Catholics, 618 259 Protestants, and 25 929 Orthodox; in addition, there is a combined total of 12 988 religious professionals or clergy from all of the registered churches in Japan.[1]

The Cultural Diversity of Christianity in Japan

In spite of the popular myth of the homogeneous Japanese and the small number of Christians, one of the defining characteristics of this minority faith in Japan is the remarkable degree of cultural diversity. This variety is rooted in the many denominations transplanted by foreign mission societies from Europe and North America, the diverse reinterpretations of the Christian faith by Japanese Christians and founders of new independent churches, and most recently the new expressions of faith and practice brought to Japan by various Protestant and Pentecostal missionaries from Korea and Catholic immigrant workers from the Philippines, Brazil, and Peru. In this chapter we will briefly sketch the historical development of this Christian diversity, introduce some Japanese appropriations and expressions of the faith, and consider the wider impact of Christians on Japanese society.

Roman Catholic Mission in Pre-Modern Japan

Although there is some evidence that Nestorian Christianity may have reached Japan in earlier times, the sixteenth-century Roman Catholic mission represents the first documented encounter between Christianity and the

Japanese. The timing of this initial mission is of critical importance. It occurred following many years of civil wars, social chaos, and famine. The established Buddhist institutions were also at a low point and less responsive to the needs of the people having become over-involved in the military and political conflicts of the day.

The Catholic mission began in 1549, when Francis Xavier, S.J. (1506–1552) and two Jesuit colleagues arrived in Kagoshima, a town on the coast of Kyushu. The fact that Japan was a divided nation, which allowed for the conversion of feudal lords and mass conversions, accounts in part for the rapid growth of the Catholic mission. It is also important to recognize that missionaries invested considerable resources in education and social welfare activities. In a half-century of mission activity, church schools were established in 200 locations in Western Japan – including a novitiate for training religious candidates, schools for primary education, a seminary and college – and numerous homes were provided to care for the sick, elderly, and orphans. The number of priests in the country never exceeded 137, which means that the ratio of priests to converts became increasingly imbalanced (1 to 412 in 1588 and 1 to 3061 in 1614). What made the rapid expansion of the church possible was the central role played by Japanese catechists and lay assistants (*dōjuku*) who lived with the priests. By 1603, over 500 Japanese lay assistants had been trained for their supportive role in mission, which included translation work, teaching, and preaching. Lay women also were active in social welfare and medical work as members of *misericordia* (which in Portugal were "brotherhoods" with membership restricted to men), and by 1614 these groups were operating seven hospitals, homes for the elderly, as well as homes for orphans and children. By this time, the number of converts had reached approximately 300 000, which means that the proportion of the Christian population was several times higher than it is today.

Persecution and Martyrdom

This so-called "Christian century" ended rather abruptly with the political unification of Japan by the Tokugawa Shogunate. The authorities issued decrees that prohibited Christianity as an evil religion (*jakyō*), ordered the expulsion of foreign missionaries, and called for a systematic persecution to force converts to abandon this subversive religion. The first edict to expel missionaries was issued in 1587, following the unification of the country by Toyotomi Hideyoshi (1537–1590). A decade later, Hideyoshi ordered the execution of 26 Christians for violating the prohibition against preaching Christian doctrine and on February 5, 1597, these individuals were led to Nagasaki and crucified on Mount Tateyama. The martyrs included six Spanish Franciscan friars, three Japanese Jesuits, and seventeen Japanese laymen (including three children). This same site was used again in 1622, the time of the "Great Martyrdom," when some 23 Christian leaders were burnt at the stake and another 22 family members were beheaded. It is estimated that between 1627 and 1636 alone there were 5000 to 6000 martyred.

During the Tokugawa period (1600–1867), the authorities designed numerous methods of social control. One was the *danka seido*, a system in which all the residents of a given area were required to register their household with a local temple and record births, marriages, and deaths. Buddhist priests were used by the Tokugawa regime to monitor and control the entire population by issuing certificates (*tera-uke*) to individuals each year attesting that the person in question was not a member of the proscribed religion (Christianity), which was often ascertained through the ritual of *e-fumi*, requiring individuals to step on a picture of Christ or the Holy Mother.

Hidden Christians

In spite of being cut off from the resources of the Mother Church and widespread persecution, small Christian communities in the area around Nagasaki and on the smaller islands off the coast of Kyushu were able to survive and transmit the Christian tradition to successive generations. These "hidden Christians" (*Kakure Kirishitan*) secretly carried on the faith largely through oral tradition, lay leadership, and confraternities. Eventually their understanding of the faith took on written form in a text known as *Tenchi Hajimari no Koto* [*The Beginning of Heaven and Earth*]. At the end of the Tokugawa period, when Westerners were once again admitted to the country and Catholic missionaries were able to resume their activities and hold religious services, many of these Christians rejoined the Roman Catholic Church. A number of others, however, felt that they could not abandon the *Kakure Kirishitan* tradition, which had been passed down to them directly from their ancestors.[2]

The Second Phase of Christian Mission: Increasing Diversity

After the two and a half centuries of national isolation, Japan was forced to reopen its ports and the second wave of Christian mission to Japan became possible. This time, however, it was a more diverse missionary enterprise that included Roman Catholics, Protestants, and the Russian Orthodox Church. Missionaries began to arrive in 1859, just six years after Commodore Perry persuaded Japan to open its doors to the West. Open missionary activity, however, was not possible until 1873, the year the government finally removed the notices proscribing Christianity, an action largely due to pressure from foreign governments. Similar outside pressures led the government to include an article on religious freedom in the Meiji Constitution (1890).

Although the Christian missionary enterprise has been broadly referred to as a Western one, it has in fact been a multinational effort. Since the mid-nineteenth century, scores of missionary societies and religious orders – representing numerous national churches and cultures – have made their way to Japan. It was the Society of the Foreign Missions of Paris that was initially charged with the mission of propagation for the Catholic Church when Japan was re-opened. Numerous other religious orders quickly followed and today some 85 religious orders from 15 different national headquarters have established work in Japan. While Protestant mission societies representing European churches and denominations from North America dominated the Protestant scene for over a century, in recent decades missionaries from Korea have also been establishing a significant presence.

During the first half of the twentieth century, the fastest growing Protestant denominations (Presbyterian, Methodist, Congregational, and Episcopal) were those that concentrated their personnel in urban areas and invested in educational work and established schools. The "slow growers" (Baptists, Disciples, and Seventh-Day Adventist) had fewer missionaries, focussed their outreach in rural areas, and, for the most part, were without educational work. While one can graph patterns of relative success of the different mission groups and churches, the minimal growth of the Christian movement as a whole is related to the difficult and complex political and religious situation of the receiving society.

State Shinto and the Christian Churches

By the time missionaries arrived in the nineteenth century, most Japanese were already integrated into a system of "layered" religious obligations related to the household (Buddhist) and community (Shinto). The restoration of the Emperor and creation of State Shinto by the leaders of the Meiji government added another layer of civil religious obligations. This left little room for Christianity and created a difficult situation for Christian mission work until the end of the Second World War. For half a century the government used this civil religion to integrate the heterogeneous population and mobilize the people for nation-building, modernization, and, eventually, military expansion. By the 1930s this civil religion became increasingly totalitarian and members of every religious group were required to conform to the state-defined orthodoxy. By the end of the war, most religious organizations – Christian churches, Buddhist organizations, and various New Religions – had been co-opted by the government and forced to promote and support militarism and nationalistic expansion.

The Place of Nagasaki in Japanese Catholicism

Nagasaki was the center of the early Roman Catholic mission and often referred to as the "little Rome of the Orient." Its importance for the Japanese church was not diminished by the many years of persecution. In fact, the accumulation of names on the long list of martyrs meant that it would become a central site for pilgrimage in the modern period. Tragically, Nagasaki was to take on even more symbolic significance in the twentieth-century. The second atomic bomb, dropped on Nagaski on August 9, 1945, destroyed the Urakami Cathedral and killed about 8500 Catholics.

The theme of suffering is a dominant one in reflections on the meaning of faith in the Japanese Catholic context. One well-known figure, Dr. Takashi Nagai (1908–1951), was a dedicated Catholic and medical doctor who responded to the needs of the dying and injured following the atomic blast. Diagnosed with leukemia just two months before the atomic blast – an illness initially caused from exposure to high doses of radiation from years of research and work as a radiologist – his condition deteriorated rapidly from the additional exposure to the fallout of the atomic bomb. After losing his wife and hundreds of friends and colleagues at the medical school of the University of Nagasaki, he struggled to come to terms with the tragic and indescribable loss and destruction. He became a prominent author in the few short years before his untimely death from leukemia, publishing both scientific documentation of the effects of the atomic bomb as well as a number of volumes of essays and spiritual reflections.

In his "Funeral Address for the Victims of the Atomic Bomb," which is included in *The Bells of Nagasaki* (1946), he explained:

> Our church of Nagasaki kept the faith during four hundred years of persecution when religion was proscribed and the blood of martyrs flowed freely. During the war this same church never ceased to pray day and night for a lasting peace. Was it not, then, the one unblemished lamb that had to be offered on the altar of God? Thanks to the sacrifice of this lamb many millions who would otherwise have fallen victim to the ravages of war have been saved. Eight thousand people, together with their priests, burning with pure smoke, entered into eternal life.

While not all Japanese could accept this interpretation of the fate of Nagasaki, for many Catholics it was a theodicy that made the pain more bearable. His book ended with a hopeful appeal that this sacrifice was not made in vain: "From this atomic waste the people of Nagasaki confront the world and cry out: No more war! Let us follow the commandment of love and work together. The people of Nagasaki prostrate themselves before God and pray: Grant that Nagasaki may be the last atomic wilderness in the history of the world."[3]

Postwar Developments

The development of Christianity in postwar Japan has been framed by the fundamental changes in the political and legal system that resulted from Japan's defeat on 15 August 1945 and the arrival of the Occupation Forces. The postwar Constitution of Japan (1947), with its principle of religious freedom and separation of religion and state, led to the disestablishment of State Shinto and created a free-market religious economy for the first time in Japanese history. These legal and political changes, accompanied by demographic changes related to postwar industrialization, helped to create a more favorable environment for Christian missionary activities. An urban population of 37.5% in 1950, for example, increased to 76.1% by 1980. Since Christian organizations were largely concentrated in metropolitan areas and the established religious traditions were concentrated more heavily in rural areas, many observers thought that church growth was assured. But it was the many home-grown New Religious Movements, such as Sōka Gakkai and Risshō Kōseikai, rather than Christian churches, which benefited most from this demographic shift. Scholars estimate that between 10 and 20% of the population belongs to one of these new religious movements.

This is not to say that churches did not benefit from the new situation. The Catholic Church, for example, whose membership had dropped to around 100 000 during the war, grew to 323 599 by 1960. Protestant churches experienced a similar expansion from a low of about 190 000 in 1942 to over 400 000 in 1960. The annual growth rate, however, began to decline gradually for both Protestants and Catholics. The largest Protestant denomination, the United Church of Christ in Japan, for example, recorded over 10 000 baptisms a year between 1947 and 1951, but this dropped to less than 3000 in 1990. While churches have continued to report baptisms and membership increases throughout the postwar period, for decades annual statistics have indicated that less than 1% of the Japanese are church members. The hard reality is that the rate of defections and the increase in the Japanese population have kept Christian churches from gaining a larger share of the market in Japan's religious economy.

The Wider Impact of Christianity: Education and Social Welfare

To understand the place of Christianity in Japan one must consider much more than church membership statistics. The significance of this minority faith extends far beyond church walls. Both missionaries and Japanese Christian leaders have been pioneers in a number of fields, including social welfare, medical work, and education. Educational work has been a particularly important area for both Protestants and Catholics. Western missionaries collaborated with their Japanese colleagues to organize numerous "mission schools" that subsequently evolved into colleges and universities over the course of a century. The significance of many mission schools, particularly in providing education for women, has also been widely noted. The problematic image and reputation of Christianity as a religion "for intellectuals," however, has been created in part by this emphasis on education.

For example, when compared with the number of private schools associated with other major religious organizations in Japan, the disproportionate role of Christians in this field is striking. By the early 1960s, for example, the number of Christian schools exceeded the number of Buddhist and Shinto-related institutions combined. While there were 652 Buddhist-related schools (10 universities, 1 junior college, 77 high schools, 68 junior high schools, 1 elementary school, 410 kindergartens, and 85 "other"), and only 92 Shinto-related schools (2 universities, 1 junior college, 5 high schools, 6 junior high schools, 1 elementary school, 45 kindergartens, and 32 "other"), there were 840 Christian-related educational institutions (22 universities, 47 junior colleges, 106 high schools, 116 junior high schools, 33 elementary schools, 445 kindergartens, and 71 "other"). The miscellaneous institutions in the "other" category include specialized schools for religious education and training (theological schools or seminaries in the case of Christian-related schools).[4] While many of these institutions struggle with the problem of secularization – in particular, the shortage of Christian faculty and staff – educational work continues to be a major area of contribution. As of 2005, for example, the Catholic Church alone had some 350,000 students enrolled in one of its 870 affiliated schools (ranging from kindergartens to universities).

The impact of Christians on Japanese society extends far beyond educational work. One concrete example may be seen in the life and work of Kagawa Toyohiko (1888–1960), a Protestant leader known for his social vision and wide range of activities. Many have regarded him as the "Saint Francis of Japan" for his identification with the poor and for his compassionate work in the slums. In his own time, however, there were others who regarded him as a dangerous social activist and rabble-rouser for his leadership in the labor movement and organization of unions for struggling farmers. Kagawa maintained cooperative relationships with missionaries and was an ordained minister in the Presbyterian Church, but he was extremely critical of the established churches and their individualistic interpretation of the faith. In 1919, Kagawa published *Seishin undō to shakai undo* (Spiritual and Social Movements), a title that captured his concern for both individual and social transformation.

Kagawa never abandoned the church and continued to serve as a pastor, but he was extremely critical of a church that failed to practice redemptive love (*shokuzai ai no jissen*), which for him meant moving outside the walls of the church to live and work with those in greatest need. The membership composition of established churches tended to be dominated by the educated or white-collar classes and those groups of people who were in most critical need – the "underside of modern Japan" – were largely missing. Kagawa reasoned that clergy were failing to cultivate lay leaders and mobilize them for ministry to the poor and the larger work of the Kingdom. To address this failure, Kagawa launched the Friends of Jesus movement in 1921, modeling his organization after the third order of the Franciscans. While personal piety and purity were central concerns, membership also involved a commitment to live fully in the "world" and work for the transformation of society according to Christian principles and values. By 1928, there were some 1300 members mobilized for social transformation through the organization of labor unions, cooperatives, and educational programs. By the late 1930s, 35 institutions and over 100 projects dedicated to relief work, social reform, and Christian education were under Kagawa's supervision.

Notwithstanding Kagawa's criticisms of the religious establishment, it is important to recognize that many other Christian leaders and churches have actively addressed pressing social problems and been responsive to the most needy in Japanese society. The Catholic Church, for example, maintains 522 institutions devoted to social welfare (including childcare facilities and nursing homes for the elderly) and some 35 hospitals and medical clinics across Japan. Similar social welfare and medical work has also been undertaken by the larger Protestant churches in Japan. In the postwar period, many Christian churches have become more aware of racial discrimination both within and outside of the churches and engaged more directly the concerns of minority groups in Japanese society, including Koreans, Burakumin (the so-called "outcastes" of Japan), and most recently the number of immigrant laborers who are largely employed in less desirable jobs often referred to in terms of the three k's: *kitanai* (dirty), *kiken* (dangerous), and *kitsui* (hard, demanding).

Christianity as a Japanese Religion: Diverse Appropriations

It is important to recognize that the Western missionary movement represents only one side of the story of Christianity in Japan. Japanese were not passive recipients of transplanted Christianity, but active agents who reinterpreted and reconstructed the faith in terms that made sense to them. Many converts both within and outside of the mission churches have felt that the faith was unnecessarily bound to Western theology, organizational forms, denominational politics, and missionary control. Although many observers note that Japanese theology has tended to remain Eurocentric in orientation, there are numerous examples of how Japanese have transformed Christianity into a religion of their own through the process of inculturation or indigenization. Standard treatments of this process of cultural appropriation often consider the work of professional theologians, such as Kitamori Kazoh and his well-known *Theology of the Pain of God* (1947). Here, however, I would like to briefly consider two highly influential Japanese interpretations that are to be found outside of established theological institutions.

From "Paternal" to "Maternal" Religion

Endō Shūsaku (1923–1996), the late Roman Catholic novelist, provides an interesting interpretation of one Japanese response to the earliest Christian mission in terms of the feminization of Christianity. Endō struggled as much as any theologian to find appropriate ways to understand and interpret the Christian faith in the Japanese context. His novels, *Silence* and *Deep River*, for example, have probably had a greater impact than any theological text and encouraged Christians and non-Christians alike to think about the meaning of this religion for Japanese.[5] In his autobiographical short story, "Mothers," Endō writes: "the missionaries long ago brought to this country the teaching of a Father God. But in the course of time, after the missionaries had been driven out and the churches destroyed, the hidden Christians gradually threw over all the elements of the religion that didn't suit them, replacing them with what is most essential in all Japanese religion, devotion to Mother."[6]

This interpretation builds on Endō's distinction between "paternal religion" (*chichi no shūkyō*) and "maternal religion (*haha no shūkyō*). While the Jesuit missionaries may have introduced the Virgin Mary along with other teachings regarding Jesus and the creeds, Endō argues that the missionaries transmitted an expression of Christianity that was overwhelmingly paternal, with an emphasis on the God who judges and punishes. In another essay, he writes that "Christianity matured in Europe as a religion not of the mother figure, but of the father figure, and this figure is considered an extremely frightening presence."[7] In this context, one is reminded of the well-known Japanese proverb, *Jishin, Kaminari, Kaji, Oyaji* (Earthquakes, Thunder, Fires, and Fathers), which suggests rather negative associations with the father image in Japan. This perception of the nature of "motherhood" and "fatherhood" in Japan shapes Endō's interpretation of why "maternal religion" is so attractive in this context and the general coldness Japanese have towards "paternal religion."

Under difficult circumstances in the Tokugawa period, it was the camouflaged Virgin Mary – in the disguise of the bodhisattva Kannon – that provided Christians with a sacred image to focus their worship and ritual. As Miyazaki Kentarō explains:

> In times of persecution during the Edo period the underground Kirishitan could not possess a figure of the Christian Virgin Mary, therefore they projected Mary's image on the gentle image of the Buddhist Kannon and venerated her in this way. . . . For the underground Kirishitan who every year trodded on the *fumie* and denied God, this Father God was a fearful divine judge. Therefore, the center of their faith shifted without notice to the gentle and limitless embrace and forgiveness of the mother deity Mariya.[8]

No doubt there are some who would challenge this interpretation, but it is undeniable that there is a longing for the divine feminine – or a more compassionate, understanding, and forgiving divine being – that has significant cross-cultural appeal.

Uchimura Kanzō and the Non-church Movement

Another example of inculturation may be seen in the dozen or so independent and indigenous movements that were organized over the past century. These movements were founded by Japanese leaders who accepted the Christian faith (on their own terms), but who rejected the missionary carriers and their particular Western and denominational understanding of religion. A recurring phrase in the Japanese Christian literature is that the transplanted Christianity of the mission churches is *bata-kusai* (literally, "reeking of butter"). In other words, missionaries were seen to be bringing too much unnecessary (and "smelly") cultural baggage with them as they sought to transmit the Gospel. These movements are indigenous not only in terms of the minimum conditions of "self-support, self-control, and self-propagation," but illustrate how Japanese have found new ways to interpret, organize, and practice the Christian faith.

Uchimura Kanzō (1861–1930) organized the first independent expression of Japanese Christianity as the Non-church movement (*Mukyōkai*) in 1901. Western church authority, the priesthood, sacraments, and the clergy-laity distinction were all rejected by Uchimura. It was the Confucian-oriented *bushidō* tradition ("the way of the samurai") that provided the foundation for Uchimura's fulfillment theology and new expression of Christianity. His interpretation of the faith had particular appeal to the educated members of Japanese society. He was a prolific writer (his collected works consist of some 50 volumes), which partially explains why so many of his disciples were well-known intellectual figures, including authors and university presidents. The literature produced by or about this movement is now so extensive that a 1990 bibliography about Uchimura and his movement exceeded 100 pages. The Non-church movement has been referred to as a "manly expression of Christianity" (*otokorashii Kirisutokyō*), but in recent years women have taken on a more active role by offering critical feminist perspectives on the conservative Confucian orientation of the movement.[9] Other charismatic leaders have produced some alternatives to both Uchimura's movement and transplanted denominations by combining their distinctive interpretations of the Christian canon with elements drawn from other native religious and cultural traditions (including Zen, Shamanism, and the ancestral cult).

Inculturation and the Ancestors in Japanese Christianity

An important example of inculturation is revealed in the way in which all Christian churches have addressed the central Japanese concern for ancestors and ritual care for the dead. It is well known that most mission churches regarded the ancestral cult as something incompatible with the Christian faith and initially instructed their members to avoid participation in traditional rites. The early history of Protestant Christianity in Japan abounds with stories of individuals being cut off from their families because of their refusal to participate in household ancestor rites. It was not uncommon for zealous new Christians, following the instructions of their missionary teachers, to burn their family Buddhist altars and ancestral tablets. In spite of their early critical stance toward Japanese ancestral traditions, over the past century many Christian churches and movements have responded to the Japanese concern for the dead and instituted a wide range of post-funerary rites that resemble Buddhist practices in many ways.

In 1985, the Catholic Church published a short pamphlet that provided "Guidelines with regard to the Ancestors and the Dead," which gave official endorsement to many of the adaptations and accommodations that had already occurred in many households and parishes for decades. In the earlier periods of Catholic mission, the faithful were often instructed to dispose of household altars or at least avoid participation in family rituals connected to the Buddhist tradition. This strict teaching has been relaxed considerably, as the faithful are now encouraged to perform rituals and memorial services before either Christian or Buddhist family altars as signs of love and respect for the deceased. Similar adaptations and accommodations that have been made by various Protestant churches and some indigenous Christian movements have also developed a "theology of hope" for the ancestors through a reconsideration of certain New Testament texts that refer to baptism for the dead (I Cor. 15: 29) and to Jesus' ministry to the world of the dead and imprisoned spirits (I Peter 3:18–22).

"Christian" Weddings and the Rites of Passage

Another development that deserves mention in the context of inculturation has been the widespread recent interest in Christian marriage rites by non-Christian couples. While most Japanese are not interested in church membership, many members of the current generation are appropriating the marriage rites provided by the church into the traditional division of labor in Japanese religions. Just as Shinto has traditionally dominated the rituals associated with birth, and Buddhism has monopolized rituals connected to death, Christian churches are becoming a significant competitor in the sacralization of weddings.

Over the past two decades, the number of Japanese choosing Christian marriage rites has steadily increased. In 1982 most weddings (90%) were still conducted by Shinto priests, and only 5.1% were performed with a Christian service. According to a 2005 survey, however, the percentage of Japanese choosing Christian wedding rites has now reached some 70%, and Shinto rites have declined to roughly 20%. For a variety of reasons, Christianity seems to be finding a niche for itself in the complex of Japanese folk religion by performing this fashionable, if compartmentalized, role. While many church representatives are critical of the "wedding business" both within churches and conducted in major hotel wedding chapels, it can be argued that wedding services provide one of the few positive points of contact between churches and younger Japanese. Whether or not this will eventually translate into higher numbers actually making a commitment to organized Christianity through baptism and church membership remains to be seen.

Inter-Faith Dialogue

Inter-religious dialogue and a posture of openness to learning from other Japanese religions is another feature of Christianity in contemporary

Japan. Numerous books and journals are devoted to inter-religious under-standing, and it is not uncommon to encounter Japanese and foreign priests and laity who have incorporated Buddhist meditation practices into their own religious life – sometimes referred to as "Christian Zen." Institutions that have made significant contributions to this area on the Catholic side include the Oriens Institute for Religious Research in Tokyo and the Nanzan Institute for Religion and Culture in Nagoya. On the Protestant side, for some decades the National Christian Council Center for the Study of Japanese Religions in Kyoto has offered seminars on Japanese religions, encouraged interfaith encounters, and published journals in both Japanese and English.[10]

Future Prospects

Although membership statistics indicate a modest growth in Christian churches over the past few decades, other indicators suggest that the church in Japan is on a trajectory of steady decline. The larger established churches in Japan – the Roman Catholic Church, the Anglican-Episcopal Church (Nippon Seikōkai), and the United Church of Christ (Kyōdan) – all report a decline in the number of annual baptisms, church attendance, and enrollment in church schools. The difficulties on the horizon are not unique to the Christian community, but faced by all religious organizations in contemporary Japan and related to basic demographic realities – the low birthrate and an aging population. In addition to evangelistic outreach, religious organizations depend on natural growth, which is based on births to members and effective religious socialization. A fertility rate below 2.1 points to population decline, and Japan's birthrate declined to 1.25 in 2005. In light of these demographic changes, it is not surprising to find that almost all churches and religious groups are facing a leadership crisis and struggling to maintain participation and involvement by children and youth. In addition, these churches are dealing with overall aging of clergy and a decline in the number of seminarians preparing to enter the ordained ministry. A recent study of the Catholic Church projects that the number of priests will decrease by one-third or one-half within the next 15 years. There are already a number of "priestless" parishes, so this is a cause for concern. The largest Protestant denomination, the United Church of Christ in Japan (Kyōdan), reported that 228 churches (13%) were "pastorless" in 2003, and that number is expected to more than double in the next decade.

The situation looks somewhat brighter for the Catholic Church due to the unanticipated and steady increase of laborers from traditionally Catholic countries. The Catholic Commission of Japan for Migrants, Refugees and People on the Move reported in 2005 that the number of foreign Catholics in

Japan had reached over half a million, which is more than the number of Japanese Catholics. Today the Catholic Church in Japan is becoming increasingly multicultural, with masses being conducted in English, Portuguese, Spanish, French, Tagalog, Korean, Vietnamese, Chinese, German, Indonesian, and Burmese. The Church in Japan, which in the past has been largely shaped by European and North American traditions and gradually transformed through inculturation, is now being reshaped by new cultural influences and ways of practicing the faith by immigrant workers from Brazil, Peru, and the Philippines. These influences include, for example, the charismatic El Shaddai Movement and Couples for Christ, both introduced from the Philippines. There are clear tensions between older Japanese members and new non-Japanese members surrounding their different expectations regarding parish life (particularly in connection with use of sacred space, church facilities, and financial matters), but declining Japanese churches could very well be revitalized by these new immigrant Catholics and their children.

Although the Church in Japan struggles with membership, it is a creative minority that seeks to function as "salt" and "light" and in recent years has been assuming a more "prophetic" role by challenging various expressions of neo-nationalism. Since the 1980s, there have been a number of attempts to re-nationalize Yasukuni Shrine and legitimize official visits by the Prime Minister of Japan. Many politicians of the Liberal Democratic Party – guided by a neo-nationalist vision – have pushed through reforms of the postwar educational system, including the adoption of textbooks that promote patriotism and white-wash Japan's imperial and colonial past, such as wartime atrocities and the "comfort women" issue. In 1999, the Kimigayo (National Anthem) and Hinomaru (flag) were officially approved by the Diet, and the government instructed public schools that they were to use these symbols for all official school events. A number of teachers have already faced disciplinary action for their alleged failure to lead students to participate appropriately in these ritual events, which for many revives memories of Japan during the Second World War. The government is now pushing to revise the "Peace Constitution."

Christian leaders and organizations – from the ecumenical National Christian Council to evangelical churches – have been actively involved in organizing protests and speaking out against all of these neo-nationalist developments. In many cases, Christians have joined hands with people of other faiths to oppose, for example, the US initiated war in Iraq and the Japanese government's decision to send members of the Self-Defense Force to Iraq in support of the war. To commemorate the sixtieth year since the enactment of the 1947 Constitution, in 2007 the Peace Network of Christians and eight other organizations held an assembly in Tokyo – attended by some 6000 people – to preserve Article 9 of the Constitution and resist the current government's proposals for revision. The freedom of religion and the constitutional separation of religion and state have a very short history and relatively weak foundation in Japanese society. As religious minorities, Christians have a great deal at stake in the current neo-nationalist environment and recognize their responsibility to work for the preservation of a pluralistic and democratic society.

Timeline	
1549	The Roman Catholic mission to Japan is initiated with the arrival of Francis Xavier, S.J., and two fellow Jesuits in Kagoshima, Kyushu.
1563	Conversion of Omura Sumitada (1533–1587), the first feudal lord to adopt the new religion.
1587	Toyotomi Hideyoshi (1537–1590) unifies Japan and issues an edict banning foreign missionaries.
1597	Twenty-six Christians are crucified in Nagasaki according to Hideyoshi's directive.
1601	The number of converts reaches approximately 300 000.
1614	Tokugawa Ieyasu orders the expulsion of all Catholic missionaries and prominent Christians; severe persecutions with 44 martyred in Arima.
1619	Fifty-two Christians put to the stake in Kyoto.
1853	Commodore Perry visits Japan to establish diplomatic relations and open ports.
1859	Catholic, Protestant, and Orthodox missionaries arrive in Japan.
1865	"Hidden Christians" reappear and meet Father Petijean at the Oura Church in Nagasaki.
1873	The Meiji government removes the public notice boards proscribing Christianity, which allows Christian missionary activity.

1889	Article 28 of the Meiji Constitution establishes freedom of religious belief.
1901	Uchimura Kanzō established the Non-church movement (*Mukyōkai*).
1922	Formation of the National Christian Council of Japan.
1929	Beginning of three-year nationwide cooperative evangelistic campaign among Protestants as a part of the Kingdom of God movement led by Kagawa Toyohiko.
1941	In compliance with government directive, Protestant denominations unite to form the United Church of Christ in Japan (*Nippon Kirisuto Kyōdan*).
1945	Atomic bombs dropped on Hiroshima and Nagasaki; end of Second World War and Occupation of Japan begins.
1947	Enactment of the postwar Constitution, which includes articles on the freedom of religion and separation of religion and state.
1967	The General Assembly of the Kyōdan issues statement entitled "Confession Concerning Responsibility of the United Church of Christ in Japan during World War II."
2007	Pope Benedict XVI signs decree approving the beatification of 188 martyrs on June 1.

Notes

1. Japanese names appearing in this chapter are given in the conventional Japanese order, which is surname followed by given name. The statistics cited throughout the text are drawn from the *Kirisutokyō Nenkan* [*Christian Yearbook*] and the *Katorikku Kyōkai Jōhō Handobukku* [*Information Handbook on the Catholic Church*], both published annually.
2. For helpful studies of the *Kakure Kirishitan*, see Harrington, A.M. *Japan's Hidden Christians*, Chicago: Loyola University Press, 1993; Whelan, C. *The Beginning of Heaven and Earth: The Sacred Book of Japan's Hidden Christian*, Honolulu: University of Hawaii Press, 1996; and Turnbull, S.

The Kakure Kirishitan of Japan: A Study of Their Development, Beliefs and Rituals to the Present Day, Richmond, United Kingdom: The Japan Library, 1998.

3. The quotations are from the English edition translated by William Johnston (Tokyo: Kodansha International, 1984), pp. 108 and 118.

4. Reported in *Nihon ni okeru Kirisutokyō Gakkō Kyōiku no Genjō* [*The Current State of Education in Christian Schools in Japan*], Tokyo: Education Association of Christian Schools, 1961, p. 133.

5. *Silence*, for example, "sold some 2 and a quarter million copies in the Japanese original alone, and *Deep River* approximately 1 million." See Williams, M. "Bridging the Divide: Writing Christian Faith (and Doubt) in Modern Japan," in Mullins, M.R. (ed.) *Handbook on Christianity in Japan*, Leiden: Brill, 2003, p. 318.

6. Endō, S. "Mothers," trans. Francis Mathy, *Japan Christian Quarterly*, Fall, 1974, p. 203.

7. Endō, S. "Religious Consciousness of the Japanese," in Kenny, D. (ed.) *Nihon no Kokoro* [*The Mind of Japan*], Tokyo: Kodansha, 1985, p. 17.

8. Miyazaki, K. "The Kakure Kirishitan Tradition," in Mullins, M. (ed.) *Handbook of Christianity in Japan*, Leiden: Brill, 2003, p. 28.

9. For more detailed treatment of independent and indigenous expressions of Christianity, see Caldarola, C. *Christianity: The Japanese Way*, Leiden: Brill, 1979 and Mullins, M.R. *Christianity Made in Japan: A Study of Indigenous Movements*, Honolulu: University of Hawaii Press, 1998.

10. On these helpful resources, see the following sites: http://www.oriens.or.jp/english/english.htm; http://www.nanzan-u.ac.jp/SHUBUNKEN/welcome.htm; and http://www.japanese-religions.jp/.

Further Reading

Breen, J. and Williams, M. (eds.) *Japan and Christianity: Impacts and Responses*, London: Macmillan Press, 1996.

Ebisawa, A. *Nihon Kirisutokyō Rekishi Daijiten* [*Historical Dictionary of Christianity in Japan*], Tokyo: Kyōbunkan, 1988.

Fujita, N.S. *Japan's Encounter with Christianity: The Catholic Mission in Pre-Modern Japan*, New York: Paulist Press, 1991.

Laures, J., S.J. *The Catholic Church in Japan: A Short History*, Tokyo: Charles E. Tuttle Company, 1954.

Mullins, M.R. (ed.) *Handbook of Christianity in Japan*, Leiden: Brill, 2003.

Mullins, M.R. *Christianity Made in Japan: A Study of Indigenous Movements*, Honolulu: University of Hawaii Press, 1998.

Mullins, M.R. and Young, F.R. (eds.) *Perspectives on Christianity in Korea and Japan: The Gospel and Culture in East Asia*, Lewiston, New York: Edwin Mellen Press, 1995.

Phillips, J.M. *From the Rising of the Sun: Christians and Society in Contemporary Japan*, Maryknoll, New York: Orbis Books, 1981.

Reid, D. *New Wine: The Cultural Shaping of Japanese Christianity*, Berkeley: Asian Humanities Press, 1991.

Turnbull, S. *The Kakure Kirishitan of Japan: A Study of Their Development, Beliefs and Rituals to the Present Day*. Richmond, England: The Japan Library, 1998.

Yamamori, T. *Church Growth in Japan: A Study in the Development of Eight Denominations, 1859-1939*, South Pasadena: William Carey Library, 1974.

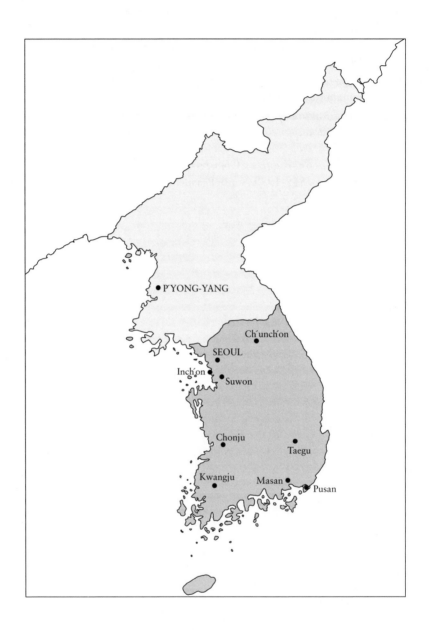

11

South Korea

Andrew Eungi Kim

Introduction

South Korea has no "official" religion – like the Anglican Church in England – nor is there one dominant religion. Shamanism, Buddhism, and Christianity as well as a whole spectrum of new religious movements co-exist peacefully in one of the most religiously pluralistic countries in the world (see Table 1). It is not hard to find expressions of shamanism in contemporary Korea: many ordinary Koreans patronize a shaman ritual called *goot* for good fortune and an estimated 3 million Koreans regularly consult modern-day shamans (fortune-tellers) whose establishments reportedly number more than 300 000 in South Korea. Confucianism, albeit more revered and practiced as a set of moral precepts, still attracts a considerable number of devotees: nearly 200 000 Koreans identify Confucianism as their religion and there are some 200 Confucian shrines that serve as the place of worship. Buddhism is the country's largest religion with nearly 11 million adherents. There are 39 Buddhist orders with more than 11 000 temples and the number of monks total over 26 000.

Protestantism, which was introduced to Korea in 1884, is the second largest religion with almost 9 million followers or about 20% of the country's 48 million people. Its growth had been particularly pronounced from the early 1960s to the end of the 1980s, the period of the country's remarkable modernization. Since the early 1960s, when South Korea's Protestants scarcely topped the 1 million mark, the number of Protestant Christians increased faster than in any other country, nearly doubling every decade (see Table 2). The dynamism of Protestantism in Korea is attested to by the fact that the nation now sends more missionaries abroad than most other countries. As of 2003, Korea had 12 000 missionaries in more than 160 countries, which was second only to the United States, which had 46 000 missionaries worldwide. Britain was third with 6000 missionaries stationed abroad. Also, five of the ten largest churches in the world, including

Christianities in Asia, edited by Peter C. Phan © 2011 Blackwell Publishing Ltd except for editorial material and organization © 2011 Peter C. Phan

Table 1. Religious population in South Korea (in thousands; percentage of total population)

	1995	2005
Buddhist	10 321 (23.2)	10 726 (22.8)
Protestant	8 760 (19.7)	8 616 (18.3)
Catholic	2 951 (6.6)	5 146 (10.9)
Confucian	211 (0.5)	105 (0.2)
Won Buddhist	87 (0.2)	130 (0.3)
Other religions	268 (0.6)	247 (0.5)
No religious affiliation	21 953 (49.3)	21 865 (46.9)

Source: *Ingumit jutaek chongjosa* [*National Census*], 1997, 2006.

the world's largest Yoido Full Gospel Church (with reportedly over a half million members), are found in Seoul, a "city of churches." In addition, there are more than 170 denominations and 60 000 churches. The largest denominations in terms of membership are Presbyterian (33%), Methodist (22%), Holiness (16%), Baptist (11%), and Full Gospel (8%). About 10% of the total number of Protestant churches comprises independent churches. Adding to the Christian presence in Korea is a large number of Catholics whose total now exceeds 5.1 million or about 11% of the population. Catholicism has

Table 2. The number of Protestant Christians, 1950–2005

Year	Number of members	Growth rate (%)
1950	500 198	—
1960	623 072	24.6
1970	3 192 621	512.4
1980	5 001 491	56.7
1985	6 489 282	29.8
1991	8 037 464	23.9
1995	8 760 336	9.0
2005	8 616 438	− 1.6

Sources: Korea Research Institute of Religion and Society's *Hanguk chonggyo yeongam* [*A Yearbook of Korean Religions*], 1993 for the 1950, 1960 and 1970 data; Ministry of Culture and Information Affairs' *Chonggyo beopin mit dnche hyeonwhang* [*Current Status of Religious Organizations*], 1977, for the 1977 data; and the National Statistical Office's *Ingumit jutaek chongjosa* [*National Census*], respective years, for the 1987 data; the 1991 data; the 1995 and the 2005 data.

enjoyed the largest increase in membership of all the religions in the last decade, soaring from 2.9 million in 1995 to over 5 million in 2005.

Together, Protestant and Catholic Christians comprise roughly 30% of the population, and Christianity as a whole is the largest religion in Korea. This is all the more astonishing given the fact that Korea is the only country in all of Asia, except for the Philippines, that has embraced Christianity en masse. Also, the Christian success in Korea contrasts sharply with the failure of Christianity to make any impact in Japan – the neighboring country with markedly similar religious and cultural traditions – where a mere 600 000 or about 0.5% of the Japanese population (130 million) has converted to the new religion. Christianity had not fared any better in China even when it had religious freedom until the Communist takeover in 1949.

The Beginning of Christianity in Korea

The Catholic beginning

Catholicism was introduced to Korea in 1784 – exactly a century earlier than Protestantism – when an envoy to China brought back books and articles on Christian doctrines. The Christian literature was distributed to a group of scholars and they began to discuss their new-found religion among friends and neighbours, thereby laying the foundations of the Catholic Church in Korea. These men, in fact, assumed certain priestly functions, including administering the sacrament of baptism. Despite the suspicion that their new religion drew upon them from the general populace, they spoke about Catholicism openly, instructing their converts in the catechism. This aspect of the history of Christian missions is noteworthy, because it was the Koreans themselves who initiated the spread of Catholicism and who first performed many functions of the church.

The first priest to arrive in Korea was Chinese and his arrival in 1795 facilitated further growth in membership, which increased from 4000 in 1795 to 10 000 in 1801. The new religion, however, was subjected to severe persecutions in the nineteenth century. Most intellectuals and government officials were against Catholicism, believing that it was a threat to the basis of a Confucian society. They thought that many elements of Christian doctrine conflicted with the basic ethical and ritual principles of Confucianism. The most controversial issue at the time was the question of *jesa*, the time-honored rituals of ancestor worship. The Catholics considered ancestor worship to be an act of idolatry prohibited by God in the First Commandment. Accordingly, the instruction from the Bishop in China was that Christians must not participate in those rites. This not only caused many Koreans to avoid Catholicism, but also provoked the government to strictly ban Catholicism. A series of persecutions in the nineteenth century followed, resulting in the martyrdom of nearly 9000 Catholics.

The Protestant beginning

The introduction and initial success of Protestantism in Korea had been much smoother. At the height of missionary expansion in East Asia in the late nineteenth century, Korea emerged naturally as a fertile ground for missionary efforts, especially as an extension of China and Japan mission fields. The major impetus for the initial missionary work in Korea came from the United States. The Board of Foreign Missions of the Presbyterian Church and the Foreign Missionary Society of the Methodist Episcopal Church were the first mission bodies to begin missionary work in Korea. While both mission bodies had arranged missionaries to be sent to Korea in the latter half of 1884, it was Dr. Horace N. Allen of the Presbyterian Church who, as physician to the American and other foreign diplomatic missions in Seoul, arrived first in September.

Over the next decade, missionaries from other U.S. mission bodies as well as from Canada and England arrived. While the arrival of the missionaries was an event in itself for a country that remained a "hermit kingdom" for centuries, even more remarkable development was the warm reception accorded to the new religion by the host society. This was in part due to the country's fear of losing its sovereignty. After centuries of self-imposed isolation, except for limited cultural and commercial contacts with China, Korea was forced open by the Japanese in 1876. That marked the beginning of Korea's vulnerability to outside forces. Its neighbors – China, Japan, and Russia – vied for the control of the peninsula and even a major war was fought between China and Japan from 1894 to 1895 in Korea. The Korean government naturally feared that the nation's sovereignty was in jeopardy and thought that the national salvation lay in courting the favour of strong Western powers, such as the United States and Britain, from which most of the missionaries came. In particular, the government concluded that it was desirable to welcome the missionaries and their religion, which were an integral part of the American presence in Korea at the time, in order to build a stronger relationship with the powerful United States. The government was also anxious to provide Western medical relief for people suffering from repeated epidemics and other physical ills. The provision of Western education, which was to inspire technological and economic progress, was likewise high on the government's agenda. The fact that the Americans were not connected with Western imperialism in the region at the time further contributed to the good will of the Korean government. As Lakgeoon

George Paik, a noted historian of missionary efforts in Korea, wrote: "the employment of American advisers to the chief departments of the government, the request for American teachers for government schools, repeated declarations of friendship and confidence by the Korean legation at Washington, and the employment of American engineers to open mines, gave proof of the amicable feeling of the peninsular kingdom toward the American nation."[1]

Indigenous Christian Leaders, Past and Present

Catholic leaders

In May of 1984 during the bicentennial commemoration of Korean Catholicism, Pope John Paul II canonized 103 of the martyrs – seven of whom were European Jesuits – making Korea the fourth in the world in the total number of saints. Out of these martyrs, the most celebrated figure is Saint Andrew Kim Tae-gon, who was Korea's first native priest. He was born in 1821 from a noble family and his family was among the early converts to Catholicism. In fact, his great-grandfather was martyred in 1814, while his father met the same fate in 1839. In 1836, when he was 15, he left Korea to study at a seminary in Macau, where he stayed for six years. Before being ordained, he left for Korea, but was unable to enter the country, for it had maintained a very strong anti-Catholic stance and had been carrying out ruthless persecutions. He finished his study under the auspices of a priest stationed in China and was ordained in Shanghai in August 1845. He then secretly returned to Korea to evangelize. On June 5, 1846, he was apprehended for teaching an "evil learning" against Neo-Confucianism. On September 16, he was tortured and beheaded. Since his martyrdom, Saint Kim has been revered as the most important symbolic figure of the resilience and vibrancy of Korean Catholicism. Unlike Korean Protestantism that was introduced and proselytized by the missionaries, Korean Catholicism has been built on the spirit of martyrdom – Korean Catholics accepted and kept their faith through their blood and death – and Saint Kim has been the core of this spirit for both the laity and priests. That is why his statue is found on the ground or inside of many Korean Catholic churches and people bow to the statue in the same pious way as they do in front of the statues of Jesus Christ and Mother Mary.

Besides Saint Kim, the other notable figure in Korean Catholicism is Cardinal Kim Suhan who received the red hat in 1969 and who served as the spiritual leader of Korean Catholics for nearly four decades. Korea's second Cardinal, Chung Jinsuk, was appointed to that rank in 2006 and has since shared the leadership of Korean Catholics.

Protestant leaders

In the history of Christianity in Korea, one of the most prominent charismatic leaders was Gil Sunjoo (1869–1935), whose influence is still widely felt in the lives of many Korean Christians. As the first ordained Presbyterian minister and as a leading revivalist throughout his life, Gil helped to shape the establishment of Christianity in Korea. He was, for example, instrumental in launching the first nation-wide revival meeting, i.e., the Great Revival of 1907, and was a leading proponent of revival meetings, for which he traveled tirelessly across the country. Gil was also very enthusiastic about prayer, rising early in the morning everyday to "wait on the Lord." The dawn prayer or *saebyeokgido* was so elating for him that he invited anyone who wanted it to join with him in prayer. The church bell rung at dawn and many came, heralding the beginning of the dawn prayer meeting which became a regular and unique feature of the Korean Christian life ever since. Another Christian tradition that Gil launched is the ever popular *tongsong gido* (speaking out one's prayer in unison with others), which was initiated in the revival of 1907. As a political activist, moreover, Gil was prominent in the movement for independence – he was one of the 33 signers of the Korean Declaration of Independence – during the Japanese colonial period (1910–1945).

Following in the footstep of the pioneering evangelist Gil Sunjoo was Kim Ikdu (1874–1950), the most dynamic evangelist during the Japanese colonial period, particularly during the 1920s and 1930s. Kim is best known for his healing ministry. After his ordination to the ministry in 1910, Kim performed a couple of healing "miracles," the first of which involved his wife who had a running sore on her neck. She had been treated at the Mission hospital for three years, but to no avail. As the last resort, Kim and his wife prayed for several days for healing, and within two weeks she was completely cured of the disease. This healing not only marked the beginning of a new era for Kim's charismatic leadership, but also forever changed and forged a new direction of evangelism in Korea, namely the institutionalization of healing ministry as one of the most effective means of evangelism. His fame spread quickly and hundreds of sick people from all over Korea came to his meetings, seeking his healing ministry. In Seoul in 1920, for example, his meetings attracted over six thousand people each day. Besides his faith-healing ministry, his preaching was sought eagerly by a wide audience. Partly out of his own life experience, his sermons usually emphasized humility, sacrifice, and the dignity of the poor. Kim's messages were also predominantly oriented toward life after death – he often commented that the end of the present social order would be the final judgment of God – and his vision of the Paradise was enthusiastically espoused by the underprivileged.

Another noteworthy pastor was Yi Yongdo (1900–1933) who, as a Christian mystic and as a revivalist, almost equalled the popularity of Kim

Ikdu. Yi's decisive Christian experience occurred during his seminary education in 1925, when he suffered a severe case of tuberculosis. After a powerful mystical experience during a revival meeting, he fully recovered from the disease. Henceforth, the concept of "a joyous living in dying" or "dying daily" guided Yi's way of life and his theology. He began to describe God's love in terms of the suffering of Jesus Christ on the cross. For Yi, his own physical suffering from tuberculosis became a symbol for the Christian suffering and for the suffering of the Korean people under the Japanese rule. To endure pain and to suffer as Jesus did was to become a Jesus-like person, truly manifesting the spirit of Christian life. In fact, Yi preached that the most assured means of salvation was to suffer like Jesus Christ, a salvation through the acceptance of pain and death. By 1925, Yi became widely popular in Korea, as the followers appreciated his suffering-Jesus mysticism because it dignified their own personal sufferings – Jesus Christ, God manifested in man, too, was poor and suffered just the same. Even today, Yi's mysticism is one prevalent form of Christian expression among the Korean churches. For example, certain features characteristic of the new Christian sectarian movement, including the Moon's Unification Church, can be traced to Yi's emphases on the dignity of the human suffering and God's unlimited love. In this sense, Yi's mysticism must be recognized not only for being one of the most unique and influential attempts to give Christianity a genuine Korean expression but also for recognizing the salvific potential of suffering.

Christianity as an Agency of Modernization

From early on, Christianity, both Catholicism and Protestantism, provided the first and most continuous impetus to modernization in Korea.[2] In education, the missionaries were the first to establish a complete system of education, from kindergarten to college, and they were the first to implement modern curriculum in schools, including modern science and medical science. Through the sponsorship of the missionaries, moreover, many Koreans were sent abroad to be educated, particularly to the United States. Many renowned scholars and politicians of modern Korea, including the nation's first president Rhee Syngman, were beneficiaries of such program. By the end of the nineteenth century, the schools established by the missionaries were found practically all over the country and numbered over 400. Taking over from the missionaries, both the Protestant and Catholic Churches have been committed to enriching the educational life of Koreans, operating dozens of schools at all levels, including some of the nation's top universities such as Ewha Women's University, Sogang University and Yonsei University. Today, local churches also operate large numbers of educational programs that amount to continuing education, offering day or night courses on subjects ranging from theology and philosophy to consumer rights and English conversation.

Socially, it was the missionaries who first provided Western medical care to the masses who had no other recourse. The administration of vaccination and provision of medical care in practically all the mission fields, i.e., nearly every town on the peninsula, easily earned the missionaries the highest respect and admiration. Christian organizations have since built a considerable number of large hospitals, many of which are affiliated with Christian universities. In addition, it was the missionaries who introduced institutional philanthropy by founding the nation's first orphanages as well as schools for the blind, and Korean churches, particularly the Catholic, have followed in their footsteps by operating an estimated two thousand-plus welfare centers all across the country, including those for the poor, orphans, abandoned children, the elderly, and the mentally- or physically-challenged. In fact, Christian organizations are the largest non-governmental contributors to philanthropic causes in Korea, operating more welfare institutions than any other organization, governmental or nongovernmental. The services they provide include, among others, meal provisions for the homeless and poor elderly, recreation and continuing education for the elderly, scholarships for poor children, free or subsidized daycare centers for the poor, vocational training, and job placement services. Christian organizations also provide an extensive array of counselling services, including those related to jobs, marital or family problems, juvenile delinquency, and teenage pregnancy. The government, unable to meet the rising demand for these welfare services, has warmly welcomed such active involvement of religious bodies in welfare services by providing financial support.

Politically, Koreans first became acquainted with several key values that mark modernity, such as freedom, human rights, democracy and equality, largely through Christianity. The prominence of Christians in politics throughout the last hundred years, either in the independence movement or in the democratic movement, have added further impetus to such a connection. Indeed, the role of Christianity in the nation's democratization process cannot be underestimated. Against the unprecedented socio- political role of the military and its oppressive rule – which goes back to South Korea's first administration of Rhee Syngman from 1948 to 1960, and which became most severe during the Park Chung Hee's regime from 1961 to 1979 – Christian organizations, especially the Catholic Church, became the strongest supporters of the democratic movement. Such prominent religious groups, as the Catholic Priests' Association for Justice and the National Council of Churches in Korea, played eminent roles in championing democracy during the 1970s and 1980s. These groups and many churches functioned as primary institutional centers for the movement, collectively questioning the regime's

commitment to human rights and democracy, and confronting the government over human rights abuses and political oppression. This is not to say that
the Christian organizations' stance against the military regimes had been
unequivocal, for many large, conservative Protestant churches had maintained neutrality or even a passive support of the authoritarian regimes.
Korean Christian groups as a whole, however, represented, along with
university student associations and labor unions, the only major organizations to oppose the policies and decisions of the authoritarian regimes. And it
was during this period of oppressive political rule that a Korean form of
liberation theology called *minjungsinhak*, literally meaning the "theology of
the people," became a towering symbol of the rally for democracy, equality,
social justice, and human rights.[3] Like other variants of liberation theology,
minjungsinhak views the struggle for democracy, justice and equality as a
spiritual struggle to realize God's kingdom on earth. Accordingly, the
proponents of the theology became engaged in a variety of religiously based
social activities to remedy social injustice and inequalities.

Because the Church provided the basic tools of modernization and assumed
a central role in the economic, political, and social modernization of South
Korea, many Koreans viewed the acceptance of the Gospel not only as a
means of entry into modern society but also as an access to what is believed to
be a more advanced civilization. In this way, Christianity held out a vision of
how things might or ought to be, and in due time, conversion to Christianity
came to mean enlightenment, inspiring the proselytized to do away with
many superstitious or backward aspects of their traditional worldview and
behavior. The identification of Christianity as a gateway to modernity and
success, both personal and national, acquired even more impetus during the
period of rapid economic development from the early 1960s and the end of
1980s. Koreans' admiration of Western culture and its economic achievements played a decisive role in encouraging such identification.

The Christianity-modernization nexus has been further strengthened by
the fact that a disproportionate number of Christians have held positions of
power and influence following the country's liberation from Japan in 1945.
From the leaders of the independence movement to the current political
leadership, Christians have always been conspicuously salient in the nation's
politics. For example, between 1952 and 1962 nearly one third of political
leadership consisted of Christian, an astonishing figure given the fact that only
about four per cent of the Korean population was Christian during the same
period. The prominence of Christians at all levels of government, paralleled
by the conspicuous presence of Christians in the academic, economic and
social leadership, continued unabated for the next three decades. In particular, the election of Kim Youngsam, a Presbyterian elder, as the nation's
President in 1993 is a compelling manifestation of the vitality of Christianity
in South Korea. His immediate successor, President Kim Dae Jung, is also

Christian, more specifically Catholic. His presidency means, among other things, that the country for the first time had a Roman Catholic president.

The Rise of Christianity Amidst Rapid Industrialization and Urbanization

As insinuated above, the period of greatest growth for Christianity in South Korea was from the early 1960s through to the end of the 1980s, during which the nation underwent a rapid urbanization and achieved remarkable economic growth. In grappling with the potential factors that account for such dramatic growth of Christianity, it is evident that social and social-psychological conditions characteristic of the modern development period, such as the breakdown of traditional values owing to modernization, the widespread anxiety due to the rapidity of social changes, and the profound sense of deprivation over continuing poverty and economic disparity, seem to have been crucial. Rapid industrialization, modernization and urbanization have engendered social chaos and produced a social-psychological condition of *anomie*, depriving the people of a feeling of community and burdening them with urban anxiety and stress, such as competition, avarice, residential congestion, and moral disorder. In particular, industrialization attracted a massive internal migration from the impoverished agrarian countryside, and subsequent massive rural-urban migration not only produced a class of people who were removed from their birthplace but also greatly undermined the traditional values and extended family structure that were the basis of rural stability and communal life.

Such feeling of urban anxiety provided the psychological stimulus for many South Koreans to seek spiritual security and fellowship in Christianity. They turned to Christianity not only because it had the most sympathetic and resourceful organization but also because it offered a network of communal support. Church attendance and involvement with church activities, such as Bible study, various intra-church groups, and "area or home service," provided communal or associational ties that furnished social solidarity and created a sense of community among the new believers. Indeed, churches became "havens for the masses," and grouping into small units (i.e., cell groups) became a very useful means of retaining personal relationships and staving off the impersonality of the wider society. Such personal networks, through which members "exchanged" help, material resources, affection and loyalty, ensured the continuation of mutual help, feelings of reassurance, and socio-psychological security. The church's provision of communal networks was significant particularly in light of the traditional proclivity of Koreans to seek "personal community" in social interactions and everyday matters. As Wan-sang Han argues, the appeal of the Church derived largely from its role as a community, particularly its provision of communal feelings, including *we-feeling* (sense of belonging), *role-feeling* (sense of role-playing), and *dependency-feeling* (sense of security) as well as *hope-feeling*.[4] Koreans' endeavor to regain a sense of identity also galvanized large numbers to accept Christianity. In this sense, we can conceptualize the rise of Protestant Christianity in South Korea as people's reaction to the complexity and the rapidity of social change in the last four decades as well as their endeavor to regain a sense of identity and community.

This-Worldly Orientation of Korean Protestantism

In addition to social factors, the rise of Protestant Christianity in Korea has been facilitated by its adoption of certain features of shamanism, a folk religion which, along with Confucianism, is often identified as having shaped the worldview and mental landscape of Koreans. In particular, its emphasis on the fulfillment of material wishes through prayers or through communication with spirits has been a key message of many Protestant churches in Korea (Kim, 2000a). Protestant churches have advanced the belief that Christianity, as a faith that believes in the omnipotence of God, is a religion that would yield prosperity for the converts. The early missionaries also portrayed the supreme deity of Christianity as a merciful god who attends to all kinds of human need. To that effect, God was most conspicuously characterized as the Savior, an image emphasized through references to biblical verses, especially the anecdotes of miracles, that asserted the omnipotence of God. Korean prayer books also largely depict God as a wish-granting entity to whom one turns to in times of need: one can be liberated from suffering, attain salvation, be healed or receive consolation through the power of God. Reiterated through biblical verses and prayer books, therefore, the image of God as the Savior, the messiah, the liberator has served as a "selling point" *par excellence* for Protestant Christianity. For many Christians, therefore, this emphasis on the fulfilment of practical wishes through faith in God has represented the essence of their religion. An acceptance of the Gospel is simply viewed as a means of improving their social and financial standing and attaining advantages in an unfamiliar social context.

The outstanding example of Korean Christianity catering to the shamanic tendencies of the traditional belief system is the Yoido Full Gospel Church, the world's largest church with more than 500 000 members today. The church's evangelical slogan that has attracted large audiences – and inspired other churches to emulate – is the threefold blessings of Christ, i.e., health, prosperity and salvation, contained within the second verse of the third Epistle of John. Preaching the "theology of prosperity," Pastor Paul Yonggi Cho and his imitators have advanced the idea that the acceptance of the Holy Spirit can mean that one is, besides being blessed with salvation in the next life, graced with health and materialistic successes in this world. These pastors have also maintained that illness, poverty, business failure or any other misfortune is simply due to sin and spiritual impurity.

Accordingly, many Christians associate the purpose of offerings with secular blessings. There are various types of offering, but most, if not all, are intimately linked with wish-fulfilment. *Sowonhongeum* or the "offering of petition" with which Protestant Christians regularly dedicate, in an envelope, money and a list of wishes to be prayed for is one of the most utilized forms of offering. *Gamsahongeum* or the "offering of gratitude" also exemplifies this-worldly orientation of Christian life, for many Korean Christians, both Catholic and Protestant, contribute money to their churches whenever "good fortunes" occur – e.g., birth of sons, sons and daughters passing the university entrance examination, prosperous business or the return of health – all in an attempt to express their gratitude to God and to ensure the continuation of God's blessings.

Individual Religiosity of Christians

As regards the religiosity of Korean Catholics and Protestants, they are second to none. For example, 1989–1991 surveys of religious activities in 18 countries, including the United States, England, Hungary and Australia, showed that about 68 percent and nearly 74 percent of Korean Catholics and Protestants, respectively, attended church each Sunday. The figure for the Protestants was the highest by far among the 18 countries, while the result for the Catholics was the second highest after Northern Ireland.[5] Korean Christians' high religiosity is also demonstrated in the frequency of prayer and scripture-reading. According to the 1997 Gallup survey, 64 % of Korean Protestants and 41% of their Catholic counterparts prayed at least once a day, and more than 50% of the former, compared to nearly 34 percent of the latter, were found to read religious scriptures more than once a week, all of which were among the highest in the world.[6]

The Future of Christianity in Korea

Statistical data show that Christian expansion may have reached a plateau in Korea after decades of remarkable growth. The question then is: What is the future of Christianity in Korea? Will it follow the way of the industrialized countries where the level of church membership, Christian organizations' political and social influence, and the level of religiosity have all declined? Based on current trends, it is safe to say that even though Koreans are likely to become less institutionally committed, the decline of Christianity will be minimal. That is because the rapid growth of Christianity in Korea in the last three decades has begun to slow down only recently, and the rapid growth of a given religion in a short period of time is usually followed by a long period of slow growth and stability. Another reason for optimism pertains to the strength and dynamism of Korean Christianity, which will continue to exert powerful influences on the people's thought and behavior. The ever-growing presence of Christian organizations and their enterprises, both charitable and commercial, is another reason to believe that Christianity in Korean society will continue to expand its influence into virtually sphere of society.

Notes

1. Paik, G.L.G. *The History of Protestant Missions in Korea, 1832–1910*, 2nd ed. Seoul: Yonsei University Press, 1971, p. 162.
2. Kim, A.E. "Christianity, Shamanism, and modernization in South Korea," *Cross Currents*, 50:1–2, 2000, 112–119.
3. The Commission on Theological Concerns of the Christian Conference of Asia *Minjung Theology: People as the Subject of History*, Maryknoll, New York: Orbis Books, 1981.
4. Han, W.-s. "A sociological study of the rapid growth of the church," in Christian Academy (ed.) *Hanguk Kyohoe sôngnyông undongûi hyônsanggwa kujo* [*A Study on the Pentecostal Movement in Korea*], Seoul: Taehwa, 1981.
5. Gallup Korea, *Religion in Korea*, Seoul: Gallup Korea, 1998, pp. 216–217.
6. Gallup Korea, *Religion in Korea*, Seoul: Gallup Korea, 1998, pp. 88–89.

Further Reading

The Commission on Theological Concerns of the Christian Conference of Asia *Minjung Theology: People as the Subject of History*, Maryknoll, New York: Orbis Books, 1981.

Gallup Korea *Religion in Korea*, Seoul: Gallup Korea, 1998.

Han, W.-s. "A sociological study of the rapid growth of the church," in Christian Academy (ed.) *Hanguk Kyohoe sôngnyông undongûi hyônsanggwa kujo* [*A Study on the Pentecostal Movement in Korea*], Seoul: Taehwa, 1981.

Kim, A.E. "Korean religious culture and its affinity to Christianity: The rise of Protestant Christianity in South Korea," *Sociology of Religion*, **61**:2, 2000, 117–133.

Kim, A.E. "Christianity, Shamanism, and modernization in South Korea," *Cross Currents*, **50**:1–2, 2000, 112–119.

Korea Research Institute of Religion and Society *Hanguk chonggyo yeongam* [*A Yearbook of Korean Religions*], Seoul: Korea Research Institute of Religion and Society, 1993.

Ministry of Culture and Information Affairs *Chonggyo beopin mit dnche hyeonwhang* [*Current Status of Religious Organizations*], 1977.

National Statistical Office *Ingumit jutaek chongjosa* [*National Census*], 1987, 1991, 1997, 2006.

Paik, G.L.G. *The History of Protestant Missions in Korea, 1832–1910*, 2nd ed. Seoul: Yonsei University Press, 1971.

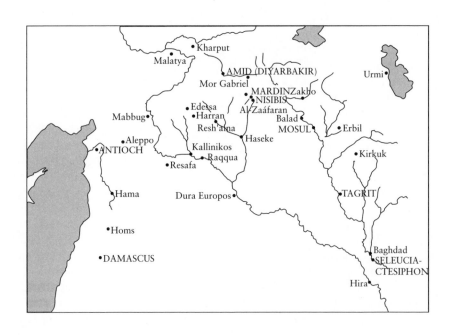

12

The Middle East

Lois Farag

Christianity is a Middle Eastern religion. Christ was born in the Middle East and the Judaic roots of Christianity are very much connected to the history of this part of the world. Christianity is indigenous to the Middle East and has a two-thousand-year history there. Christians of the Middle East are the Christians of the birthplace of Christianity. The culture, history, and identity of the region shaped and were shaped by Christianity.

Christians of the Middle East were and are multi-lingual and multi-cultural. They spoke Aramaic in its different dialects together with Greek, and after the Arab invasion, they speak Aramaic and Arabic. Thus, the early church in the Middle East is an Aramaic-speaking church. As a native of Palestine, Christ spoke primarily Aramaic in his daily life. The early Christian converts were Aramaic-speaking and the first churches, Jerusalem followed by the church in Antioch-Syria, were made up of Aramaic speakers. Christians, Jews and other religious groups in the region all used dialects of Aramaic. There are surviving documents in Jewish Aramaic, with Palestinian and Babylonian dialects, Samaritan Aramaic, Christian Palestinian Aramaic, and the Aramaic of Edessa which later came to be called Syriac. Syriac was the Aramaic dialect that came to be associated with Christianity. In the Middle East, Syriac Christians are found in present-day Syria, Lebanon, Israel, Palestine, Jordan, Iraq, southern Turkey, and Iran. These political divisions are recent and I hope the reader will think about the Christians of these countries beyond the modern political boundaries. The Syriac-speaking Church in its various traditions is the primary subject of this chapter. Under this heading I will discuss the Syriac Orthodox Church of Antioch, the Church of the East, the churches in Arabia, and the Maronite Church. I will also briefly discuss the Armenian Church in the Middle East.

One final note. "Middle East" as understood in this chapter encompasses the countries listed above. It should be noted, however, that Middle East-erners and the Middle East Council of Churches consider Christians of the Middle East to include The Coptic Orthodox Church in Egypt, with the

Christianities in Asia, edited by Peter C. Phan © 2011 Blackwell Publishing Ltd except for editorial material and organization © 2011 Peter C. Phan

closely related Ethiopian Orthodox Church, and the Armenian Churches of Lebanon and Jerusalem. The artificial elimination of the Coptic Orthodox Church, the largest Christian Church in the Middle East, is to conform to the subject matter of the book and limit the Middle East to its Asian component. It is artificial because the theology of the Coptic Orthodox Church strongly influenced the history and structure of the Syriac Church as we will observe in this chapter. Another artificial elimination is of the Syriac Churches in India, which are strongly rooted in the Syriac tradition. There are six of these Syriac Indian Churches: The Malankara Syrian Orthodox Church, the Malankara Orthodox Syrian Church, and the Malabar Independent Syrian Church, all affiliated with the Syriac Orthodox Church of Antioch; the Malankara Catholic Church, affiliated with the Syrian Catholic Church; and the Syro-Malabar Church affiliated with the Roman Catholic Church. The chapter is limited to the Syriac Churches in the Middle East, leaving the Churches of India to be part of the Indian historical mosaic. In addition, this chapter will not discuss the various Melkite Churches in the Middle East, which are affiliated with Constantinople. Their religious history belongs more to Byzantine than to Middle Eastern history. Interest in these churches can be pursued through the history of the Byzantine Church.

The Syriac Orthodox Church of Antioch

Christianity began in Jerusalem on the day of Pentecost. Apostolic evangelization beginning from Jerusalem spread to Ceasarea Palestine and other minor cities such as Ascalon and Gaza, thus laying the foundation of the Church of Jerusalem, which included present-day Israel/Palestine in its jurisdiction. From Jerusalem, Christianity spread to Antioch. According to the historian Eusebius of Caesarea and Syriac Church tradition, Peter the Apostle evangelized in Antioch in the year 37 and instituted the Antiochian Apostolic See, one of the first apostolic churches in Christianity. The first nucleus of the Church was among the Aramaic speaking population. The Book of Acts tells us that "it was in Antioch that the disciples were first called 'Christians.'" (Acts 11:26) Antioch was a major city and the capital of the Syriac-speaking region. From Antioch, the rest of the Syriac-speaking provinces received the Christian message, in addition to Cyprus, Asia Minor, and Greece. We know that by the year 325, when the Council of Nicea convened, the Syrian province was represented in the Council by 23 bishops. These bishops represented rural as well as urban areas, an indication of the spread of Christianity beyond urban centers. Legend maintains that Christianity spread east of the Euphrates through Addai, a disciple of Thomas the Apostle, who converted King Abgar V of the Osrhoene Kingdom to Christianity after healing him from leprosy.

From the early missionary activities and because of the political structures of the ancient world, the Syriac-speaking church was divided into an East Syriac tradition with its ecclesiastical leadership in Seleucia-Ctesiphon – the capital of the Persian Empire and east of the Euphrates – and a West Syriac tradition whose ecclesiastical leadership was in Antioch, within the Roman Empire. This political division would later be aggravated by divisions along theological lines. Theological debates have always been part of church history. Beginning with the fourth century, the theological debates about the nature of Christ, especially the Nestorian, Eutychian, and Chalcedonian debates, became defining moments in the history of the Syriac Church.

Nestorius was a monk from Antioch who acquired fame for his preaching. When in 428 the see of Constantinople became vacant, Theodosius II invited Nestorius to be the bishop of the capital city. Nestorius gave a series of sermons in Constantinople asserting that the Virgin Mary could not be called *Theotokos* – Bearer and Mother of God. His theological reasoning was that the divine person, the Word, was indwelling the human person of the man named Jesus. The Virgin Mary gave birth to the human person Jesus, not the Incarnate Son of God, and hence should be called *Christotokos*. This was based on his understanding of Christ as two separate persons, the divine person and the human person. The two persons were in conjunction and had one will. Soon these teachings reached Cyril, pope of the Church of Alexandria in Egypt, who responded with a letter, accompanied by 12 anathemas, explaining the faith of the church. Nestorius refused to reconsider his teachings. The Emperor Theodosius called for a council to convene at Ephesus in 431. Basing itself on the orthodox theological articulation of the letter of Cyril of Alexandria, the council condemned Nestorius and his teachings. Nestorius was exiled. Segments of the Syriac Church, especially east of the Euphrates, did not accept the Council of Ephesus and became very active in Persian territories. The debate sometimes became violent and led to the separation of what came to be known historically as "The Nestorian Church," which is now known as "The Church of the East." "East" in the title indicates east of the Roman Empire. This marked the first division along theological lines within the Syriac-speaking church.

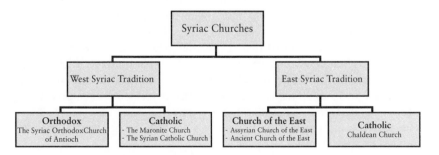

Eutyches (378–454) was the archimandrite (head) of a large monastery in Constantinople. In response to the Nestorian teachings, he sought to assert the unity of the person of Christ by teaching that there is one nature in Christ and this one nature is not consubstantial with humanity. This teaching was condemned by the universal church and came to be dubbed "Monophysitism." There are no churches at present that follow such teachings. In response to Eutyches' teachings Leo, the pope of Rome, in a famous letter (*The Tome of Leo*) proposed the formula of two natures united in the one person of Christ. In 451 the Emperor Marcian called the Council of Chalcedon, which unanimously condemned Eutyches' teachings. The council wrote a statement of faith that came to be known as the "Chalcedonian Definition." This definition proposed two natures in the one person of Christ in accordance with Leo's teaching. The Church of Alexandria (The Coptic Orthodox Church of Egypt) and the Church of Antioch (the West Syriac Church) rejected such a definition and asserted instead Cyril of Alexandria's formula of "the one nature of God the Word Incarnate." These churches wanted to ensure the unity of Christ against Nestorianism. They taught that after the incarnation and the unity of the two natures in the one person of Christ, we should not separate or divide (against Nestorius) or confuse (against Eutyches) the natures. The Alexandrian and the Antiochian Churches accused the Churches of Rome and Constantinople of asserting Nestorian theology by dividing the Son into two. The Churches of Rome and Constantinople accused the Alexandrian and the Antiochian Churches of confusing the natures like Eutyches. This marked the second major division in the Christian Church; essentially it was a division between the major apostolic churches of Christianity.

The following two centuries witnessed many attempts to reconcile the two groups, which we now call Dyophysite Chalcedonian churches (Rome and Constantinople) and Miaphysite non-Chalcedonian Churches (Alexandria and Antioch). The Miaphysite churches are sometimes referred to as Monophysite or Jacobite. These terms are pejorative and are not used anymore. The Chalcedonian churches came to be called Melkite (following the king) because they were affiliated with the see of Constantinople, were strongly supported by the emperor, and followed imperial theology. Because of imperial opposition, the Syriac Orthodox faithful suffered oppressive persecutions in which the hierarchy along with thousands of believers suffered imprisonment, exile, or martyrdom. This oppressive situation lasted from 451 until 636, when Arab Muslims invaded Mesopotamia and ended Byzantine rule with the accompanying persecution. This marked the beginning of a new era for the Syriac churches (in their diverse traditions), which has lasted up to the present day: to be under Islamic rule. Christians under Islam became isolated from Christians of the West. Eventually, the West came to disregard the existence of the ancient apostolic Syriac church that was founded by Peter himself.

The Islamic era had its own challenges for Christians. The Syriac Christians were no longer facing an oppressive Byzantine rule that challenged their theological understanding, but rather a new political system that challenged their faith itself. Within a few decades of Islamic rule, Christians were reduced to dhimmitude (indigenous non-Muslims given certain protection under Islamic law) in their own native lands. They suffered from oppressive conditions such as excessive taxation, as well as a loss of political rights and religious freedom. The suffering was compounded when in the eleventh century the First Crusade (1095–1204) invaded Antioch (1098) and Jerusalem (1099). The Muslim rulers accused native Christians of treason, suspecting them of collaborating with the invading coreligionist armies; on the other hand, the Crusaders did not recognize any Christian not submitting to Rome. The Syriac Christians suffered excessive loss of life from both armies in addition to the plunder of church treasures by the Crusaders. The Crusades marked the beginning of continuous attempts by Rome to subordinate all Christians in the East to the pope of Rome.

The Arab invasion began a series of Islamic dynasties. The Arab Umayyads (661–750) ruled from Damascus, followed by the Abbasids (750–1517) ruling from Baghdad, who in turn lost their power to the Ottomans. Even while the Abbasids were officially in power, different, competing dynasties were the actual rulers, including the Fatimids (969–1070), the Seljuks and the Crusaders (1099–1187), the Ayyubids (1171–1250) and the Mamluks (1250–1517). Further catastrophes hit the Syriac Orthodox Church in the fourteenth century with the massacres by the invading Mongul armies led by Timur Leng (Tamerlane). The Church was further weakened when in 1783 the Roman Catholic Church ordained a patriarch in Aleppo, who in 1830 was recognized by the Ottomans, creating a separate Syriac Catholic Church. The Catholic Syriac Patriarch presently resides in Beirut.

While the Ottomans were in power, the British and the French colonials were exercising their authority in the region. All these competing powers grabbed as much wealth as possible from the indigenous population, who were further impoverished with each new ruler. It should be observed that from 451 on, non-Chalcedonian churches never found an ally in the state; rather the church was a persecuted church for more than 15 centuries. This is demonstrated by the continuous relocation of the seat of the Patriarchate of the Syriac Orthodox Church, mostly for political reasons. It was first instituted in Antioch by St. Peter and remained there till 518. Continuous conquests and hardships forced the Patriarchate to relocate in monasteries in Mesopotamia; it moved to the Monastery of Mor Barsaumo during the twelfth and thirteenth centuries, and then in 1293 to the Monastery of Al-Za'afaran, five kilometers east of Mardin in Turkey, where it remained until 1933, when it moved to Homs, Syria. In 1961 it moved to its present location in Damascus, Syria. The last two relocations of the Syriac Orthodox patriarchal seat are an indication of the hardships the Christians of the Middle East endured during the twentieth century. For more than fourteen centuries the ecclesiastical hierarchy was never allowed to exert any power, political or otherwise. Because the political situation has not allowed the eastern churches to be involved in or influence political power, issues of political or social justice are not part of the theological vocabulary of eastern churches. Politics has affected the Church, but differently than its Western counterpart.

Though the political situation was not favorable to the indigenous Syriac Christians, their religious and intellectual achievement is commendable. Syriac literary production began in the first century and continues to the present. This literary activity is diverse and is the pride of the Aramaic-Syriac community. Its most significant achievement is the translation of the Old and New Testament into Syriac during the formative years of Syriac Christianity. This translation, known as the *Peshitta*, came to be the official Biblical text of Syriac Christians. The most commonly used form of the Gospel texts was the *Diatessaron*, which is the four gospel texts harmonized to form a continuous narrative. Later translations of the Bible into Syriac, from the sixth and seventh centuries, are still extant, such as the Gospels of Rabbula. These Syriac translations of the Bible became invaluable for modern Biblical scholars.

Ephrem the Syrian (306–373) is the most notable Syriac writer of the fourth century and his writings are still influential in the Syriac Church. He wrote in Syriac and his writings are characterized as representative of the Aramaic heritage without any Greek influence. He wrote primarily in verse and many of his poems are chanted to this day in Syriac liturgical services. He encouraged the establishment of a women's choir in the church to chant his hymns. He wrote in verse on various topics. His prose writings include apologetic writings against heretics and Biblical commentaries on Genesis and the *Diatessaron*. By the fourth and fifth centuries, Syriac literature was gaining prominence among the Greeks and some of the writings of Ephrem the Syrian were translated into Greek and other languages during his lifetime.

Severus of Antioch (465–538) was Patriarch of Antioch and is a pivotal theologian in the Syriac Orthodox Church. His writings include apologetic works, homilies, letters, hymns or poetry, and some liturgical compositions. His caring pastoral activity is demonstrated by his prolific letter production. He wrote more than 3759 letters, though less than 300 survived. His writings are an important expression of the Syriac theology defending the Miaphysite Christology. His homilies (124 homilies still extant) were cut short by his banishment to Egypt for the sake of the faith. Another towering figure is Jacob of Serug (451–521), who also wrote in Syriac verse, primarily on Biblical themes. He also wrote prose homilies and some of his letters are still extant. Another monumental figure is Bar Hebraeus (1226–1286), the Maphrian (metropolitan) of the East who is buried at the Monastery of Mor Matti near Mosul, Iraq, where he also resided. He wrote primarily in Syriac with a few works in Arabic. His knowledge was encyclopedic. He wrote a theological compendium, an encyclopedia of Aristotelian philosophy, a scholia on the whole Bible, an ecclesiastical history, a book of grammar, and books on the monastic life and church discipline, among many other topics. Syriac writers were most instrumental in translating and transmitting the heritage of Late Antiquity from Greek into Arabic.

The fourteenth through the nineteenth centuries were very difficult for Christians of the Middle East and literary production was very limited. The twentieth century saw an escalation in literary activity facilitated by the use of the press and modern technology. With the restrictions on printing in the Middle East, Syriac presses are now located in the West. Especially noteworthy is the press set up in 1986 at the Syriac Orthodox Monastary of St. Ephrem in Holland, which publishes Syriac liturgical texts as well as other texts.

The major means of preserving the spiritual and cultural heritage of the Syriac Orthodox Church has been monasticism. The School of Edessa was the theological center of early Syriac Christianity. When glory of the school faded because of its association with East Syrian theology, monasteries became the rallying center of the faithful. By the sixth and seventh centuries they had become the centers of learning. If all Syriac monasteries had survived, they would amount to more than a thousand. Of the remaining monasteries, the most important are the Monastery of Mor Gabriel, the Monastery of Mor Mattai, the Monastery of Al-Za'afaran, and the Monastery of St. Mark in Jerusalem.

In 1997, the Monastery of Mor Gabriel in Tur Abdin, Turkey celebrated its sixteen-hundredth anniversary. The monastery is well known as a center for manuscript copying and scholarly activity. When Simeon, the great renovator of the monastery, died in 734, there were 180 volumes in the library. Though none of these volumes survived, the library boasted many other volumes, especially during the eleventh to the thirteenth centuries. The monastery suffered from two raids (in 1393 and 1413) by Timur Leng, during the second of which only one monk survived. Raids and devastation continued to plague the monastery and by the seventeenth century it was deserted. The monastery was revived in 1834, but was again abandoned during the 1915 holocaust. It was revived again in 1919. Now, the monastery is a center for Syriac learning and provides many teachers of Syriac language.

The Monastery of Mor Mattai is located north-east of Mosul in northern Iraq. It originated in the fourth century but became prominent in the sixth and seventh centuries when it was an important center with a massive library and a residing bishop. During the Abbasid Caliphate it was the center of a substantial translation effort from Syriac and Greek into Arabic which eventually affected western civilization when these texts were in turn trans-lated into Latin. It also suffered from the Mongol raiders in 1269.

The Monastery of Al-Za'afaran is located east of Mardin, Turkey. The monastery served as the residence of the Syriac Orthodox Patriarch from 1293 to 1932. This monastery was also a literary center where many manu-scripts on various subjects were copied. In 1875, Patriarch Peter IV imported a printing press from England and installed it in the monastery. The press published many liturgical and other Syriac books.

The Monastery of St. Mark in Jerusalem is located at the site of the Last Supper. When Saladin took Jerusalem in 1187, the Syriac Orthodox Church lost all its properties. The Syriacs later regained the monastery and since the fifteenth century it has been the seat of the Syriac Orthodox Metropolitan of Jerusalem as well as a center for manuscript copying and other literary activities. There is also a monastery for nuns in Jerusalem dedicated to Mary, the Mother of God.

Monasteries are not only places of literary activity but strong spiritual centers that sustain the church spiritually and theologically. One of the important monks that the Syriac Church is especially proud of is Symeon the Stylite. He was a fifth-century saint who lived his ascetic life on a pillar, attracting many pilgrims seeking his advice. The remains of the pillar is preserved in Qal'at Sim'an. He was very influential in his time and many ascetics emulated him, especially in the West. The survival of monasticism and its role in preserving Syriac literary heritage and spirituality were due to the efforts and perseverance of generations of dedicated Syriac Orthodox Christians. The surviving literary heritage with its magnificent illuminated Bibles and other manuscripts testifies to the dedication of these Christians.

The Church of the East

The Church of the East is known as the Persian Church and also as the Nestorian Church, though the latter is considered a pejorative term and is not used any more. According to the tradition of the Church of the East, Christianity reached Mesopotamia through Addai, who arrived in Edessa and miraculously healed Abgar, the king of a small buffer state between the Roman and the Parthian Empires. Another tradition claims that Thomas the Apostle sent Addai to Edessa before traveling to India to preach the faith. One factor that might have contributed to the spread of Christianity in Mesopotamia is the presence of a strong Jewish population in Arbela (present day Erbil in Iraq). There is strong evidence of the presence of a Christian community in Arbela by 170. By the year 300 the bishop of the Persian winter capital of Seleucia-Ctesiphon (south of present-day Baghdad) was granted primacy in the Persian Church. In 410, a synod met in Seleucia-Ctesiphon and reorganized the church into six provinces. Another synod in 424 claimed independence for the church with the bishop of Seleucia-Ctesiphon assuming the rank of Catholicos. Independence, and not schism, from the Patriarch of Antioch, who was located in the Roman Empire, was asserted for good reason. The Christians of the Persian Empire were always accused of treason and siding with their coreligionists in the Roman Empire, which resulted in many persecutions and horrific massacres, in which Christians died by the thousands.

Nestorius, whose teaching was condemned in 431 at the Council of Ephesus, was a student of Theodore of Mopsuestia. The Church of the East revered the teachings and writings of Theodore as well as those of his teacher Diodore of Tarsus. The teachings of Theodore of Mopsuestia continued to be taught in the School of Edessa until 489, when Roman imperial authorities closed the school. The students and teachers who insisted on the study of Theodore of Mopsuestia fled to Persia and established a school in Nisibis, which became a theological center for the Persian Church. Because of its adherence to Theodore the Church of the East was accused of the duality of Nestorius, which the Church of the East denies. Babai the Great (551–628), the illustrious Assyrian teacher, wrote the definitive East Syrian Christology in his *Book of the Union*, which teaches that the two *qnoma* (hypostases) are unmingled but united in the *parsopa* (prosopon) of Christ. The Nestorian controversy marked the schism between the Western and Eastern Syriac Churchs, actually between the Church of the East and the rest of the Christian churches.

The sixth century witnessed a monastic revival on Mount Izla (close to Nisibis). The monastic revival was accompanied by the flourishing of monastic writers such as Sahdona, John Saba, and Isaac of Nineveh, whose writings inspired many in the Orthodox Church as well as the Roman Catholic Church. During the Abbasid rule (749–1258), the Patriarchate moved to Baghdad where Christians contributed to the advancement of the new Islamic state with monumental translations into Arabic, by Hunayn ibn Ishaq (d. 873) and others, of Greek philosophy, scientific and medical work, which would impact European knowledge of Aristotle and Greek philosophy in later centuries.

The greatest blow to the Persian Church came in the fourteenth century with the massacres by the invading Mongol armies of Timur Leng. The Church was further weakened by a division in the sixteenth century by the creation of the Chaldean Church affiliated with Rome. The twentieth century was even more dramatic. After the First World War and the murder of the Catholicos – the head of the Church of the East – the Christians fled to Baghdad seeking protection from the British mandate. After the British left (1933), the Catholicos was exiled and settled in the United States. Many members of the Church of the East followed. There are now more members of the Church of the East in the United States than in Iraq. With the current war in Iraq, we hope that there are still members of the Church of the East remaining in their homeland.

Missionary Activity of the Syriac Church

For most Christians today, regardless of denomination, the word 'missionary' conjures up images of European or North American Catholics and Protestants working – often in a culturally insensitive way – amongst the peoples of Africa, Asia, and South America. Indeed, many of the Christians of Europe and North America presume that all branches of Christianity other than their own are the products of such missionary activity, and that such churches thus date back to the sixteenth century at the earliest, but more probably to the nineteenth and twentieth centuries. Such perceptions are not only politically dangerous (allowing ancient, often pre-Islamic, communities to be caricatured as the remnants of European colonial interference), and theological detrimental (depriving world Christianity of a wealth of profound insights into the relationship of humanity with the divine), but they are also fundamentally flawed. By the early fourteenth century the most widespread church on earth was not that of Latin Christianity, which is still largely confined to western Europe, but Syriac Christianity....[1]

According to Syriac Church tradition and the apocryphal acts, St. Thomas was the first to preach Christianity in India in the year 52. Scholarly skepticism of this story dwindled with the recent discovery of Roman settlements and Roman coins in Kerala State in southwest India. By the second century there were significant Christian communities in Kerala and in the fourth century more than 70 families migrated from Edessa to Kerala. By the eighth century Persian merchants immigrated to India. With the increasing number of immigrants two Persian bishops arrived to serve the flourishing congregations. By 1504 there were 1400 churches with distinct Syriac theology and liturgical practices. Vasco da Gama arrived in India in 1498; by 1560 an inquisition was established in Goa followed by a campaign of Latinization of the Syriac Church in India. In 1599, the synod of Daimper imposed Latin theology on the Indian Church and destroyed its Syriac literary and liturgical heritage. However, by the seventeenth century some Indians separated from the Latinized church, some affiliating themselves with the Church of the East, others with the Syriac Orthodox Church of Antioch.

Christianity spread to central Asia and China through the missionary activity of the Persian Church. Bardaisan (154–222) mentions the presence of

Christians around the Caspian Sea and in northern Afghanistan. A more organized missionary activity can be found in Merv, Turkmenistan, where by the fourth century there was a well established bishopric with churches and an organized clergy offering liturgical as well as social services to local communities. We know of similar missionary activities east of the River Oxus, east of Samarkand, among the Huns of northern Bactria, Mongolia, and even among some of the Turkish tribes. Bishop Timothy I, bishop of Baghdad during the Islamic Abbasid rule, was one of the most energetic missionary bishops of the eighth century. He sent missionaries accompanied by bishops and clergy to establish and serve churches along the Silk Road and among the Turks.

The mission to China is documented on a stone monument erected in Sian-fu in 781. The Chinese account (with a few portions in Syriac) informs us of the arrival of the Syriac monk Alopen from the Church of the East at the Chinese court in 635. Emperor T'ai-Tsung granted permission for the spread of Christianity. Scripture was translated into Chinese, and monasteries were established within the imperial city. In 845, however, Emperor Wu-Tsung ordered the secularization of all monks and nuns and Christianity was no longer a favored religion. Christianity could not recover from this blow. An eleventh century traveler mentions the presence of Christians in Sian-fu, but not much was heard later about Christianity in China.

A Syriac document preserves a very interesting account of Rabban Sauma, a Uighur monk. He was sent as an emissary of the Mongolian il-Khan to Europe to safeguard an anti-Muslim alliance. When he arrived in the Middle East at the end of the thirteenth century he made a pilgrimage to Jerusalem. His companion Mark was consecrated as Yabhallaha III, patriarch of the Church of the East in Baghdad. Rabban Sauma describes his journey to Europe and his celebration of Mass, during which Pope Nicholas IV received communion. His political mission was not successful, however.

Christianity flourished in all the churches founded by the Church of the East until the Mongol invasion of Timur Leng annihilated Christianity in these areas. What survived the Mongols did not survive the Black Death of the fourteenth century.

Churches in Arabia

The Book of Acts mentions the presence of Arabs witnessing the work of the Holy Spirit on the Day of Pentecost (Acts 2:11). The establishment of churches in Arabia, however, came about through the efforts of the Syriac churches. The Arab tribes were never part of either the Roman or the Persian Empires, thus they received their Christian faith from both the West Syriac

(The Syriac Orthodox Church in the Roman Empire) and the East Syriac traditions (The Church of the East in the Persian Empire). The Roman Empire employed the Syriac Orthodox Arab tribe of Banu Ghassan to protect its frontier with Persia. The Persian Empire employed the tribe of Banu Hira, some clans of which were affiliated with the Syriac Orthodox Church while the majoritywere affiliated with the Persian Church.

We have knowledge of specific Arab tribes that were totally Christian and we also know of Arab bishops who attended various councils. The famous tribes of Banu Tanukh, Banu Taghlib, Banu Salih, Banu 'Abd al-Qays, and Jurajima (in the present day Bahrain) were all Christians. As early as the mid-third century, we hear of the bishop of Bostra who attended the trial of Paul of Samosata held at Antioch in 264. Another synod held in Antioch in 363–364 records the presence of Arab bishops. The minutes of the Council of Chalcedon (451) indicate that 18 Arab bishops were present. The Persian Church in Adiabene had a Persian bishop at Beit Katraye, which is the present-day Qatar. We also know that the Arab churches were not isolated since Eusebius of Caesarea mentions that in the third century a heresy among the Arabians led a synod to send Origen to them to discuss the points of contention.

In 542, the Arab Ghassanid King, Harith bar Gabala, requested two bishops from Empress Theodora. Theodora sent Theodorus, Bishop of Arabia, and Jacob Baradaeus, Bishop of Edessa (d. 578), who would be one of the most influential bishops of the Syriac Church, securing its survival by building up the clergy when imperial persecution after the Council of Chalcedon threatened its very existence. To secure the survival of the church, Jacob Baradaeus worked relentlessly to consecrate bishops and clergy. (It is said that he consecrated 27 bishops and 100 000 priests.) From this account we understand that the Ghassanid were affiliated with the Syriac Orthodox Church.

The Syrians are famous for their trade and Yemen was an important port linking Syria to India by trading routes through Arabia. The majority of the Christians of Yemen were Syriac Orthodox. The strategic position of Yemen led the Persian Empire to instigate some Jewish Yemenites to persecute the Christians in 519 and 523. The Christians appealed to the Orthodox king of Ethiopia who came to their rescue and in 525 appointed an Ethiopian governor over Yemen, who remained until 576 when the Persians took over. Christians in Yemen affiliated with the Persian Church were mentioned by Marco Polo in the fourteenth century.

The churches of the Arabs have contributed some saints and martyrs. The famous saints Cosmas and Damian (martyred, 303) are patron saints of medicine and pharmacy. We also have records of the martyrdom of the 300 martyrs of Najran in 520 and the persecution of the Banu Taghlib and martyrdom of their chief, Sham'ala, by Al-Walid, the Muslim caliph.

With the rise of Islam in the mid-seventh century, many of the Arab tribes, such as the Arabs of Kufa, Banu Taghlib, and Banu Tamukh, kept their faith for a century or more. With the increasing persecution, however, Christianity could not survive in the Arabian Peninsula.

The Maronite Church

The Maronites are Syriac Christians. The origin of the name "Maronites" is debated, even among the Maronites themselves. Among the many propositions, some suggest that they are named after St. Marun – a fifth-century ascetic saint – or the monastery named after him. Not much is known about St. Marun and there is not enough evidence that indicates that he founded a monastery during his lifetime, though later several monasteries were named after him.

In the seventh century, in an attempt to re-unite the empire, divided into Dyophysites and Miaphysites since the Council of Chalcedon in 451, the Emperor Heraclius (610–641) enforced the idea of Monothelitism, which attempted to attract the Dyophysites by asserting that even if there are two natures, Christ has only one will and one energy. Dyophysites, it will be remembered, adopted the definition of Chalcedon, which asserted two natures in the one person of Christ, while Miaphysites rejected Chalcedon in favor of Cyril of Alexandria's formula of "One Nature of God the Word Incarnate." Monothelitism failed to unite the two parties, but the monks of the Monastery of Marun accepted it in 629. It is still debated whether these monks were Chalcedonians or non-Chalcedonians before accepting Monothelitism.

Monothelitism remained the theology of the Byzantium Empire from the time of Heraclius until the Third Council of Constantinople in 680, when it was anathematized. By the time the Council of Constantinople convened, the Muslim Arabs had invaded the territories of all churches of Syriac tradition and the long history of isolation from churches in the West had begun. Melkite Syriac churches, cut off from Byzantium, were not fully aware of the changes happening in Constantinople, whether political or theological, and continued to follow the Chalcedonian faith with a Mono-thelite understanding. The monks of the Monastery of Marun staunchly defended Monothelitism even after it was condemned by the council in 680. During this period of isolation, the monks of the Monastery of Marun began to ordain patriarchs from their own monastery; however, they cannot be a distinguished as a separate group before the eighth century, when the Chalcedonian Melkite Church in Syria accepted the two-will doctrine of Maximus the Confessor. The Maronites began having their own leadership by 745. They later moved from Syria proper to Lebanon.

Contact between the Maronite Church and the Church of Rome began during the time of the Crusades. The Crusaders arrived in Syria in 1099. The Maronites welcomed them as allies and coreligionists and offered help, anticipating in return that the Crusaders would save them from the hardships they suffered from the Fatimids and the Seljuk Turks. In the thirteenth century, we have the first indication of direct and formal contacts between the Maronites and the Church of Rome. In 1204, Pope Innocent III (1198–1216), knowing the good relationship that existed between the Maronites and the Church of Rome, sent Cardinal Peter to Lebanon. Peter was well received and the Maronite Patriarch together with the lay people pledged submission to the Church of Rome. In 1213 al-Amshiti, the Maronite Patriarch, received an invitation to attend the Lateran Council and during his trip he gained an audience with the Pope. The Maronites received frequent envoys from Rome. But when the Crusaders were defeated and withdrew from the Middle East, contacts between Rome and the Maronites were cut off.

In the sixteenth century Rome sent Giovanni Eliano on a mission to the Maronite Church to conform the Maronite theology to that of Rome. The Eastern Syriac liturgy was replaced with the Latin-rite liturgy, Maronite liturgical books were printed in Rome, and a Maronite school was established in Rome in 1584. Jerome Dandini (1554–1634) led a second mission to the Maronites. The result of these missions was the Latinization of the Maronite Church. This Latinization included, among many other changes:

(1) Acceptance of the Chalcedonian faith and the *filioque* (the insertion of the words "and the Son" of the procession of the Holy Spirit in the Nicene-Constantinopolitan Creed).

(2) Acceptance of the idea of original sin, a notion alien to Eastern theology.

(3) The sacrament of confirmation administered separately from the sacrament of baptism. Baptism not by immersion but by pouring water over the head. Confirmation administered only by bishops.

(4) Acknowledgment of purgatory.

(5) Children no longer permitted to partake of the Eucharist. The use of unleavened bread in liturgical services.

(6) No divorce, even in the case of adultery, as was the practice of the Maronites.

(7) The name of the pope of Rome was to be mentioned in the liturgy.

(8) The Maronite patriarch could not administer any disciplinary actions without prior consent of the pope.

In 1649, Patriarch Yuhanna al-Safrari (d. 1650) placed the Maronites under French protection. The French established a consulate in Beirut. Other Christian Churches suffered a backlash from the Maronite decision. The Ottoman government became suspicious of all Christians, accused all unprotected indigenous Christians of being traitors and pro-Western, and increased persecution of these churches. In 1736, the Maronites assembled a synod in the Monastery of Louisa in Lebanon and proclaimed total submission to the Church of Rome. The political move to be under French protection and the religious move of complete submission to Rome helped preserve the Maronites and spared them much of the anguish of a persecuted minority church. At present, however, the Maronites are in search of their early Syriac identity, which was lost in the Latinization of their church. This search was encouraged by the Second Vatican Council (1962–1965).

The seventeenth century witnessed the increasing power of the Maronites. This was clear during the power struggle of Amir Milhim (d. 1568), who secured his power from the Ottoman Sultan through the intervention of the Maronite Patriarch Jirgis Amira (d. 1644). Amira pleaded to the pope of Rome on behalf of Milhim. The pope in turn contacted the king of France to assert his influence at the Sublime Porte to secure the position for Milhim. With their increasing power, the Maronites began purchasing land from the Shiites. They began moving south towards the Druze region and soon they became the majority of the population in Lebanon. The increasing political power of the Maronites was expressed by the increasing number of Maronite consuls appointed by the French kings. These consuls began to assert their power even over the Patriarch and the clergy.

In 1754, the Shihabis and the Druze Lam'i Muslim princes converted to Christianity. This enhanced the power of the Maronites even more, to the point where the chief counselor in Lebanon began to be appointed from among the Maronites. From the time of the conversion of the Shihabis, the Maronites considered Lebanon their homeland; being Lebanese began to be synonymous with being Maronite. The Maronite Church began to be the main institution reflecting the religious and even the secular ethos of Lebanon.

The Muslim Druze were also struggling to assert their power in Lebanon. With the retreat of Muhammed Ali and his Egyptian troops from Syria and the abdication of the loyal Amir Bashir II in 1840, there was a power vacuum. The Druze took the opportunity to massacre the Maronites for almost 20 years. The Ottomans were unhappy with the unrest in Lebanon and they placed Lebanon under their direct control. With the intervention of European powers, the Ottomans divided Lebanon into the northern Maronite and southern Druze regions. The discontent with this division led in April 1845 to another civil war in the south. The unrest continued and resulted into another civil war beginning on April 29, 1860. The 1860 civil war was exacerbated by foreign involvement. The French supported the Maronites, while the British, who wanted to counter France's increasing influence in the region, supported the Druze. This conflict resulted in increasing power for the Maronites. During that time they became more financially secure and politically mature. A nationalistic vision appeared of a Lebanon as the exclusive homeland of the Maronites.

During the First World War, France occupied Lebanon in accordance with an agreement with the British signed in 1916. The peace conference of 1919 discussed the destiny of the Ottoman provinces. The Lebanese demanded an autonomous rule under the French and thus were separated for the first time from Syria. In 1926 the State of Greater Lebanon was established with a constitution that diminished the power of the Maronite Patriarch in favor of the secular power of the Lebanese president. The Muslim groups in Lebanon favored union with Syria, the Greater Syria, and held a conference in 1933 to discuss this issue.

On December 25, 1935 the Maronite Patriarch Arida called for independence from France. This was welcomed by the Muslims who wanted unity with Syria. In 1936 Peirre Jumayyil established a group of Maronites called the Kata'ib (military battalion), which launched the struggle for an independent Lebanon. The situation became more complicated in 1948–1975 with the increasing number of Muslim Palestinian refugees in Lebanon and, after the Iranian revolution, with increasing influence of Shiites from Iran.

Lebanon is not religiously homogeneous. Other than the majority Maronites, there are other non-Catholic Christian churches, such as the Syriac Orthodox and Armenian Orthodox, in addition to Shiites, Sunnis, and Druze Muslims. In 1943, a National Pact was signed by all parties to establish sectarian equality in the new republic with a Christian Maronite President, a Sunni prime minister, and a Shiite president of parliament. The pact also included Lebanon as part of the Arab fold, while the Muslims had to abandon the idea of unity with Greater Syria. This pact affirmed Lebanon as a Christian nation in the midst of a majority Islamic Arab region. The pact instituted a secular Maronite entity that represents the secular aspirations of the Maronites. Since the establishment of the Maronite Church in the eighth century, it had always been the patriarch who was the leader, spokesman, and representative of the Maronites. The following decades witnessed the struggle between the secular and religious leadership of the Maronites.

The presence of a Palestinian refugee population in Lebanon, which increased with the continuous conflict in Israel, led to conflict in Lebanon. The Cairo Agreement of 1969 recognized the Palestinians as a military entity with the right to acquire arms without the knowledge of the Lebanese government. They began working to take over the Lebanese government and establish a military base in Lebanon to attack Israel. In April 12, 1975 the Palestinians attempted to assassinate the Lebanese president; the Maronite Battalions responded on the spot, beginning a civil war in Lebanon.

The Maronite Battalions attacked Palestinian strongholds in Lebanon and the Arab league sent armed forces, mostly from Syria, to settle the war. The Syrians never left. Lebanon became the battleground between different Maronite factions, the Arabs (represented by Syria), the Palestinians, and Israel. This all culminated in the destruction of Lebanon and the weakening of the only Christian state in the Middle East. The Maronite Church is the only indigenous Middle Eastern Christian Church that is supported by the state and influences the state.

The position of the Patrirach as a spokesman of a Lebanese nation has been weakened. Decades of continuous civil war made many Maronites leave their homeland. This continuous, massive emigration of Maronites has led to decreasing numbers in the Christian population, which is leading other groups to demand greater rights. The increasing power of the Iranian militia and Palestinian jihadists in Lebanon is worrying to the decreasing number of Christian Maronites who call Lebanon their homeland.

The Armenians in the Middle East

The Armenians have a long history in the Middle East, especially in Jerusalem. Their presence is felt when one enters the Church of the Resurrection (Church of the Holy Sepulcher) or when one moves around in the compound of St. James Monastery. The Armenian Quarter occupies about one sixth of the Holy City within the walls. I will begin with the inception of Christianity in Armenia and then follow its connection to the Middle East, specifically in Lebanon and Jerusalem.

Christianity arrived in Armenia during apostolic times through the preaching of St. Bartholomew and St. Thaddeus. It was Gregory the Illuminator in the fourth century, however, who transformed Armenia. Gregory healed King Triddates III (298–330) from a serious disease, which led the king and the whole Armenian nation to be baptized, making Armenia the first Christian nation. Gregory was consecrated bishop by Leo, the metropolitan bishop of Caesarea in Cappadocia, in 314. Sixty years later, however, the Armenian Church became independent of Cappadocia and the head of the Armenian Church had the title of Catholicos. The Armenians did not attend the Council of Chalcedon in 451, mostly for political reasons. In 555, however, the Armenian Church rejected the teachings of the Council of Chalcedon and thus became part of the non-Chalcedonian Miaphysite churches.

The Christianization of Armenia was accompanied by a vibrant intellectual and theological development. Mesrop Mashtots (361–440) invented the Armenian alphabet and immediately set about translating the Bible into Armenian, most probably from an Old Syriac version. An extraordinary translation campaign resulted in the translation of major patristic texts from Syriac, Greek, Coptic, and Georgian. Some of these texts survive only in their Armenian translation. For this significant Armenian literary production we are primarily indebted to the Armenian monastic movement. Armenian monasteries had scriptoriums that produced literary work with great illuminations. Many of these manuscripts are presently preserved in the Catholicosate of Antelias, the monastery of Bzoummar in Lebanon, and in Jerusalem. Christianity was the cohesive glue that united the Armenians though their difficult history and the church was the upholder of the Armenian culture and language.

Because of its geographical location, Armenia was divided between the Persian and the Roman Empires. After suffering from the Persians, the Armenians suffered from the Arabs, Turks, and Russians. The Armenian Church is divided into Catholicates, a division based on jurisdiction and not on any theological difference. Among them are the Catholicos of Jerusalem, and the Catholicos of Cilicia, in the capital Sis in modern-day Turkey. The Armenian Genocide inflicted by the Ottoman Turks in 1915 led to massive migrations of Armenians to Syria, Lebanon, Egypt, and Cyprus. The Catholicos of Cilicia is now in Antelias, which is a suburb in Beirut, Lebanon. The Armenians in these countries come under the jurisdiction of the Catholicos of Antelias and the jurisdiction of the Catholicos of Jerusalem is limited to Israel, the West Bank, and Jordan.

The presence of Armenians in Palestine has a longer history and is closely connected with pilgrimage to the Holy Land. Since the Christianization of Armenia in the first decade of the fourth century there was a constant presence of Armenian pilgrims in the Holy Land. The Armenian Church of Jerusalem and the Monastery of St. James functioned as hospices, providing accommodations and food for Armenian pilgrims. The pilgrims usually stayed three months, from the beginning of Lent till after the Feast of the Ascension. With the presence of a constant flow of pilgrims there developed strong monastic communities in Palestine, dating from the fifth century. The number of Armenian monastics in the monasteries of St. Sabbas, St. Theodosius, and St. George, led the superiors of these monasteries to establish special chapels for the Armenian monks and nuns.

This tradition of pilgrimage lasted from the fourth century till the early decades of the twentieth century when pilgrimage was hampered by the Armenian Genocide of 1915 followed by the annexation of Armenia by the Bolshevik Soviets in 1917. In the nineteenth century, Patriarch John (1850–1860) recognized the signs of the times and understood the patriarchate could not survive on pilgrimage alone, so he invested heavily in real estate. Real estate investment helped sustain the patriarchate and the strong presence of Armenians in the Middle East partially helped sustain the pilgrimage. It was completely halted by the Six Day War of 1967, however.

With the unstable conditions of the Middle East, the number of Armenians has drastically dwindled in the last three decades.

The Last Century

In the late nineteenth and early twentieth-centuries, more than 4 million Christians in Turkey fled to the Middle East, including Syriac Orthodox, members of the Church of the East, and Armenians. The massacres of 1895–1896 in Turkey affected Armenian and Syriac Orthodox Christians. It is estimated that about 105 000 Christians were killed. In 1915 another holocaust was set against the Christians in Turkey. One and a half million Armenians, one third of the Syriac Orthodox population, and over 100 000 members of the Church of the East were killed.

The last half-century has witnessed changes in the Middle East more dramatic than in all its previous history. The above-mentioned massacres, the present political instability, and continuous war in the area have led to massive emigration of Christians as never before. The conflict in Israel and Gaza, the war in Iraq, and the turmoil in Lebanon are not only daily headlines but also a reality directly affecting the Christians of the Middle East. The land that witnessed the first Christian communities in history is the land that is presently witnessing the flight of its Christians. Some of the Christian churches mentioned above have larger communities in Europe, Australia, and in North and South America than in the Middle East. Though the political situation is dire for the Christians, the spiritual revival in these lands is a story beyond belief. The Middle Eastern Christians are strengthened in their faith just as the early Church grew and flourished through the age of persecution. The story of the Christians of the Middle East is the story of a hope, perseverance, and faith that has survived and will survive against all odds.

Timeline	
37 AD	Establishment of the Syriac Church of Antioch.
154–222	Bardaisan.
306–373	Ephrem the Syrian – greatest of the Syriac Fathers and theologians.
397	Founding of the Monastery of Mor Gabriel.
424	Independence of the Church of the East.
431	Nestorius condemned.

451	Council of Chalcedon.
459	Symeon the Stylite.
459–460	Earliest Biblical Syriac manuscript – *Peshita* of Isaiah.
489	School of Edessa closed.
Sixth century	Syriac writers and theologians: Severus of Antioch and Jacob of Serug.
586	Gospel of Rabbula.
636	Arabs take over Middle East.
661–750	Umayyad Islamic rule.
750–(1517)	Abbasid Islamic rule.
Sixth to ninth centuries	Revival of East Syriac monasticism – Isaac of Nineveh, John Saba.
781	Sian-fu Syriac inscription documenting Syriac mission to China.
Eighth to ninth centuries	Syriacs lead translation movement in Baghdad.
Eleventh century	Crusades – Fatimid Islamic rule – Seljuk Islamic Turkish rule
Twelfth century	Ayyubid Islamic rule.
1258	Mongols capture Baghdad.
1286	Bar Hebraeus represents Syriac renaissance- wrote in Syriac and Arabic.
1280	Rabban Sauma and Yahbalaha III travels to the West from Beijing.

1293	Al-Za'faran becomes seat of the Syrian Orthodox Patriarchate.
1360–1405	Timur Leng invades the Middle East.
1517	Beginning of Ottoman Empire (until twentieth century).
1498	Vasco Da Gama in India.
1599	Synod of Diamper in India: beginning of Indian Church Latinization.
1895–1896	Holocaust in Turkey.
1915	Holocaust in eastern Anatolia – Turkey.
1920	French and British mandate in the Middle East.
1946	Greater Syria divided into Syria and Lebanon.
Twentieth century	Syriac massive emigrations to Europe.
1961	Seat of Syriac Orthodox Patriarchate moves from Homs to Damascus
2000	Syriac Orthodox Patriarch celebrates liturgy in the ancient church at Antioch, Turkey.

Notes

1. Bablicka-Witakowski, E., Brock, S.P., Taylor, D., and Witakowski, W. *The Hidden Pearl, The Heirs of the Ancient Aramaic Heritage*, Rome: Trans World Film Italia, 2001, p. 167.

Further Reading

Bablicka-Witakowski, E., Brock, S.P., Taylor, D., and Witakowski, W. *The Hidden Pearl, The Heirs of the Ancient Aramaic Heritage*. Rome: Trans World Film Italia, 2001.

Baumer, C. *The Church of the East, An Illustrated History of Assyrian Christianity*, London: I.B. Tauris, 2006.

Bell, G.L. *The Churches and Monasteries of the Tur 'Abdin*, London: Pindar, 1982.

Budge E.AW. (ed.) *The Monks of Kublai Khan, Emperor of China*, London: Religious Tract Society, 1928.

Der Nersessian, S. *The Armenians*, New York: Praeger, 1970.

Hollerweger, H. *Turabdin*, Linz, Austria: Friends of Turabdin, 1999.

Jansbury, M. *Jacob of Serug, On the Mother of God*, Crestville, NY: St. Vladimir Seminary Press, 1998.

McVey, K. *Ephrem the Syrian, Hymns*, Mahwah, N.J.: Paulist Press, 1989.

Mathews, E. and Amar, J. *St. Ephrem the Syrian, Selected Prose Works*, Washington, DC: The Catholic University of America Press, 1994.

Moffett, S.H. *A History of Christianity in Asia, 1, Beginnings to 1500*, San Francisco, HarperCollins, 1992.

Montgomery, J.A. *The History of Yaballaha III and of his Vicar Bar Sauma*, Piscataway, NJ: Gorgias Press, 2006.

Moosa, M. *The Maronites in History*, New York: Syracuse University Press, 1986.

Murray, R. *Symbols of Church and Kingdom, A Study in Early Syriac Tradition*, Cambridge: CUP, 1975.

Sarkissian, K. *The Council of Chalcedon and the Armenian Church*, New York: Publication of the Armenian Church Prelacy, 1975.

Shahid, I. *Byzantium and the Arabs*, 4 volumes, Washington, DC: Dumbarton Oaks Center for Byzantine Studies, 1984–1995.

Trimingham, J.S. *Christianity Among the Arabs in Pre-Islamic Times*, London: Longman Group, 1979.

Wigram, W.A. *An Introduction to the History of the Assyrian Church 100–640 A. D,*Piscataway, NJ: Gorgias Press, 2004.

Conclusion: Whither Asian Christianities?

Peter C. Phan

At the end of this book readers will no doubt wonder about the future of Asian Christianity. Even those whose concerns lie more in politics and economics than in Christianity may also be interested in this question, given the emergence of China and India as "superpowers," not to mention the important role Japan and the other "Asian Tigers" continue to play in the global economy. But even if one does not give much credit to the breathless predictions about the imminent demise of the United States as the world's only superpower and the equally breathless projection of the impending demographic explosion of Christianity in Asia, especially in China, the question of "whither Asian Christianities?" still arouses much interest and bears a close examination.

A Prospective Glance

Unfortunately a straightforward and unambiguous answer to the question about the future of Christianity in Asia is hard to come by. Asia is too vast and its Christianity too diverse to permit a comprehensive prognostication. Perhaps it is more helpful to speak of Christianity country by country. Demographically, the Philippines and East Timor will remain overwhelmingly Christian, and more specifically, Roman Catholic. The Christian population in Pakistan, Bangladesh, Burma/Myanmar, Indonesia, Malaysia, Cambodia, Laos, Thailand, Mongolia, Taiwan, and Japan will remain very small for the foreseeable future, especially in countries where religious freedom is curtailed. In India, Sri Lanka, Vietnam, Hong Kong, and Macau the presence of Christianity, albeit a minority, will remain influential in many sectors of the society, especially in education and social services, though mass

Christianities in Asia, edited by Peter C. Phan   © 2011 Blackwell Publishing Ltd except for editorial material and organization © 2011 Peter C. Phan

conversions to Christianity appear extremely unlikely. In the Republic of Korea Christianity, already about 30% of the population, is expected to enjoy a vigorous growth.

The future of Christianity in the People's Republic of China is harder to gauge. For the Catholic Church the major challenge is to unify the state-approved "Chinese Catholic Patriotic Association" and the so-called "Underground Church" that professes loyalty to the pope, in particular with regard to the appointment of bishops. Recently relations between the Holy See and the Chinese government seem to have taken a turn for the better, with the appointment of the bishops of Shanghai and Guiyang approved by both sides and with the Vatican's overtures toward establishing full diplomatic relations with China. Even though the proportion of Catholics to the total population in mainland China is still minuscule (estimated at 13 million, out of 1.3 billion, about 1%), their absolute number is still quite significant. The China Christian Council, a government-approved umbrella organization founded in 1980 for all Protestants, claimed in 2005 to have 10–15 million members, while the unofficial house churches claimed to have 30 million. Thus, the total number of Christians in China is an important factor in World Christianity, especially if the presence and activities of Evangelicals, on which statistics are notoriously unreliable, is taken into account.

Christianity in the Middle East is in an alarming situation. Because of poverty, war, and oppression the number of Christians, especially in Iraq and Israel, has dwindled precipitously. The current political, military and economic conditions in the Middle East do not bode well for Christianity. A Christian renascence appears quite unlikely in the near future.

Future Directions: A Triple Dialogue

In spite of this rather bleak prognostication, the attitude of Asian Christians is not one of resignation, much less despair. On the contrary, foreign visitors have often remarked that in the Asian churches there is a spiritual vibrancy and vitality, and where there is persecution, courage and perseverance, that are unmatched in their own churches. Comments have also been favorable on Asian Christians' church attendance and religious practices. In the Roman Catholic Church biblical and liturgical spirituality is also nourished by popular devotions. Furthermore, in a "reverse mission," many Asian churches, like the African ones, are sending missionaries abroad, especially to the West, where there is a shortage of clergy and religious.

The impact of Christianity on the world cannot of course be measured in terms of its size, just as the success of Christian mission cannot be quantified by the number of conversions. Many Asian theologians have recently reminded their fellow Christians that the essential task of Christianity is announcing and bearing witness to the reign of God, as Jesus' ministry was, and not expanding its membership and influence through conversion. Planting the church is only the means, not the end of Christian mission, the center and goal of which is the reign of God. The future of Asian Christianity then depends on how well Christians perform its basic task of witnessing to the kingdom of God. But how should this task be carried out? What concrete directions and approaches must Asian Christianity take?

Asian Christians' answer to this momentous question has been of course manifold and diverse. For some, perhaps a minority, the main and perhaps only method of Christian mission is preaching (mostly through the Bible) and its goal is conversion and baptism. For others, mainly members of the so-called mainline churches, oral preaching (proclamation) remains an essential task of Christian mission, but the modality in which it is done is dialogue, indeed a triple dialogue, that is, dialogue with the Asian peoples, especially the marginalized and impoverished among them; dialogue with Asian cultures (contextualization or interculturation); and dialogue with Asian religions (inter-faith or inter-religious dialogue).

The foremost proponent of this triple dialogue as the future directions of Asian Christianity is without doubt the Federation of the Asian Bishops' Conferences (FABC), a Roman Catholic organization.[1] Through its plenary assemblies and its various committees, the FABC has repeatedly affirmed the necessity of this triple dialogue as the way for Asian churches to become truly Asian churches. At its Seventh Plenary Assembly (Samphran, Thailand, January 3–12, 2000), with the general theme of "A Renewed Church in Asia: A Mission of Love and Service," the FABC took a retrospective glance over a quarter of a century of its life and activities and summarized its "Asian vision of a renewed Church." It is said to be composed of eight movements which constitute a sort of Asian ecclesiology. Given its central importance, the text deserves to be quoted in full:

1. A movement toward a Church of the Poor and a Church of the Young. "If we are to place ourselves at the side of the multitudes in our continent, we must in our way of life share something of their poverty," "speak out for the rights of the disadvantaged and powerless, against all forms of injustice." In this continent of the young, we must become "in them and for them, the Church of the young" (Meeting of Asian Bishops, Manila, Philippines, 1970).

2. A movement toward a "truly local Church," toward a Church "incarnate in a people, a Church indigenous and inculturated" (2 FABC Plenary Assembly, Calcutta, 1978).

3. A movement toward deep interiority so that the Church becomes a "deeply praying community whose contemplation is inserted in the context of our time and the cultures of our peoples today. Integrated

into everyday life, "authentic prayer has to engender in Christians a clear witness of service and love" (2 FABC Plenary Assembly, Calcutta, 1978).

4. A movement toward an authentic community of faith. Fully rooted in the life of the Trinity, the Church in Asia has to be a communion of communities of authentic participation and co-responsibility, one with its pastors, and linked "to other communities of faith and to the one and universal communion" of the holy Church of the Lord. The movement in Asia toward Basic Ecclesial Communities express the deep desire to be such a community of faith, love and service and to be truly a "community of communities" and open to building up Basic Human Communities (3 FABC Plenary Assembly, Bangkok, 1982).

5. A movement toward active integral evangelization, toward a new sense of mission (5 FABC Plenary Assembly, Bandung, Indonesia, 1990). We evangelize because we believe Jesus is the Lord and Savior, "the goal of human history...the joy of all hearts, and the fulfillment of all aspirations" (GS, 45). In this mission, the Church has to be a compassionate companion and partner of all Asians, a servant of the Lord and of all Asian peoples in the journey toward full life in God's Kingdom.

6. A movement toward empowerment of men and women. We must evolve participative church structures in order to use the personal talents and skills of lay women and men. Empowered by the Spirit and through the sacraments, lay men and women should be involved in the life and mission of the Church by bringing the Good News of Jesus to bear upon the fields of business and politics, of education and health, of mass media and the world of work. This requires a spirituality of discipleship enabling both the clergy and laity to work together in their own specific roles in the common mission of the Church (4 FABC Plenary Assembly, Tokyo, 1986). The Church cannot be a sign of the Kingdom and of the eschatological community if the fruits of the Spirit to women are not given due recognition, and if women do not share in the "freedom of the children of God" (4 FABC Plenary Assembly, Tokyo, 1986).

7. A movement toward active involvement in generating and serving life. The Church has to respond to the death-dealing forces in Asia. By authentic discipleship, it has to share its vision of full life as promised by Jesus. It is a vision of life with integrity and dignity, with compassion and sensitive care of the earth; a vision of participation and mutuality, with a reverential sense of the sacred, of peace, harmony, and solidarity (6 FABC Plenary Assembly, Manila, Philippines, 1995).

8. A movement toward the triple dialogue with other faiths, with the poor and with the cultures, a Church "in dialogue with the great religious traditions of our peoples," in fact, a dialogue with all people, especially the poor.[2]

This eightfold movement describes in a nutshell a new way of being church in Asia. Essentially, it aims at transforming the churches *in* Asia into the churches *of* Asia. Interculturation, understood in its widest sense, is the way to achieve this goal of becoming local churches. This need for interculturation in the church's mission of "love and service," according to the FABC's Seventh Plenary Assembly, has grown even more insistent in light of the challenges facing Christianity in Asia in the next millennium, such as the increasing marginalization and exclusion of many people by globalization, widespread fundamentalism, dictatorship and corruption in governments, ecological destruction, and growing militarization. The FABC sees these challenges affecting special groups of people in a particular way, namely, youth, women, the family, indigenous people, and sea-based and land-based migrants and refugees.[3] To meet these challenges fully, the FABC believes that it is urgent to promote the "Asianness" of the church which it sees as "a special gift the world is waiting": "This means that the Church has to be an embodiment of the Asian vision and values of life, especially interiority, harmony, a holistic and inclusive approach to every area of life."[4]

The FABC's vision for the future of Christianity in Asia is of course a Roman Catholic one. But it is neither sectarian nor denominational. Most Christian churches can readily subscribe to its basic orientations. The triple dialogue – with Asian peoples, especially their impoverished and marginalized, with Asian cultures, and Asian religions – can offer useful directions for building up a vigorous Asian Christianity in its mission of bearing witness to the reign of God.

Asian and Pentecostal

Finally, no prognostication of contemporary Christianity, in Asia as well as elsewhere, particularly in Africa and Latin America, is complete without mentioning the presence of the Pentecostals who, now estimated to be over half a billion worldwide, form the second largest and fastest-growing Christian tradition (after the Roman Catholics).[5] Pentecostal and Charismatic movements have often been divided into five groups: (1) "Classical Pentecostalism," with roots in the nineteenth-century Holiness Churches and historically connected with the Azusa Street Revival in Los Angeles, California, 1906–1909, emphasizing speaking in tongues (glossalalia) as an initial evidence of the baptism in the Spirit; (2) "Charismatic Movement," especially in mainline churches such as the Episcopal Church and the Roman Catholic Church after the 1960s, which connects the gifts of the Spirit with sacramental life in the institutional church; (3) "Third-Wave Movement," which arose in the 1980s and is composed of evangelical Christians who refuse the label of "Pentecostal" and "Charismatic" but continue to insist on prophetic, healing and exorcism ministries; (4) "Nondenominational Movement," composed of classical Pentecostals who reject denominational hierarchy and insist on congregational autonomy and freedom of worship; and (5) "Indigenous/

Independent Churches Movement," which have been created in the Third or Majority World by blending historic Christianity with local cultures and religions.

All of these five forms of Pentecostalism are present in Asia. While some forms of Asian Pentecostalism are historically connected with Western, especially North American, revival movements (e.g., the Azusa Street Revival), many are indigenous and even predate the Los Angeles event. For example, in the Khasi Hills of north-east India the Welsh Presbyterian mission experienced a great awakening in 1904–1906. At about the same time, a number of girls at the Mukti Mission, founded by Pandita Ramabai (1858–1922) in Kedgaon, near Pune in south-west India, were reported to have received the gifts of the Spirit such as speaking in tongues. While the above-mentioned categorization of Pentecostalism into five groups is a helpful guide to understand the many and diverse types of Pentecostal churches, it is important to note that in Asia they do not exist as distinct and separate groups. Rather, in the Asian churches, as Hwa Yung has persuasively argued, they are blended together and co-exist in a unique configuration as independent churches, with emphasis on the presence of demons and spirits and of miraculous "signs and wonders" and with indigenous leadership.[6]

Asian countries where Pentecostalism is gaining a phenomenal and rapid expansion include China (The True Jesus Church, The Jesus Family, The Little Flock, The "Yeller"), South Korea (Yoido Full Gospel Church), Myanmar/Burma, the Philippines (Jesus Is Lord Church, The Pentecostal Missionary Church of Christ, Keys of the Kingdom Ministries, The Bread of Life), Malaysia (Full Gospel Church, Full Gospel Businessmen's Fellowship, The New Testament Church), and Indonesia (Persatuan Pendeta-Pendeta Aliran Panyekosta Deluruh Indonesia).

With their exclusive emphasis on the Bible and Jesus (Jesus as the Savior, the Baptizer, the Healer, and the Coming King) and on the gifts of the Spirit, in particular glossalalia, healing and exorcism (also at times on the "Prosperity Gospel"), Asian Pentecostal churches seem to respond to the economic, emotional and spiritual needs of Asian peoples. Two additional elements will play a key role in the spreading of Pentecostalism, namely, the role of women as leaders in these grass-roots churches and their predominantly missionary orientation. Through the leadership of women, especially in the household church movement, and mission outreach to other countries (especially from the Korean churches), the face of Asian Christianity is changing radically, and with it, the future of World Christianity itself is at stake.

Notes

1. The FABC was founded in 1970, on the occasion of Pope Paul VI's visit to Manila, Philippines. Its statutes, approved by the Holy See *ad experimentum* in 1972, were amended several times and were also approved again each time by the Holy See. For the documents of the FABC and its various institutes, see Rosales, G. and Arévalo, C.G. (eds.) *For All The Peoples of Asia: Federation of Asian Bishops' Conferences. Documents from 1970 to 1991*, Vol. 1, New York/Quezon City: Orbis Books/ Claretian Publications, 1992; Eilers, F.J. (ed.) *For All the Peoples of Asia: Federation of Asian Bishops' Conferences. Documents from 1992 to 1996*, Vol. 2, Quezon City: Claretian Publications, 1997; Eilers, F.J. (ed.) *For All The Peoples of Asia: Federation of Asian Bishops' Conferences. Documents from 1997 to 2002*, Vol. 3, Quezon City: Claretian Publications, 2002; and Eilers, F.J. (ed.) *For All The Peoples of Asia: Federation of Asian Bishops' Conferences. Documents from 2002 to 2006*, Vol. 4, Quezon City: Claretian Publications, 2007.
2. Eilers, F.J. (ed.) *For All The Peoples of Asia: Federation of Asian Bishops' Conferences. Documents from 1997 to 2002*, Vol. 3, Quezon City: Claretian Publications, 2002, pp. 3–4.
3. See Eilers, F.J. (ed.) *For All The Peoples of Asia: Federation of Asian Bishops' Conferences. Documents from 1997 to 2002*, Vol. 3, Quezon City: Claretian Publications, 2002, pp. 6–12.
4. Eilers, F.J. (ed.) *For All The Peoples of Asia: Federation of Asian Bishops' Conferences. Documents from 1997 to 2002*, Vol 3, Quezon City: Claretian Publications, 2002, p. 9.
5. For an introduction to Pentecostalism, see Hollenweger, W. *Pentecostalism: Origins and Development Worldwide*, Peabody: Hendrickson, 1997 and Anderson, A. *An Introduction to Pentecostalism: Global Charismatic Christianity*, Cambridge: CUP, 2004.
6. See Yung, H. "Pentecostalism and the Asian Church," in Anderson, A. and Tang, E. (eds.) *Asian and Pentecostal: The Charismatic Face of Christianity in Asia*, Oxford: Regnum, 2005, pp. 37–57. This volume is currently the best work on Asian Pentecostalism.

Index